ARGENTINA'S NORTH
CLASSICAL CIRCUITS

Photographs, Ossian Lindholm
Text, Ana Inés Figueroa Alexander

MAIZAL
EDICIONES

Introduction

Argentina's North is a perfect mixture of landscapes, history, colours, flavours and music.

Since Pre Hispanic times it has been inhabited by advanced cultures, which the Incas began conquering circa 1480 AD, when they came down from Cuzco and entered through the Quebrada de Humahuaca. They found a densely populated region rich in resources, upon which they exerted their organization and culture. The Spaniards attested to this when they came in from Peru half a century later, in 1536, using the Inca roads and the Quechua language that was, by then, the general language throughout the hole empire.

To travel throughout these places so full of history, we have to drive along roads that twist around sedimentary coloured mountains, in the Calchaquí Valleys or the Humahuaca Gorge.

We can follow roads that pass under laurel, walnut and cedrella trees, important species of the Mountain Forest that nestles on the eastern slopes of different mountain ranges.

On the other hand, we can drive up the Andes to find the vast Puna, where trails that seem unending take us to surreal corners.

Argentina's North is crossed by mountain ranges that run mainly in a North South direction.

Between each of these ranges, there are valleys with a unique ecosystem and culture. If traveling from East to West, one gains altitude and meets a dryer climate. This happens because the Trade Winds that blow in from the Atlantic collide into each mountain range leaving their moisture on the eastern slopes, which are covered by dense vegetation. Then the wind travels on to the West, dryer and dryer.

There are two marked different seasons. A dry winter with many cloudless days and almost purple skies. The riverbeds turn dusty and dry.

Summer paints the mountainsides with lush dark green vegetation. The rivers rush down torrentially with their waters tinted with reddish sediments.

Here in the North one will find the most advanced Pre Hispanic cultures, the first Spanish towns, Inca shrines, and lonely churches. All set amongst coloured landscapes, gorges and valleys, all decorated by jungle, deserts, red rivers and clear waterfalls.

Wine, woolen crafts and colonial silverware. Locro, empanadas, humitas and tamales. Guitars, sikus, quenas and charangos; that sing zambas, vidalas, carnavalitos or bagualas. Gauchos on horseback. All are words that bring to mind this part of the world.

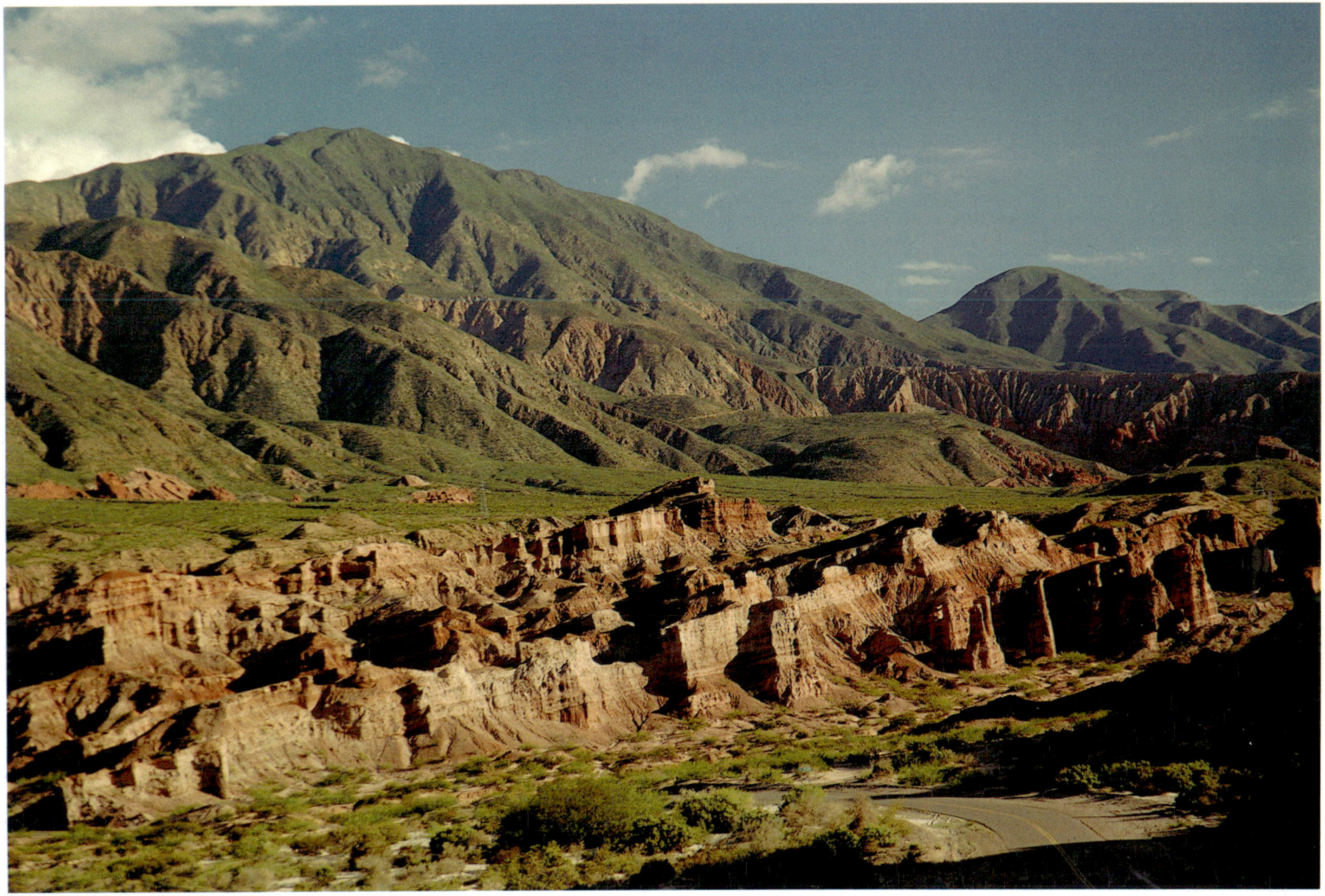

Salta, road to Cafayate.

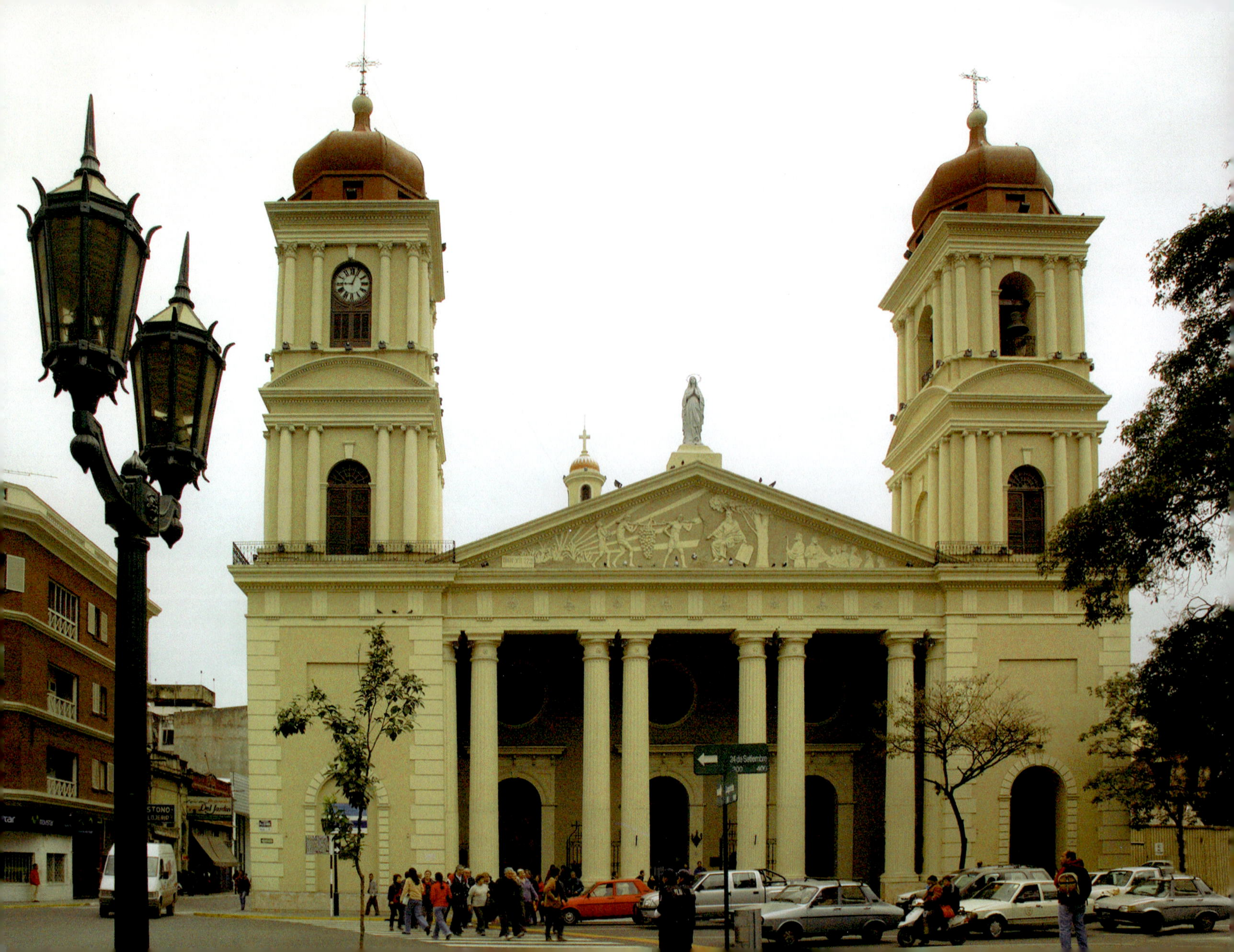
24 de Setiembre

From the City of Tucumán to Quilmes via Tafí del Valle

San Miguel de Tucumán is the usual starting point when visiting northern Argentina, getting there either by land or by air.

In this city, we will find centuries of history that have strongly influenced Argentina as we know it today.

Plaza Independencia is at the centre of the city's lay out, designed as a typical Hispanic city: in square blocks with straight streets. Walking around this main plaza, we will find the Government House, that combines French and modern architecture. The Cathedral that guards the images of St. Simon and St. Judas, the city's vice patrons. Across the plaza, a French styled building houses a social club; and at the corner, we find the Church and Convent of the Order of San Francisco.

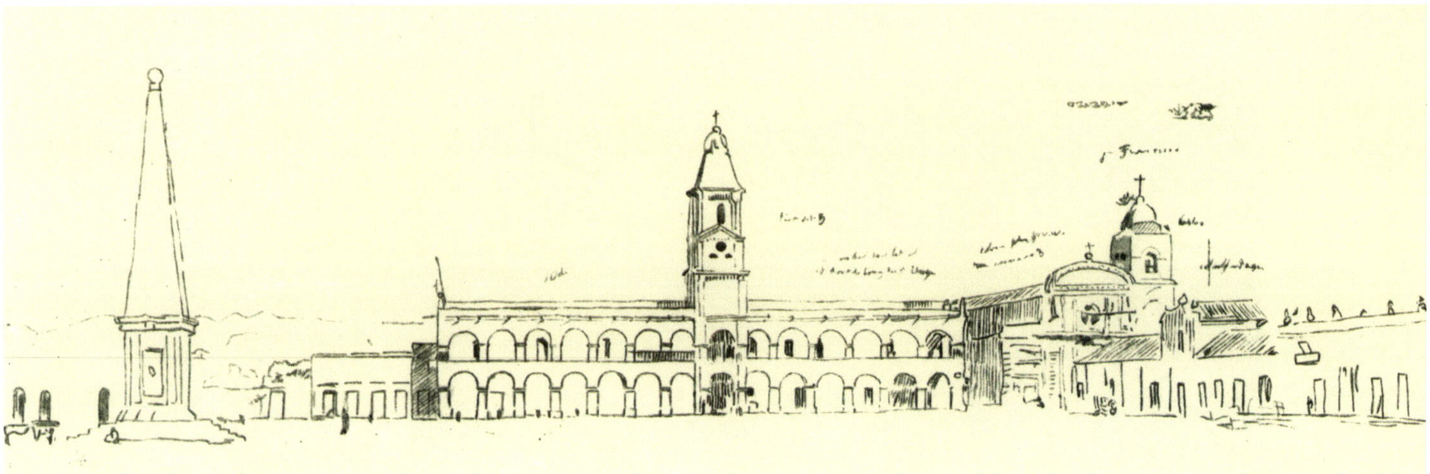

Independence Square, Juan León Palliere (1823–1887).

San Miguel de Tucumán Cathedral. (p. 4)

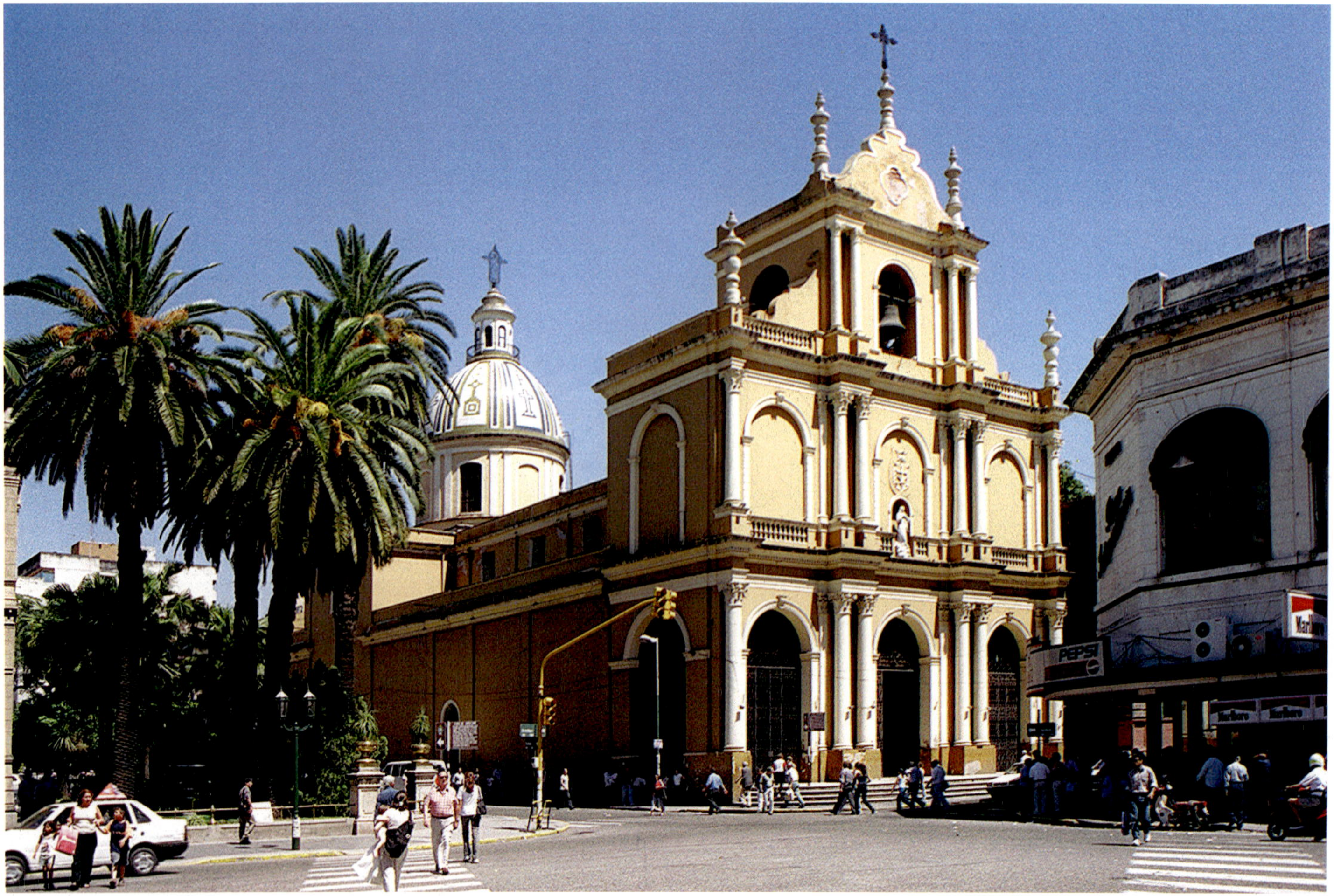

San Francisco Church and Convent.

San Francisco Church and Convent.
In this same place the Jesuit church and school stood until the Society of Jesus was expelled from America in the late 18th century. Then the Franciscan Order took over. Inside we find the first flag to be hoisted in Tucumán in 1814.

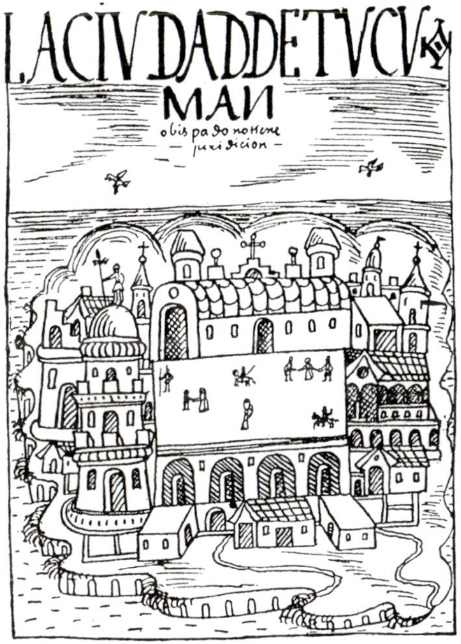

Tucumán, Guamán Poma de Ayala, 1587.

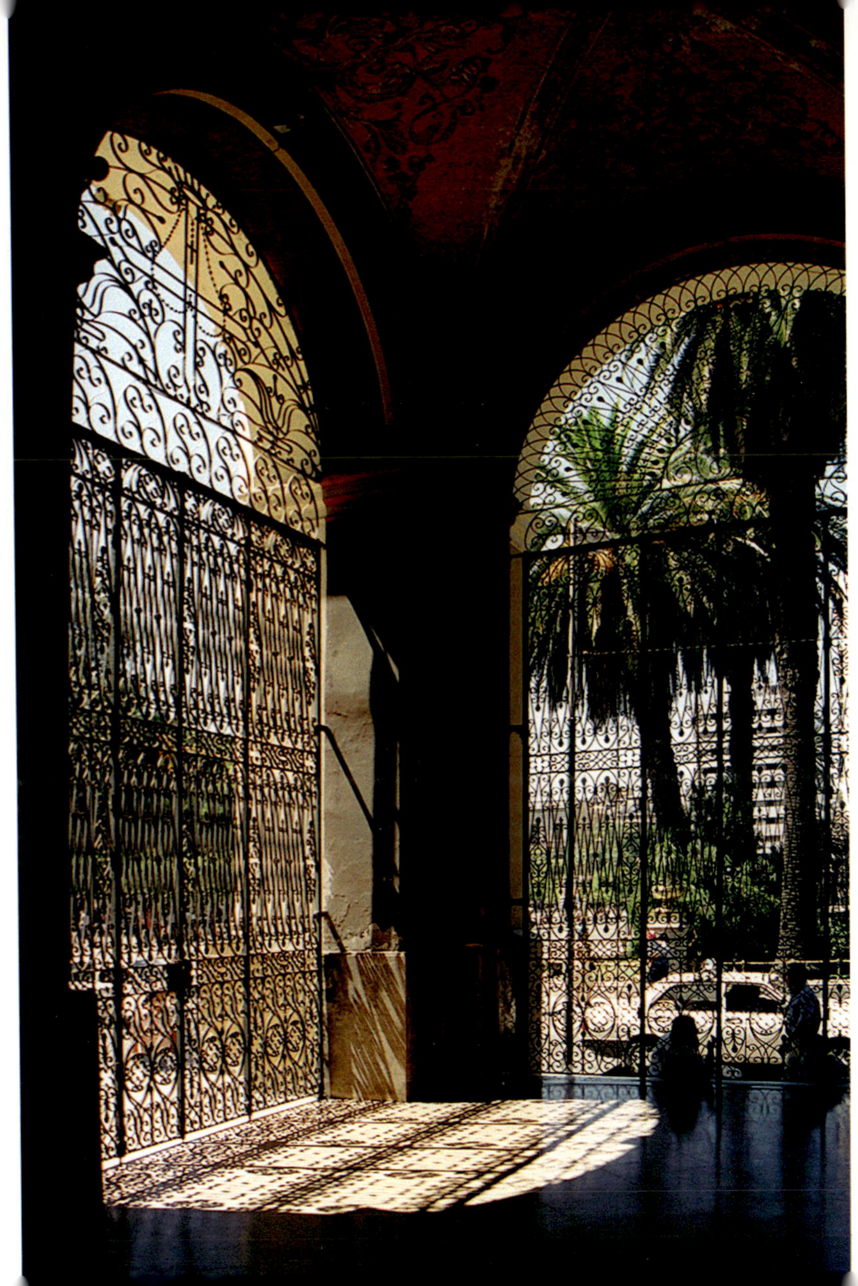

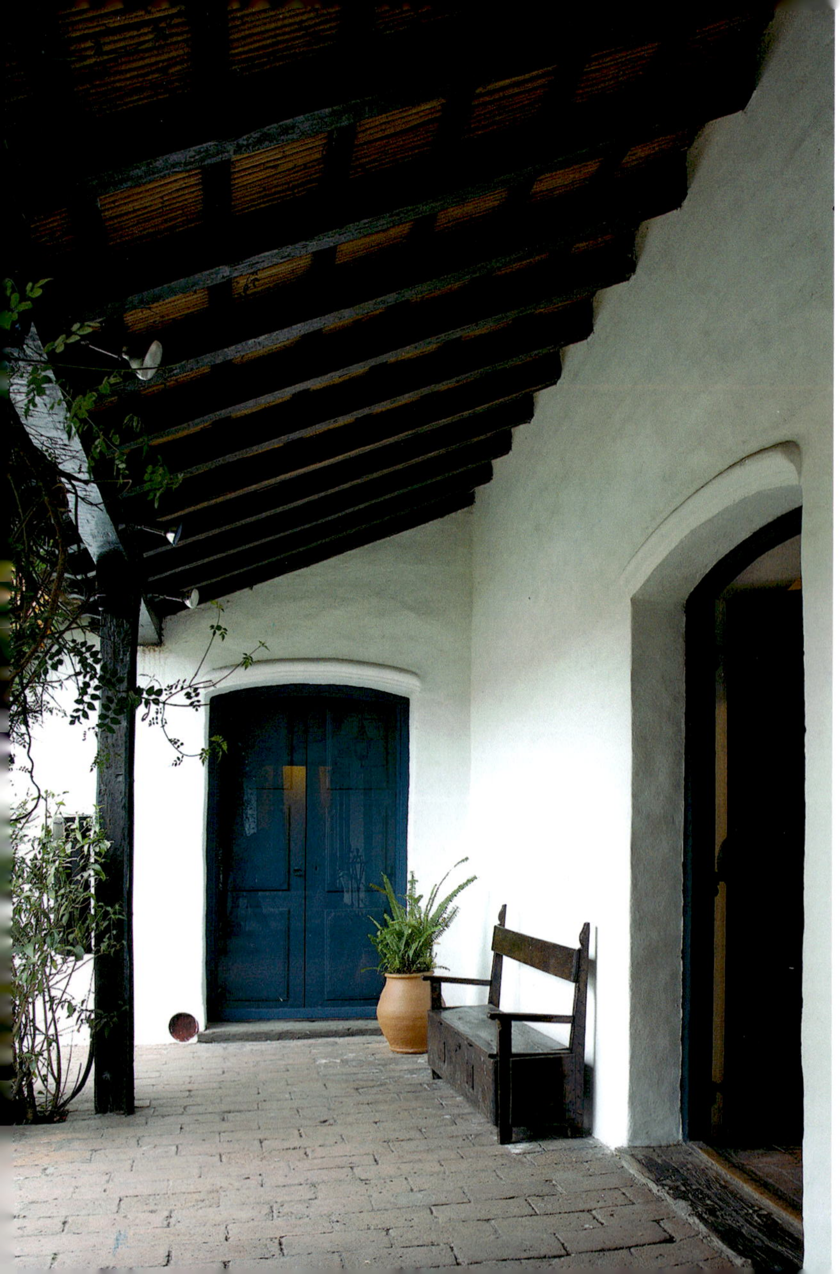

A couple of blocks away, the Casa Histórica de Tucumán, gives us a chance to walk around the rooms and patios where on July 9th, 1816 Argentina declared its Independence.

Tucumán is a city of creoles and immigrants. Sugar cane plantations and mills set in the outskirts create a singular way of life. It is a city of commerce and agriculture. In addition, it is full of students, due to the famous Tucumán National University, the fourth to open its doors in Argentina.

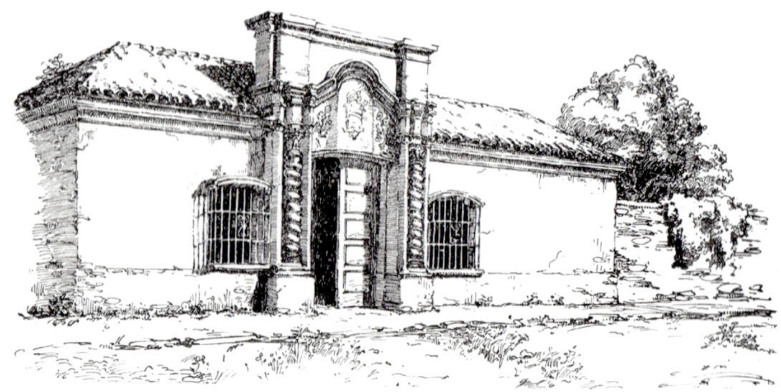

House of Independence.
It is a good example of colonial time architecture. Its historical assembly room was witness to the proclamation of Independence of the United River Plate Provinces. Its back patio exhibits lovely Lola Mora embossments.

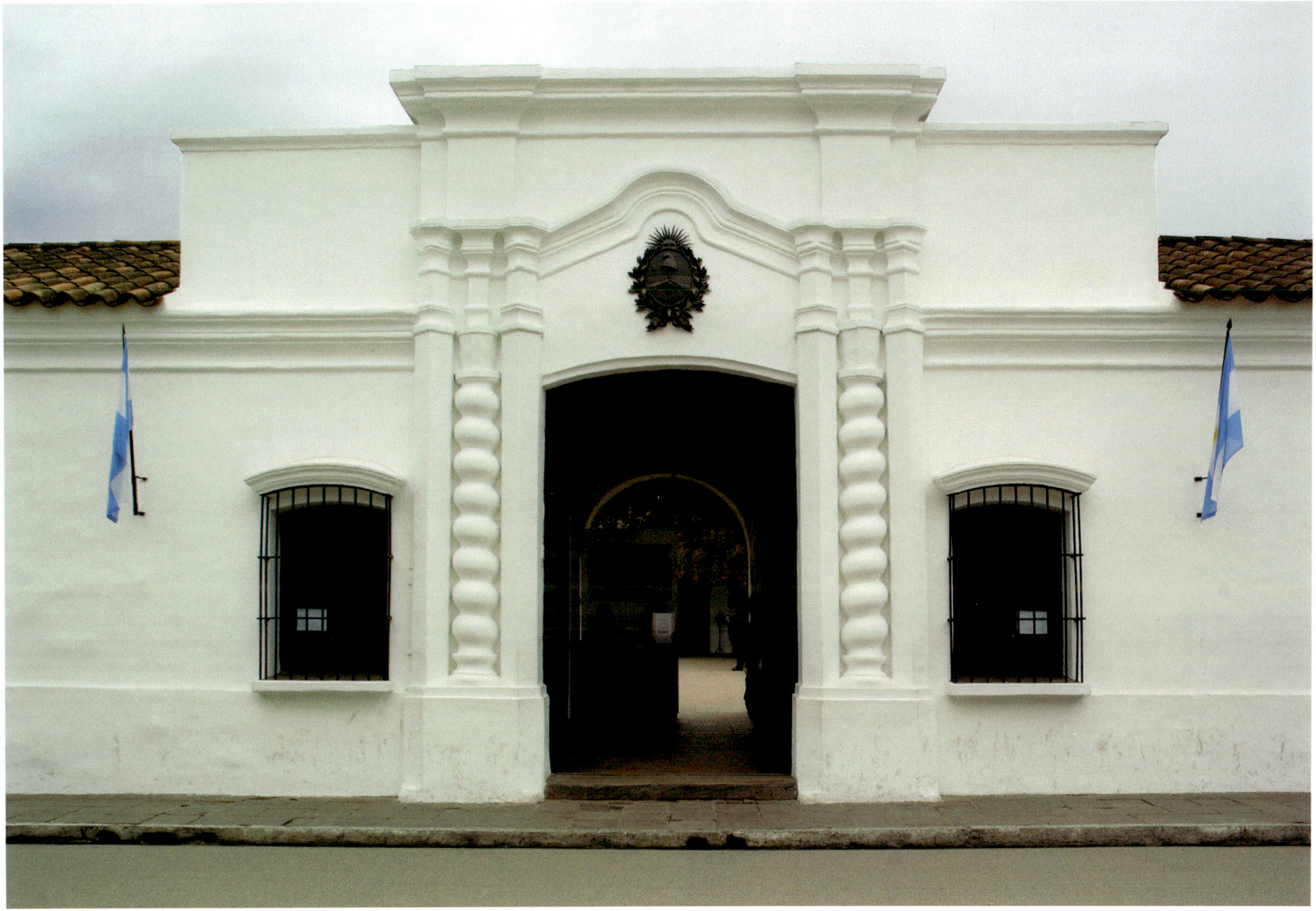

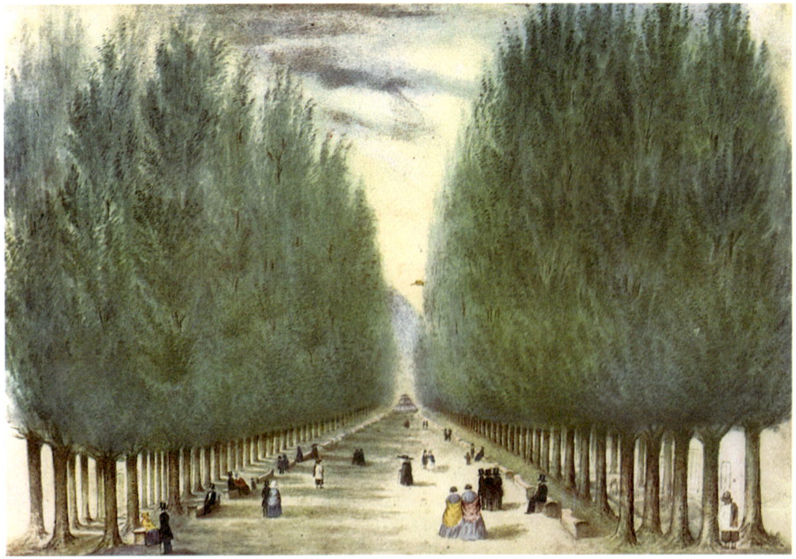

Promenade in Tucumán, Ignacio Baz (1820–1887).

Bishop Colombres' House – Museum of the Sugar Industry. Here we find the first trapiche or sugar mill that was used in the province in 1821, together with other testimonies of the sugar industry. It is located in what is today the 9 de Julio Park.

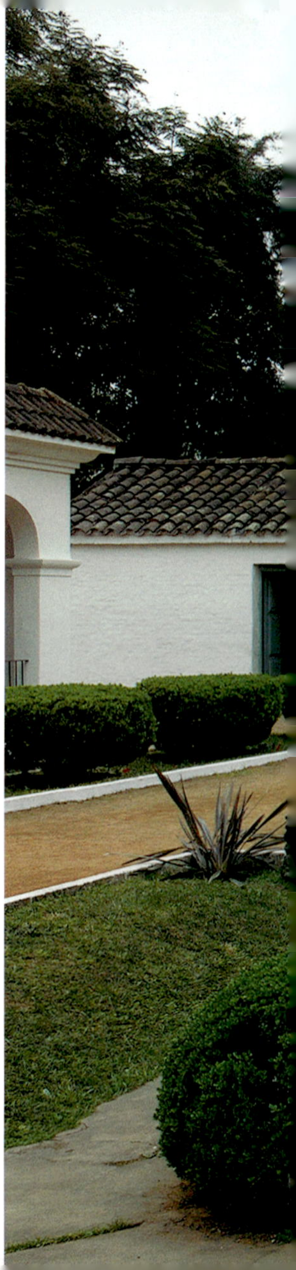

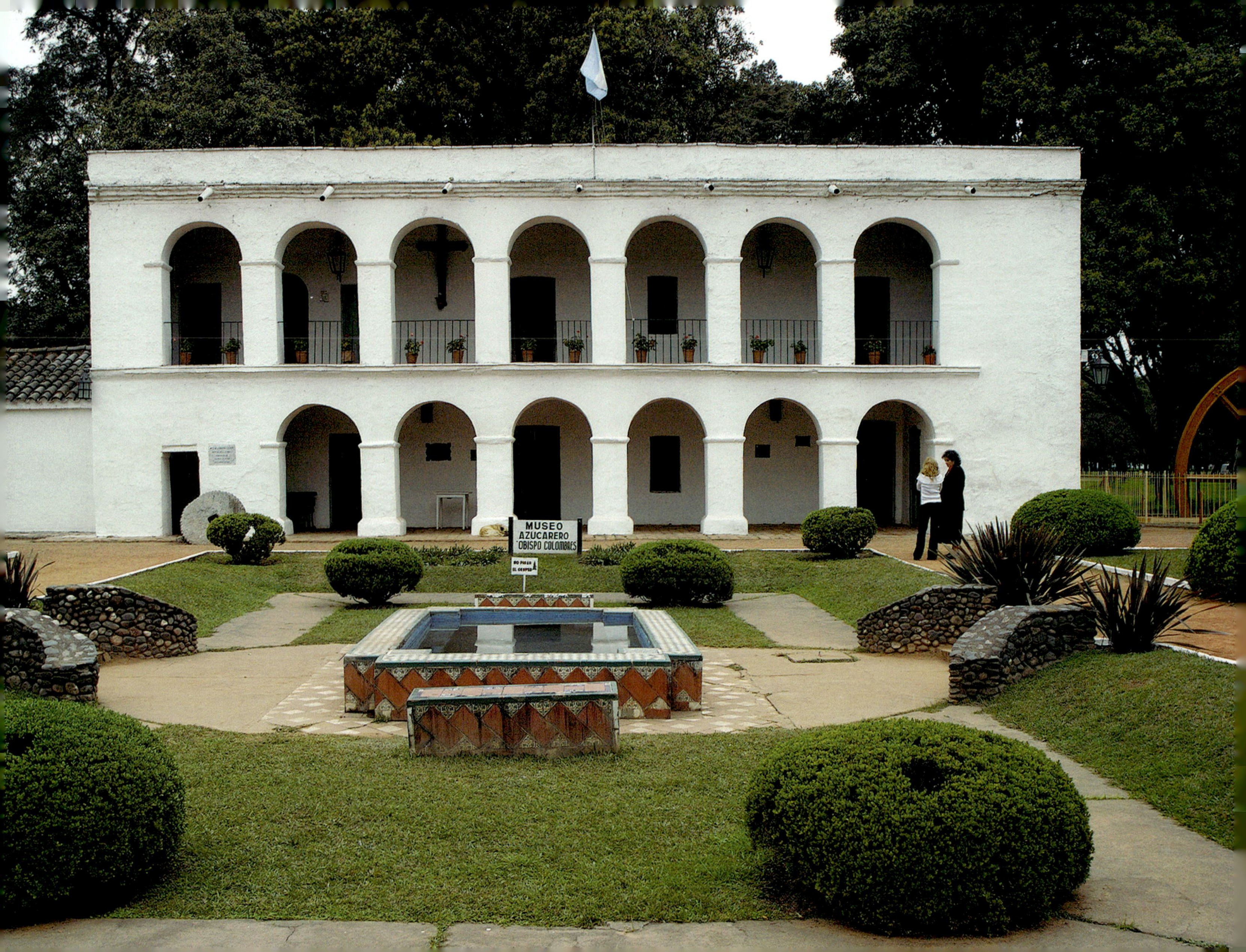
MUSEO
AZUCARERO
"OBISPO COLOMBRES"

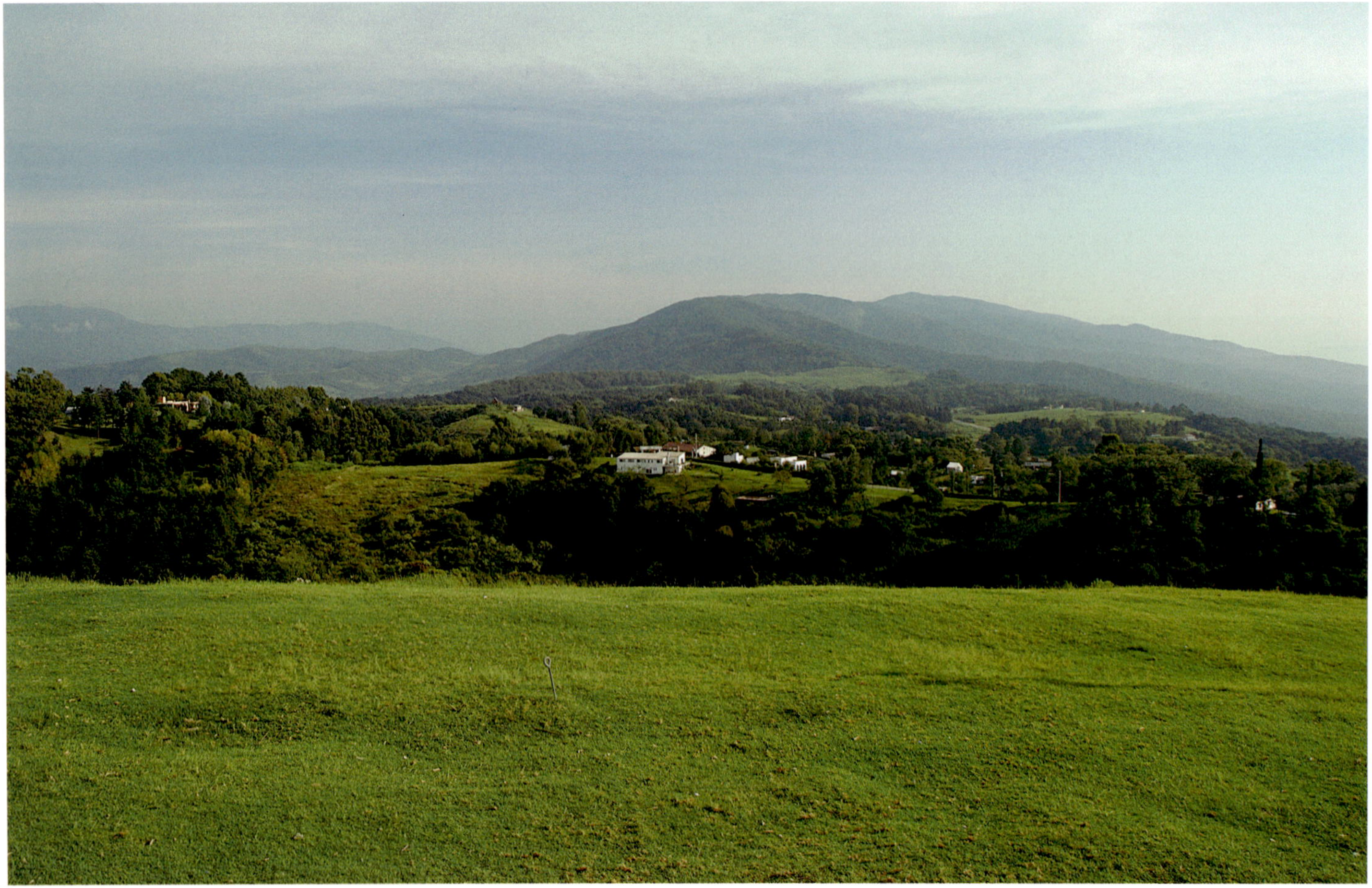

El Taficillo as seen from the San Javier Christ.

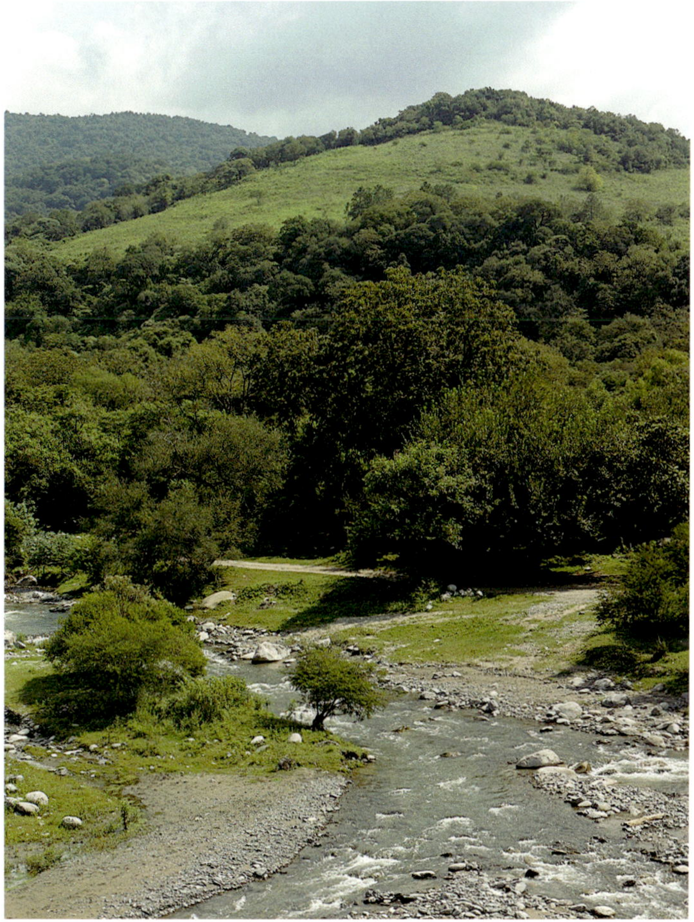

Tucumán. Río Grande, just a few minutes away from El Siambón.

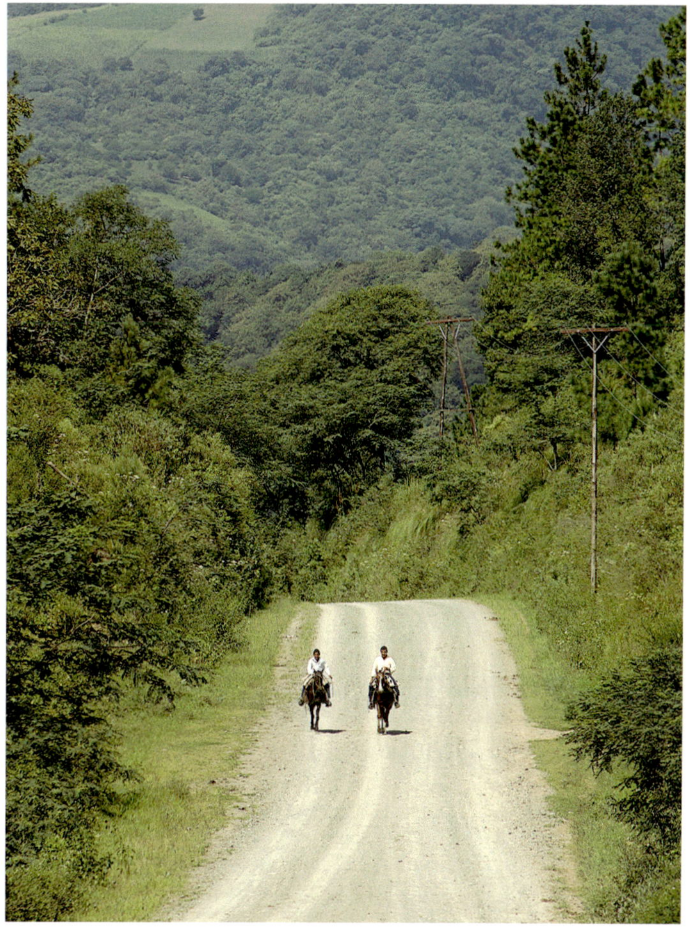

Gauchos on horseback.

Its vegetation is green all year round, earning it the name of *Garden of the Republic*. It has a subtropical climate with a hot and damp summer, and the only city of those we are going to visit in the North, that is located on a plain.

Behind the city, the Aconquija Range rises as the first barrier the Trade Winds find as they blow in from the Atlantic.

We head for these mountains in the southwest, and driving through sugar cane and lemon trees, we leave San Miguel de Tucumán.

Horco Molle Experimental Reserve.
The North West fauna is represented in this Reserve, where scientists find a natural lab to develop environmental research.
Tapir (Tapirus terrestris).

Aquila Mora (Geranoaetus melanoleucus).

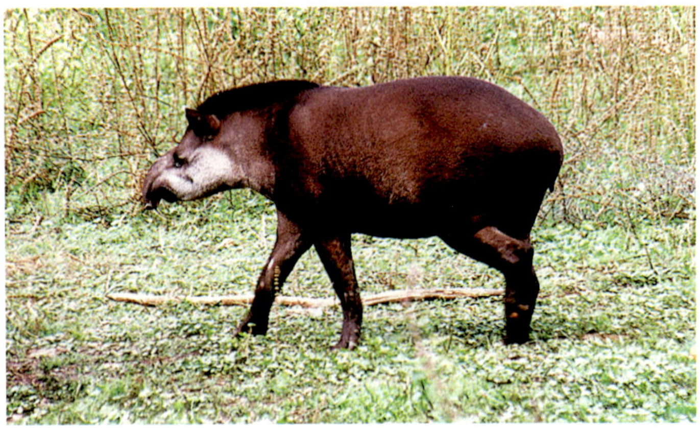

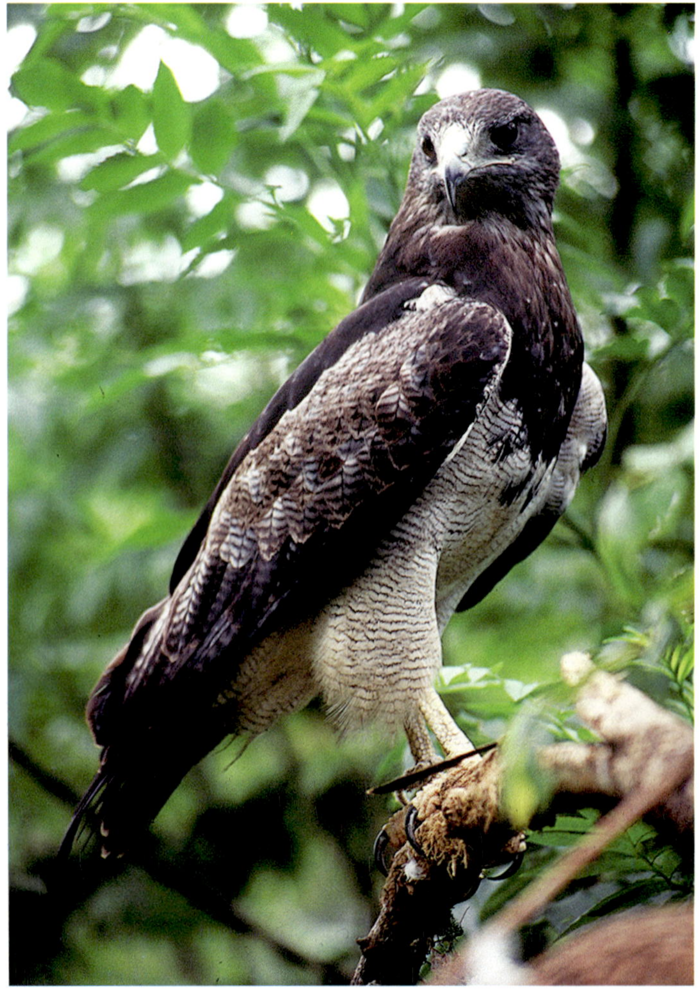

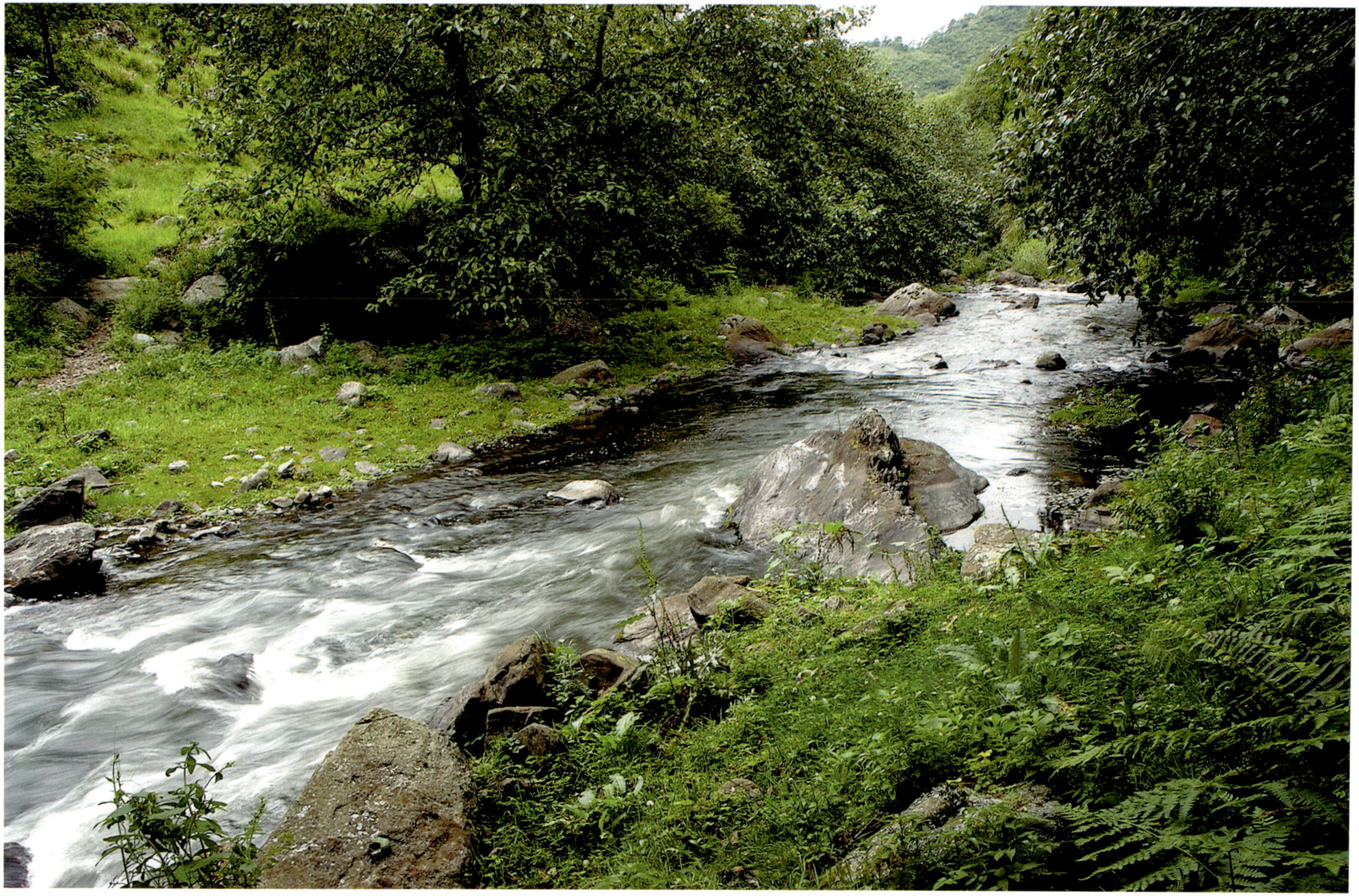

Tucumán, Quebrada Los Sosa.

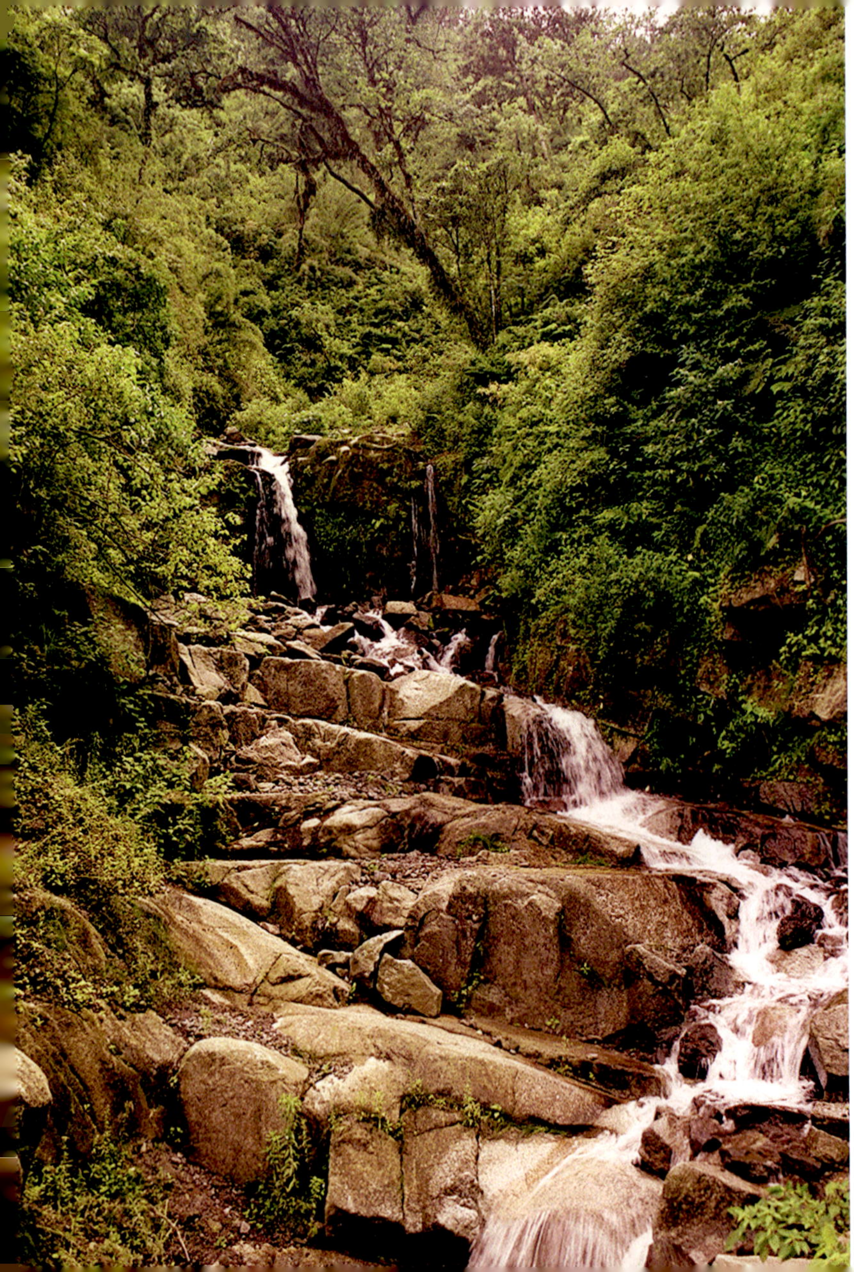

Near Acheral, we turn west and start climbing up mountains that from a distance seemed black since they are covered by forest. At first the slope is easy, but once in the Quebrada de Los Sosa we go up a winding road that takes us through all the different strata of the mountain forest.

At the bottom of the gorge, the river pours over huge boulders that have been dragged here during summer river floods. The vegetation increases, the under bush is full of a kind of solid cane (Chusquea boliviana) and ferns.

After near 50 kilometers of mountain road we are near the top, the river is now a stream, indicating we are near the pass. Vegetation thins, the trees here are the alisos (Alnus jorullensis), that grow at 2000 m.a.s.l. (6560 ft) and mark the line between the thick mountain forest and the high mountain pastures. The trees end as abruptly as they began; we drive through the pass and find ourselves in the Valley of Tafí.

Tucumán,
Quebrada Los Sosa.

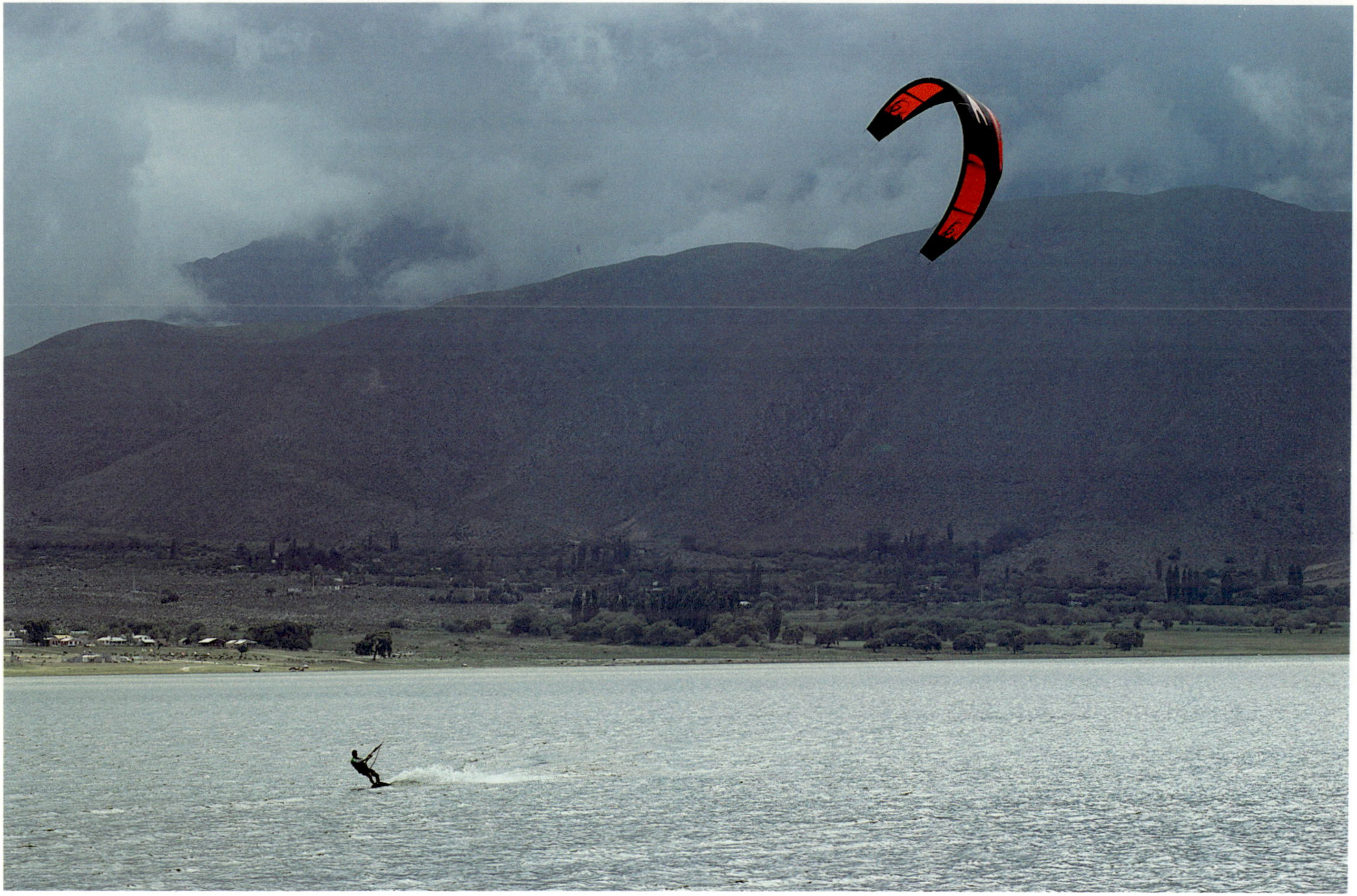

El Mollar, water sports in the Angostura Dam.

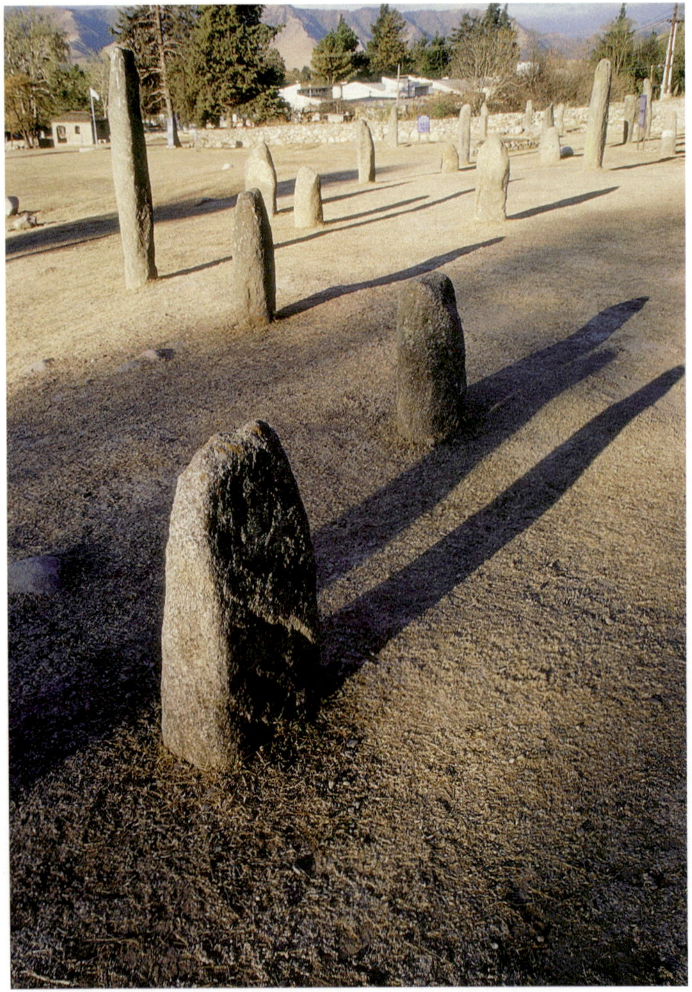

El Mollar is a summer village set in front of La Angostura, a dam that usually reflects the clouds resting on the mountains in its water. This is usual since Tafí has a transitional microclimate between the hot and fertile plains to the East and the dry valleys to the West. Its cool climate made the Valley popular amongst the people from Tucumán who built their summerhouses here to escape from the heat of the city.

This cool environment allowed the Jesuits to establish dairy farms that today continue making unique cheeses with the Order's original recipe brought from Spain.

To discover incredible sights, one must climb the mountains surrounding the valley on foot or horseback.

In general, to leave a valley there are two options: one is through a gorge, following a river course; and the other is to climb up to a pass, which is a high point between two valleys without water running through it. Instead new rivers are born at this point, each flowing down opposite sides of the mountain.

El Mollar, Parque de Los Menhires.
This archeological reserve displays menhirs belonging to the Tafí culture that flourished between the years 300 BC to 800 AD. They are engraved with symbols, specially snakes and human figures. It is thought they were magical and had ceremonial purposes.

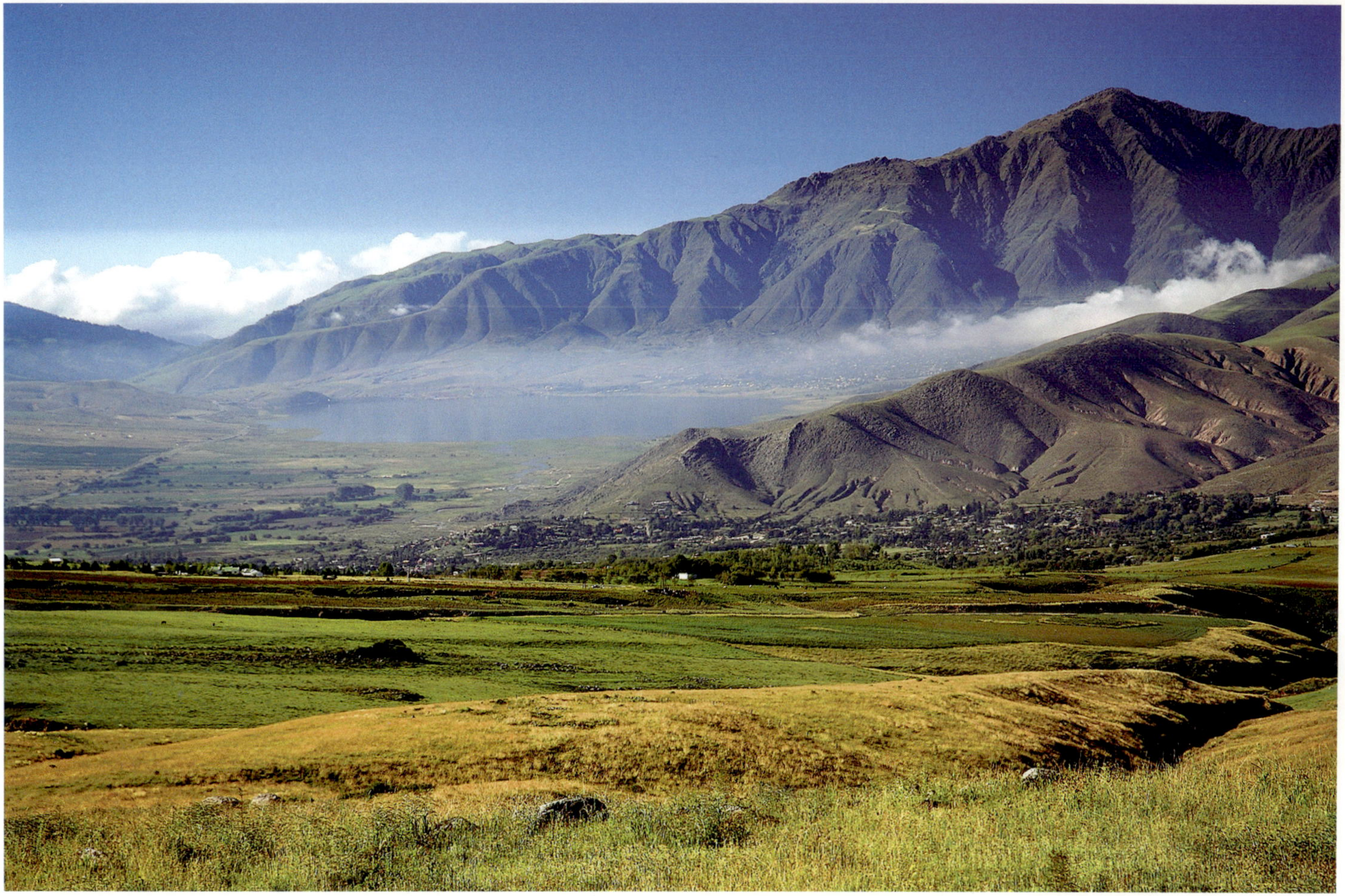

Tafi del Valle .View from the road that leads up to the Abra del Infiernillo. Potato seed crop.

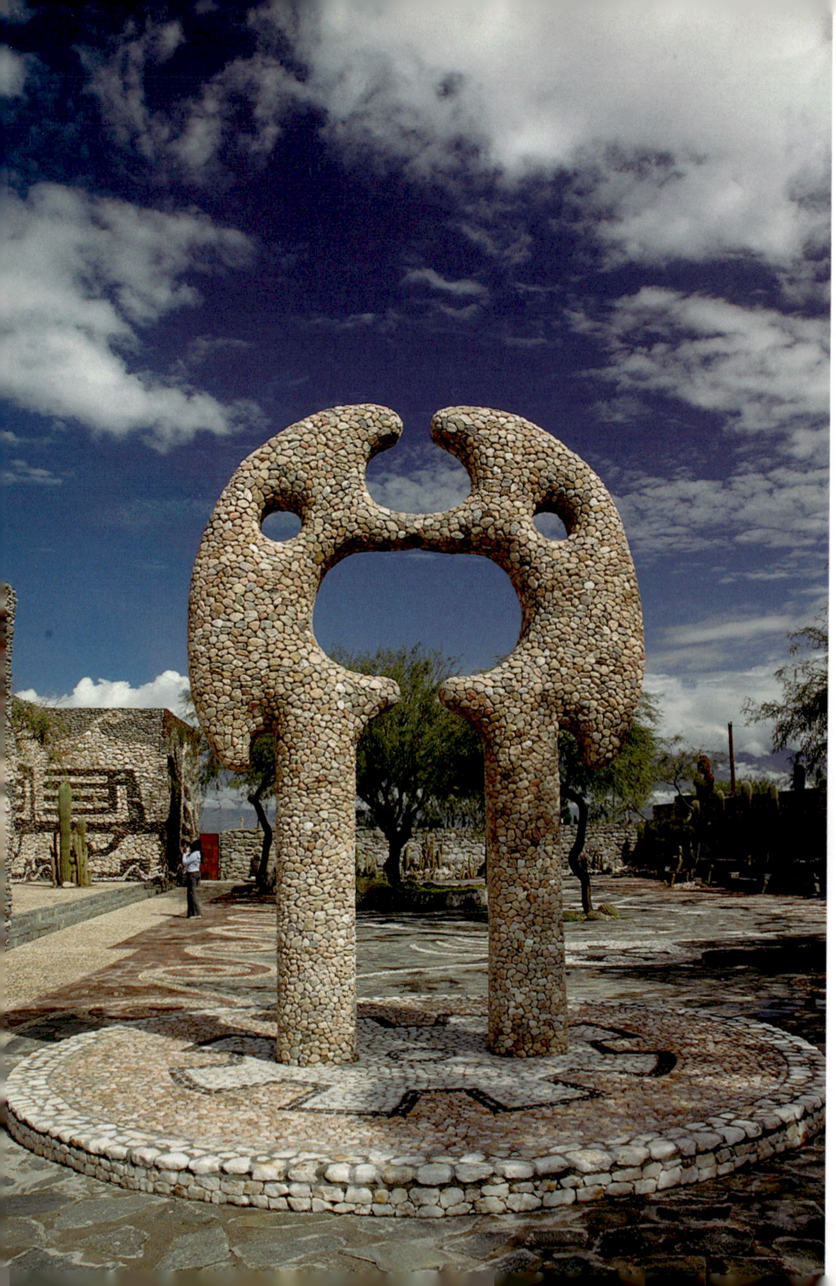

This time, to leave the Valley of Tafí we climb to the Abra del Infiernillo, a pass just above 3000 m.a.s.l. (9840 ft). On the way up, if one looks carefully it is easy to see that the groups of rocks set across the mountainsides are circles, belonging to ancient dwellings of the people of the Tafí Culture.

As we start our descent, the scenery changes, and we find rocks, shrubs and lower, the first cardones *(Trichocereus sp.)*, standing superb against the arid landscape.

We are on our way into the Calchaquí Valleys, and from the top of the Aconquija Range, the view seems like a picture taken from an airplane.

Down below awaits the small village of Amaicha, and we are surprised to find sculptures on the side of the road that link native and modern art. They belong to the Pachamama Museum.

Looking down from the mountains the river seems a white strip at the bottom of the valley. Now we discover it is wide and sandy, with a greater part of its waters flowing under the surface. It is the Santa María or Yocavil River, born in Catamarca behind the Quilmes or Cajón Mountain Range, on its way to Cafayate.

Amaicha del Valle. Pachamama Museum. Moon Warrior.
This complex shows ethnological, geological and textile art samples belonging to the different pre Hispanic cultures. Its patio is decorated with sculptures made by the local artisan Hector Cruz, the museum designer.

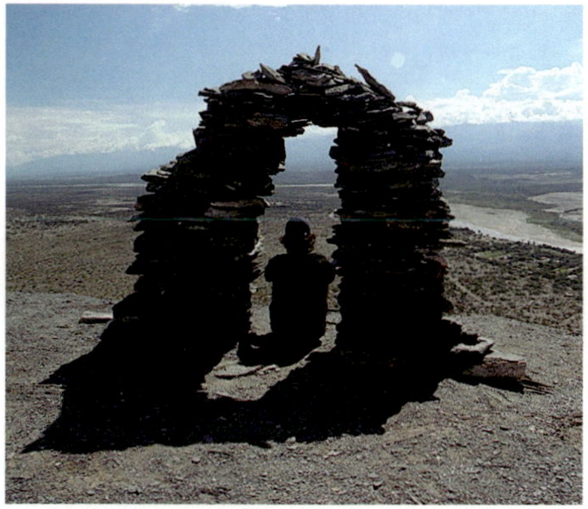

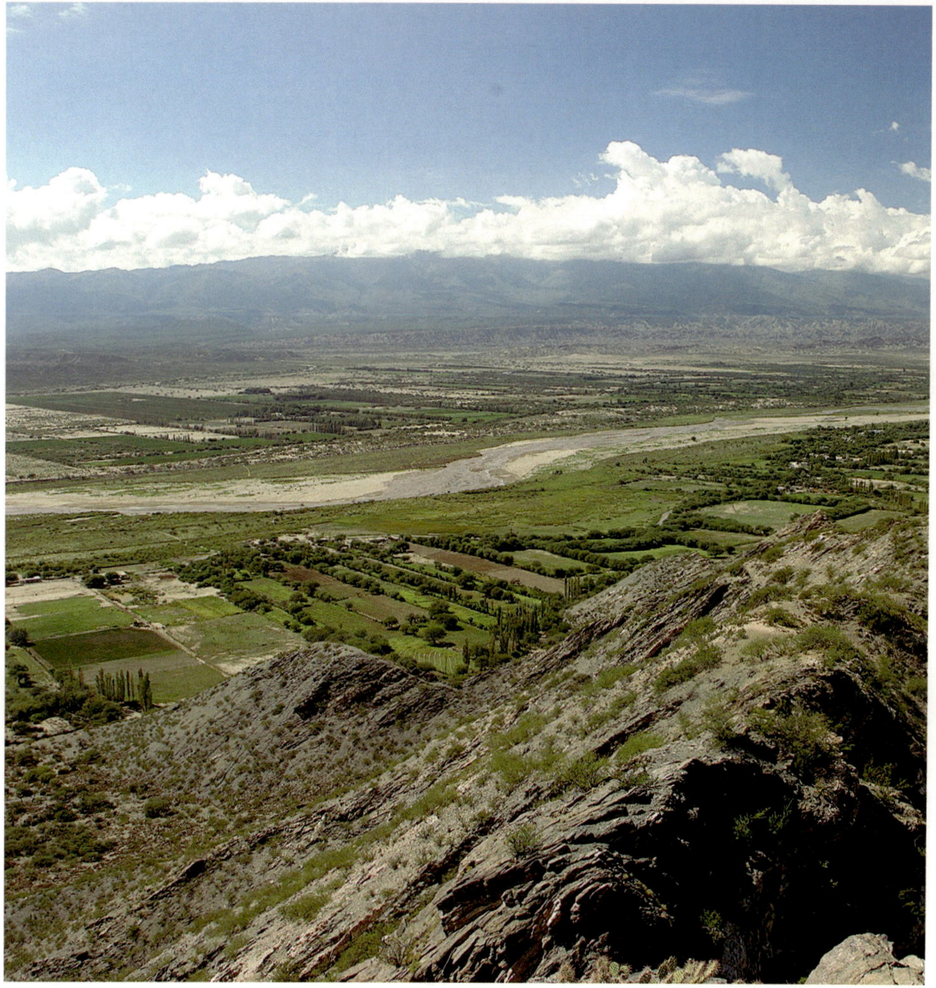

Fuerte Quemado – Intihuatana (Solar Observatory). Archeological site occupied from the late Santamaría Period and up to the Hispanic–Aboriginal one.

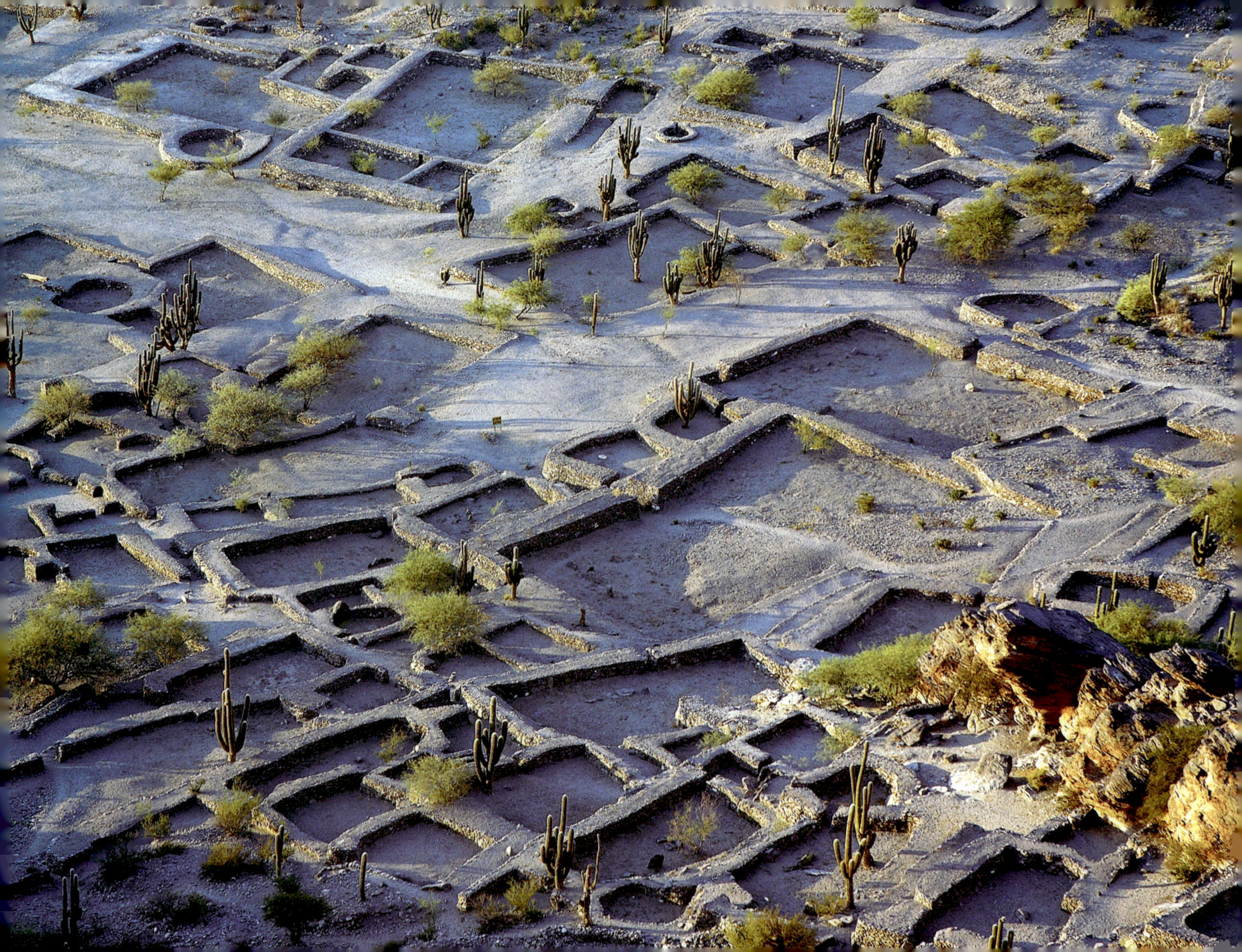

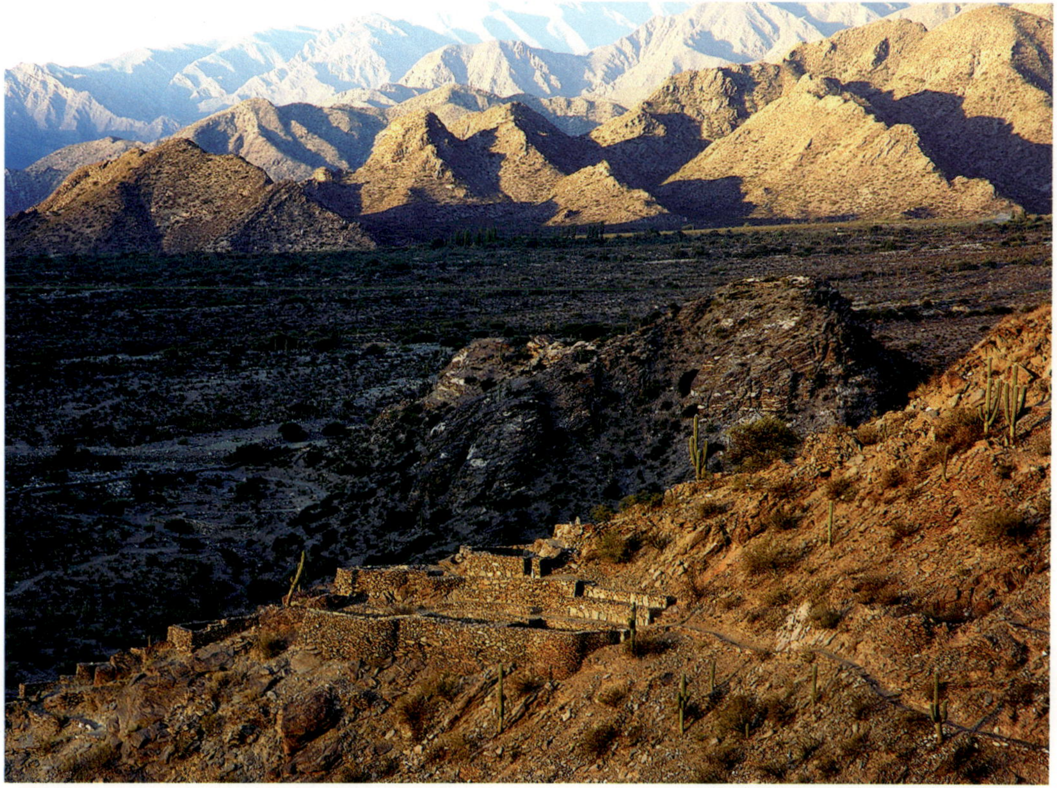

Quilmes Ruins. View towards the southern Pucará.
Pucará is the name used to express a fortified lookout.

View of a partially reconstructed area. Andean constructions are notorious, very adequate for the dry climate of the Valley. The city shows an irregular layout with houses set amongst open spaces, all interconnected by stairways and passages. *(p. 22)*

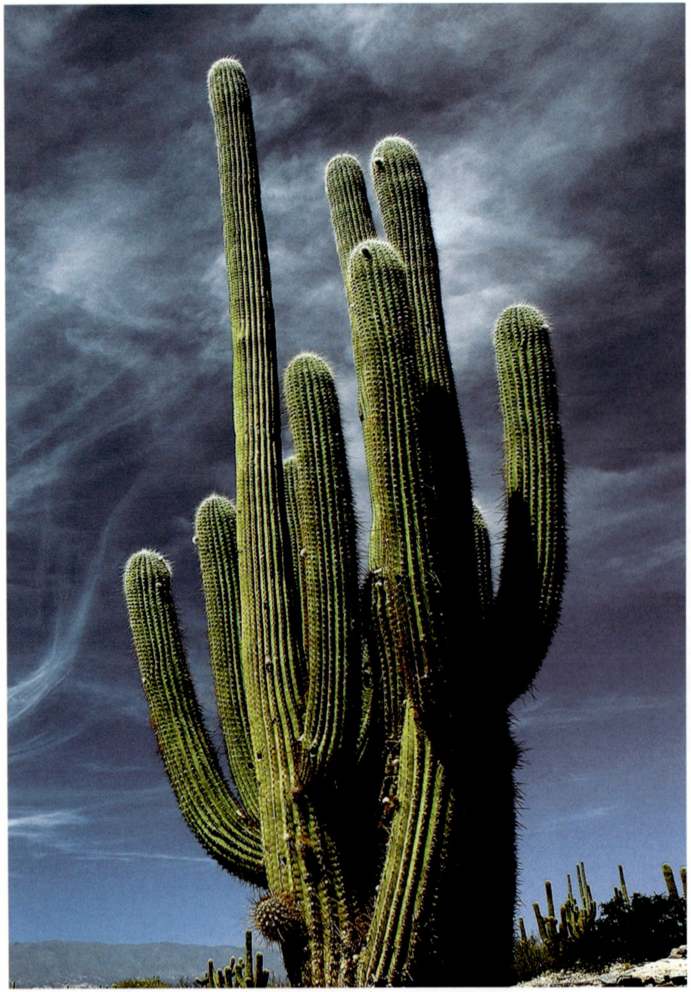

One of the most important archeological sites in Argentina are the Quilmes Ruins, located in the southern part of the Calchaquí Valley. They are strategically set on the side of the Cerro del Rey, a natural unreachable fortress, that the natives used to their advantage. From National Route 40, up to the entrance of the ruins one drives through a forest of ancient algarrobos *(Prosopis sp.)*, where the Quilmes people hunted and gathered its fruit, a nutritious pod still eaten in many ways by the local Calchaquí inhabitants.

It is evident that the location of this ancient city is not casual but the logical consequence of the work of experts, who knew the area, and wanted to accomplish an inaccessible citadel. So much so, that they were the last tribe to fall under Spanish rule. However, Spain achieved this, only at the end of the Third Calchaquí War, in 1664.

To walk through the ruins of this once important town, and climb to its Pucarás or lookouts on either side of the mountain and look out at the big Calchaquí Valley, gives one a chance to carry oneself to another time and, with some luck, to see all this with new eyes.

Cardón
(Trichocereus sp.).

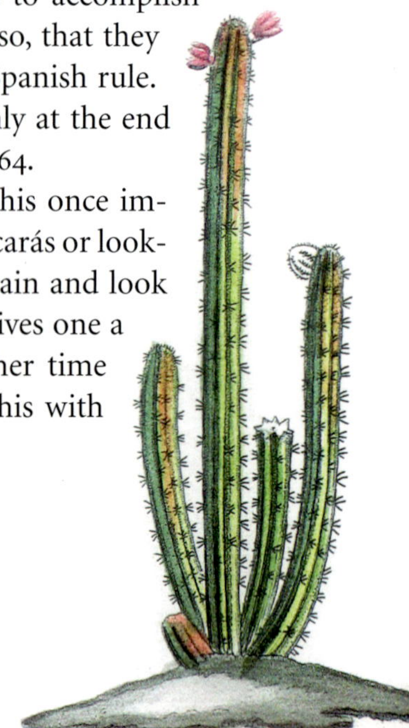

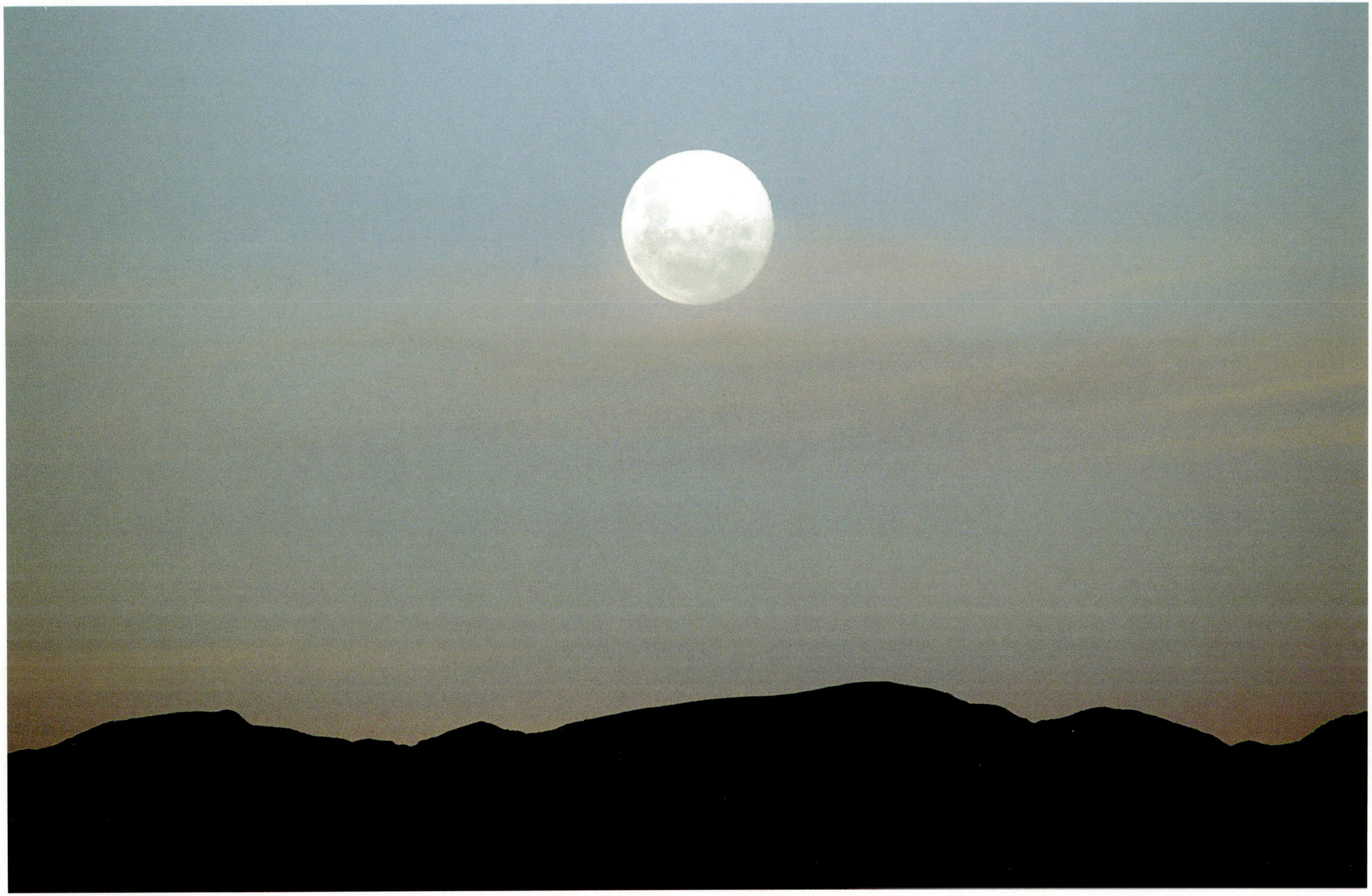

Full moon above Calchaquí heights.

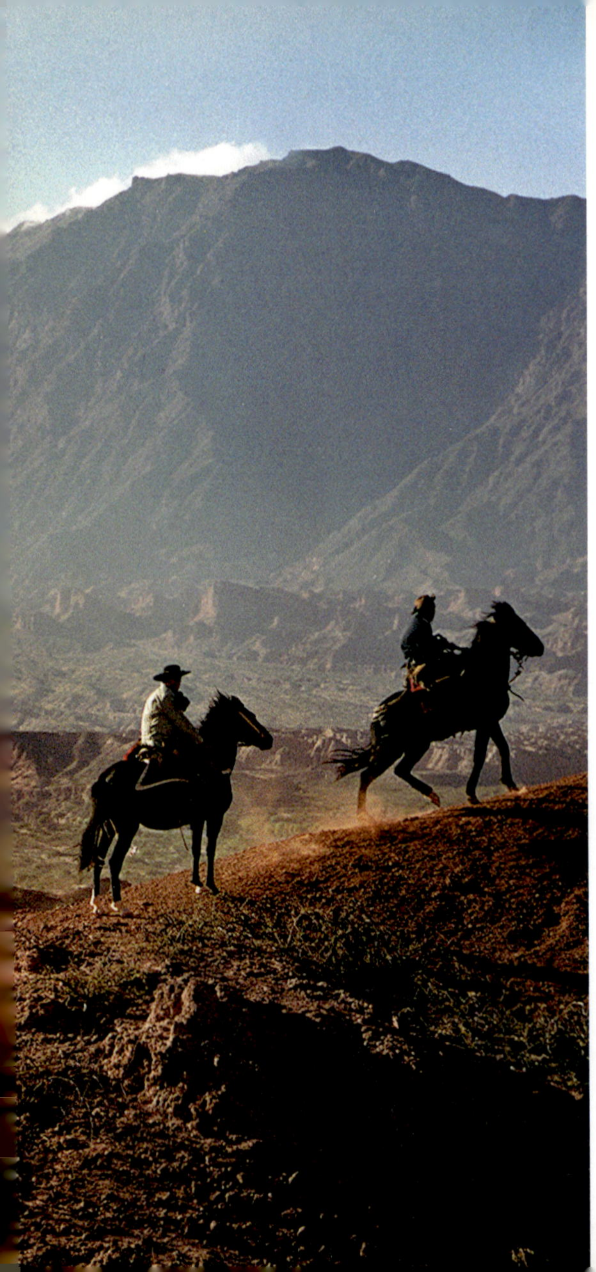

From Cafayate to Salta via La Quebrada de Las Conchas

We leave Cafayate on route 68 that starts under the shade of old poplar trees. We are driving towards a wall of red mountains. There are sand dunes on either side of the road, that lie in between the mountains and the first vineyards planted in the outskirts of the town. Local plants are growing on them to avoid them from flying on to the vine plantations.

This is the lowest part of the Calchaquí Valleys, 1660 m.a.s.l (5446 ft), and where the Calchaquí River, born up North in the snow capped peaks of the Acay Mountain, collides with the Santa María or Yocavil River that runs in the opposite direction from Catamarca. The River Las Conchas is born when these two come together, whose water then travels down to the Valle de Lerma where it is one of the main tributaries of the Cabra Corral Dam. River and road do this trip through the Cafayate Gorge, a place to go trough slow and with open eyes, since it is a landscape that will fulfill the senses.

The colours surprise us, formations are unending. The Andean rise gave birth to these mountains, and water and wind worked as a team during milliards of years to create this gorge full of natural sculptures.

There are formations that have names, such as El Fraile (the monk), El Sapo (the frog), El Anfiteatro (the amphitheatre) or La Garganta del Diablo (the devil's throat); each kilometer is festooned with masterpieces of erosion.

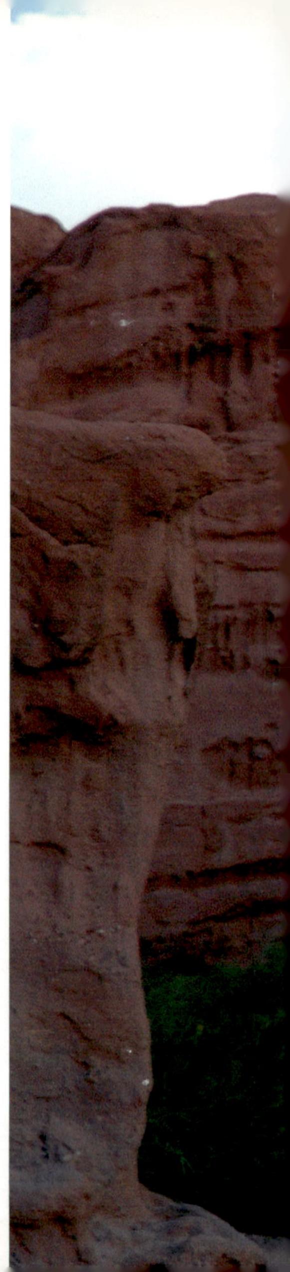

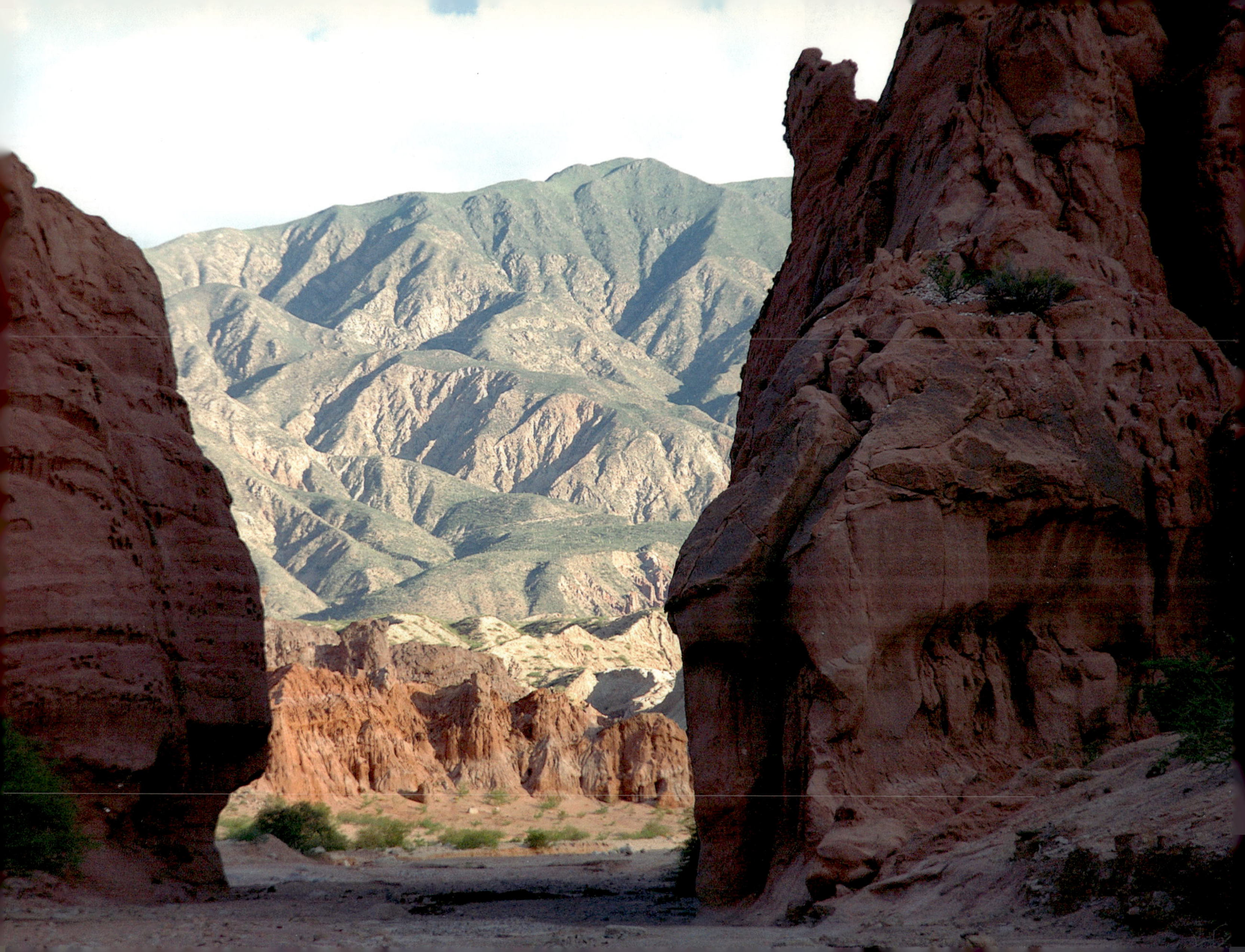

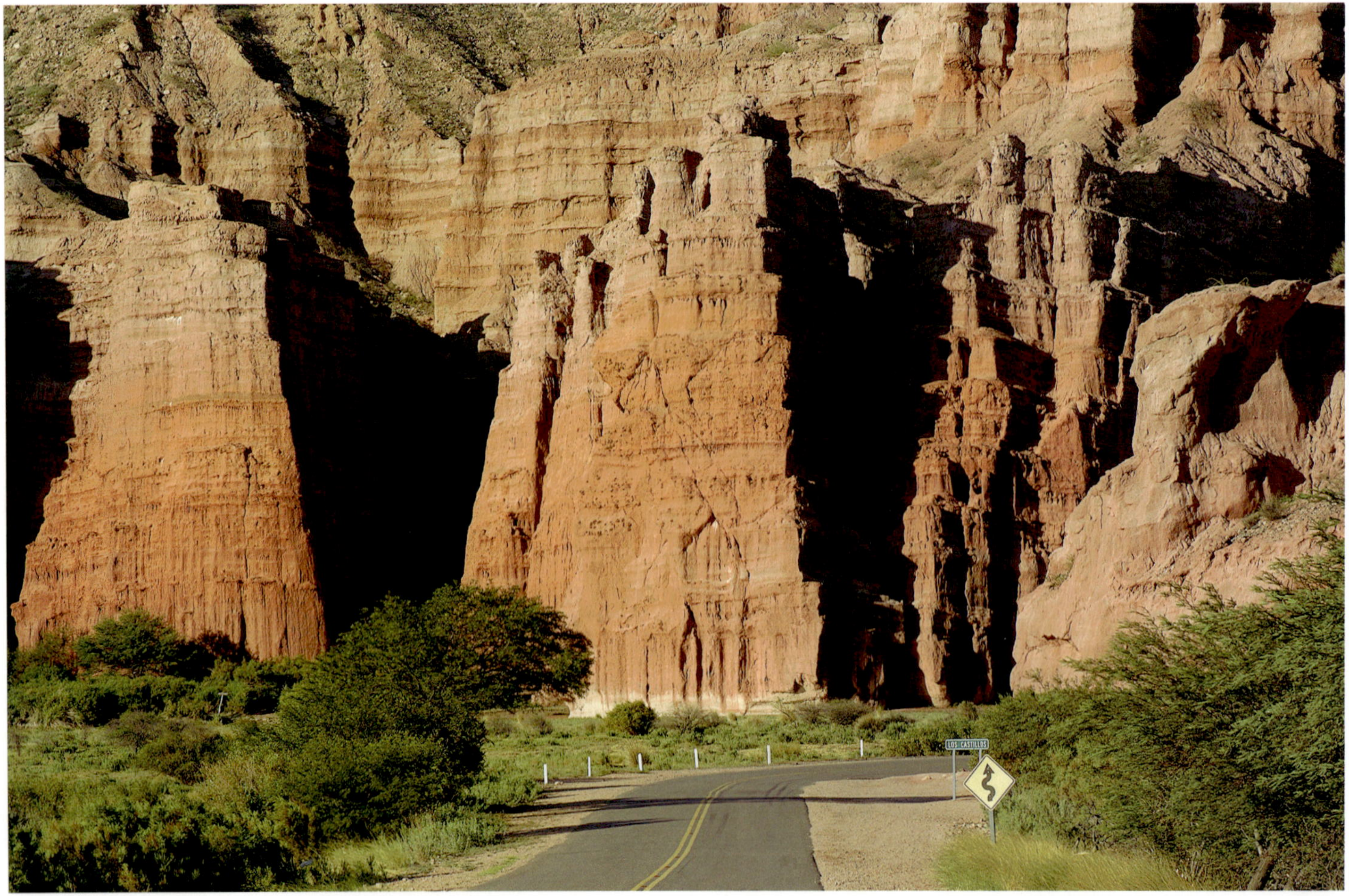

Los Castillos (The Castles).

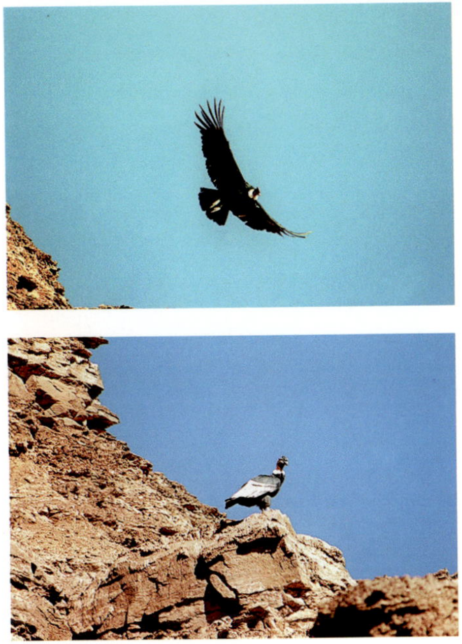

Cóndor (Vultur gryphus).

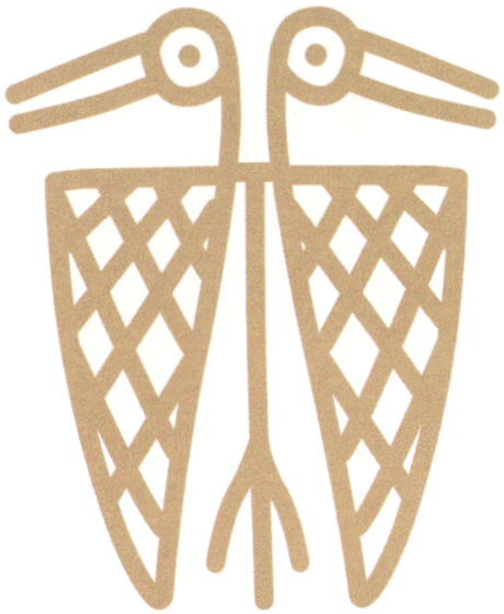

The Amphitheatre. An ancient waterfall, nowadays nonexistent, made this formation.

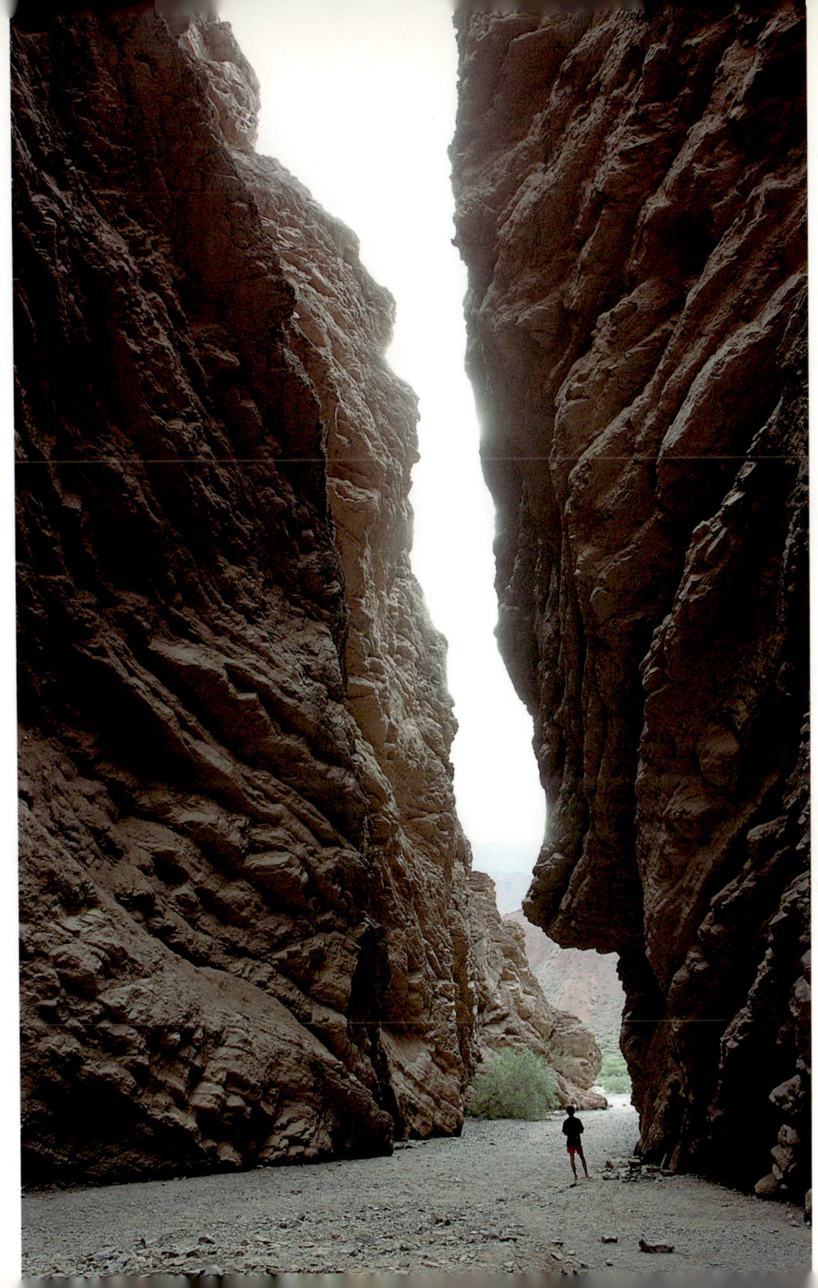

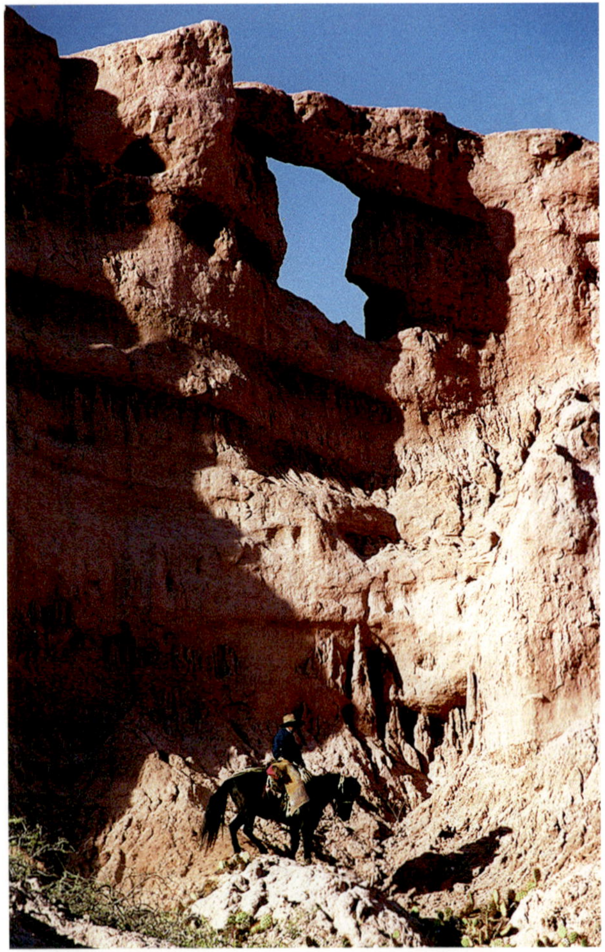
Gaucho on horseback near Las Ventanas (The Windows).

After driving through mountains for some 100 kilometers, we reach Alemania, a near abandoned village that was the last train station belonging to the train that went south from Salta. From there on passengers traveled by cart, horse or in latter days by bus.

The gorge comes to an end and we are in the southern end of the Valle de Lerma. This is its driest part, good for growing olives and *criollo* tobacco.

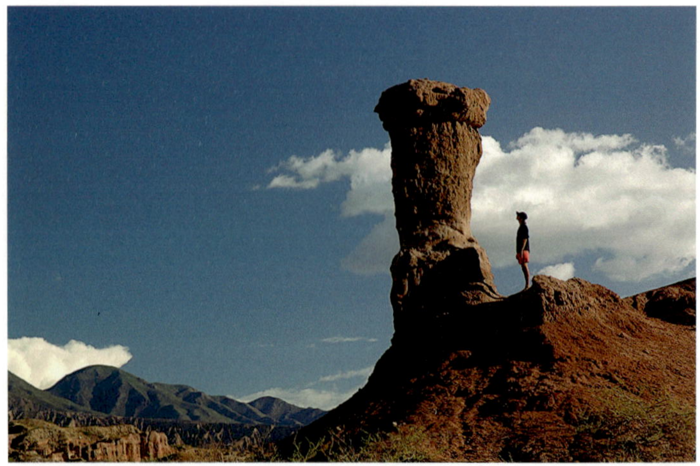
El Clavo (The Nail).

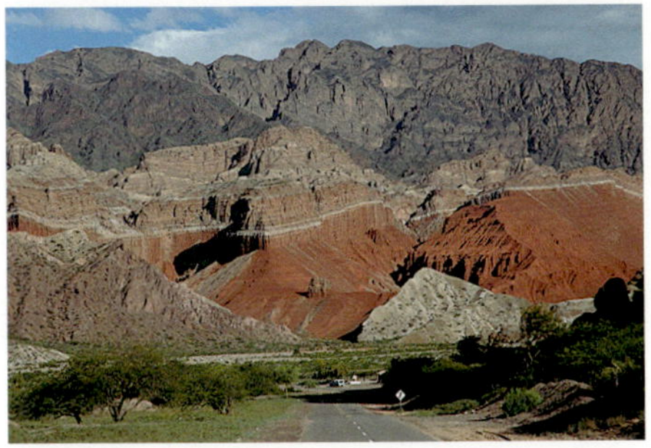

La Yesera.

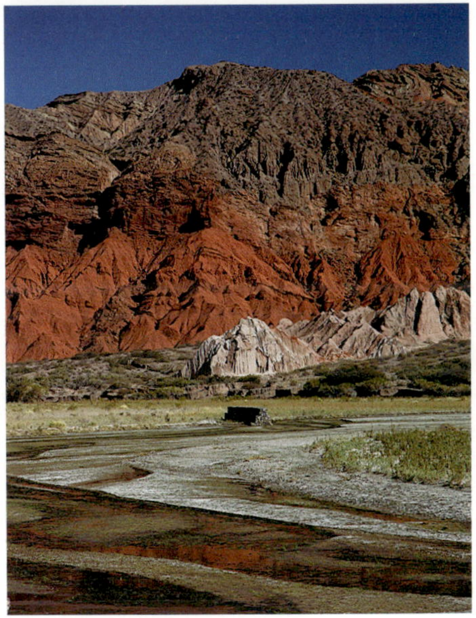

River Las Conchas.

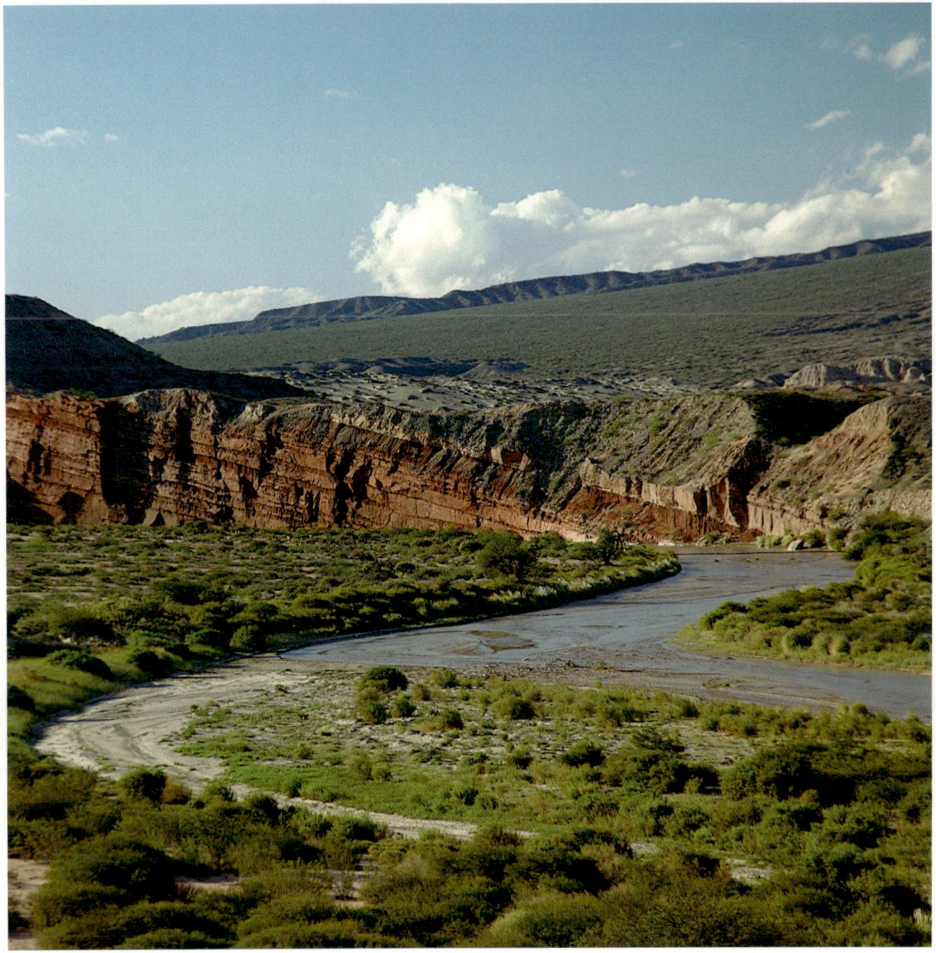

River Las Conchas.

The Lerma Valley has farms that produce tobacco, beans, fodder, vegetables, peppers and corn. There is cattle, and with it: the gaucho.

All agricultural activities in the valley are determined by two different seasons, winter is dry, with frosts and clear blue skies. Summers are rainy with thunder storms and hail at the beginning of the wet season.

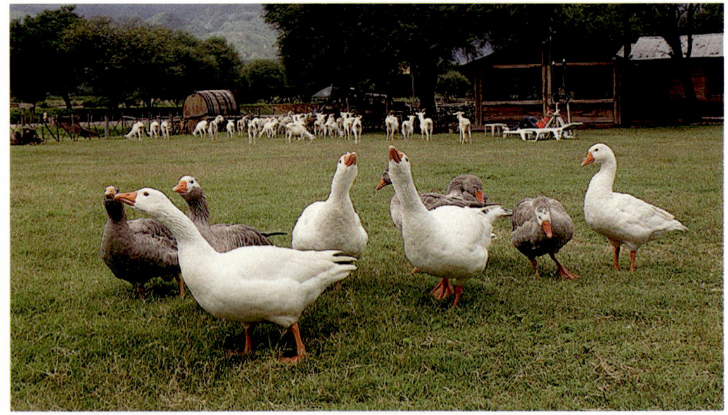

Geese at the Posta de las Cabras, a goat cheese farm.

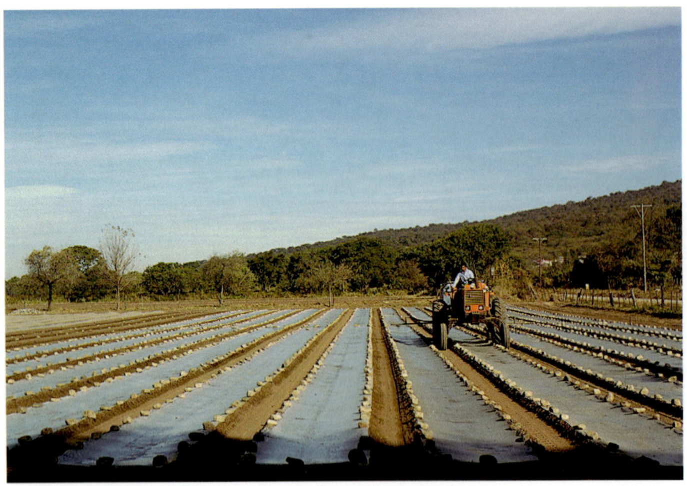

Virginia tobacco seedlings awaiting transplant.

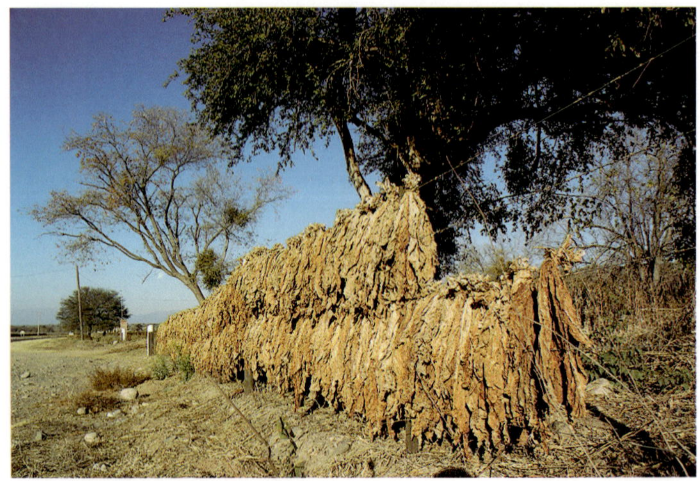

Criollo tobacco drying in the sun.

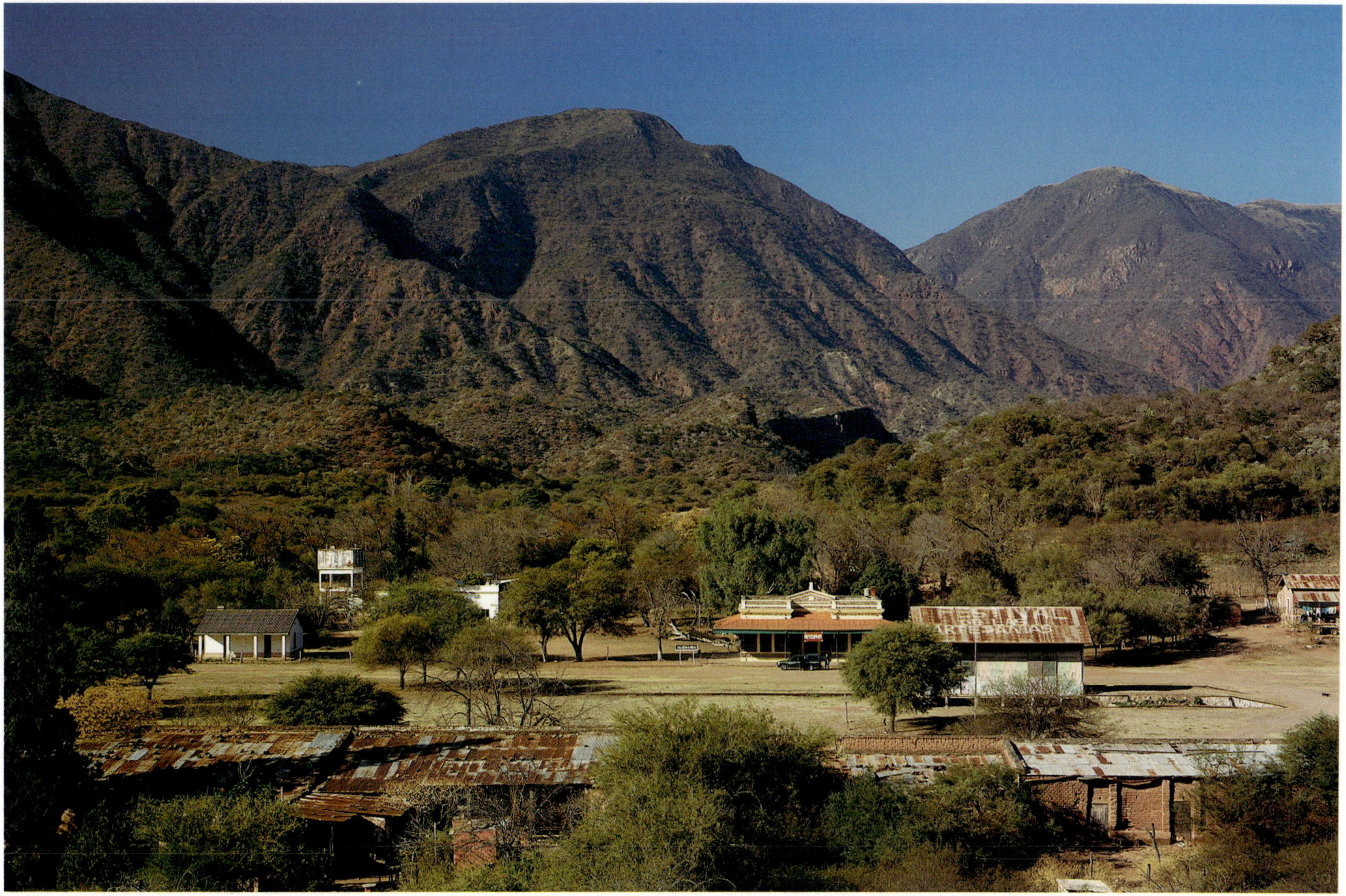

Alemania. This was the last station the train that went to the south of the Valle de Lerma reached. Then one went on to Cafayate on a red dust trail.

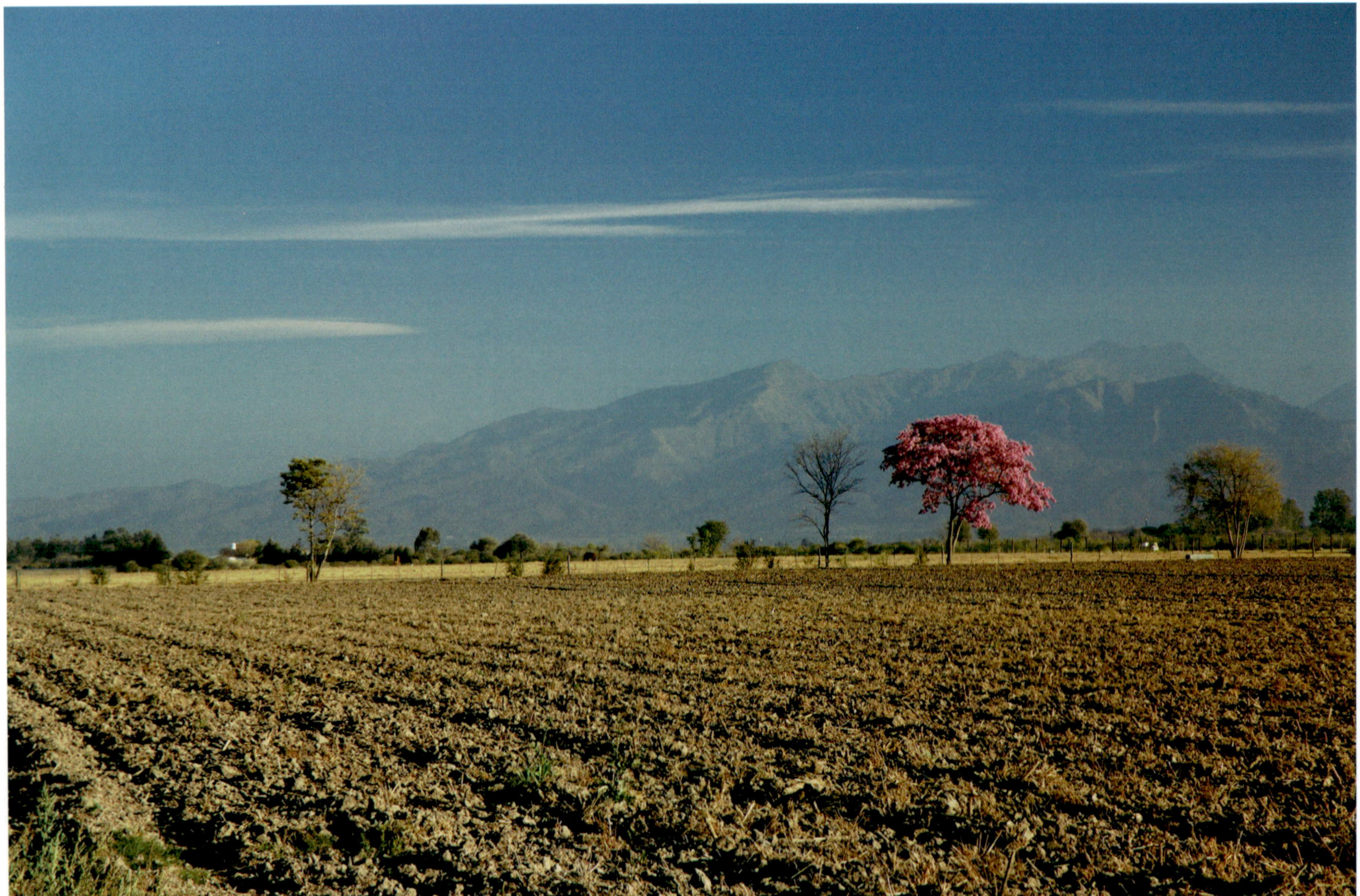

Lapacho (Tabebuia avellanedae) in Valle de Lerma.

Red peppers drying in the sun before grinding. Chicoana. (p. 35)

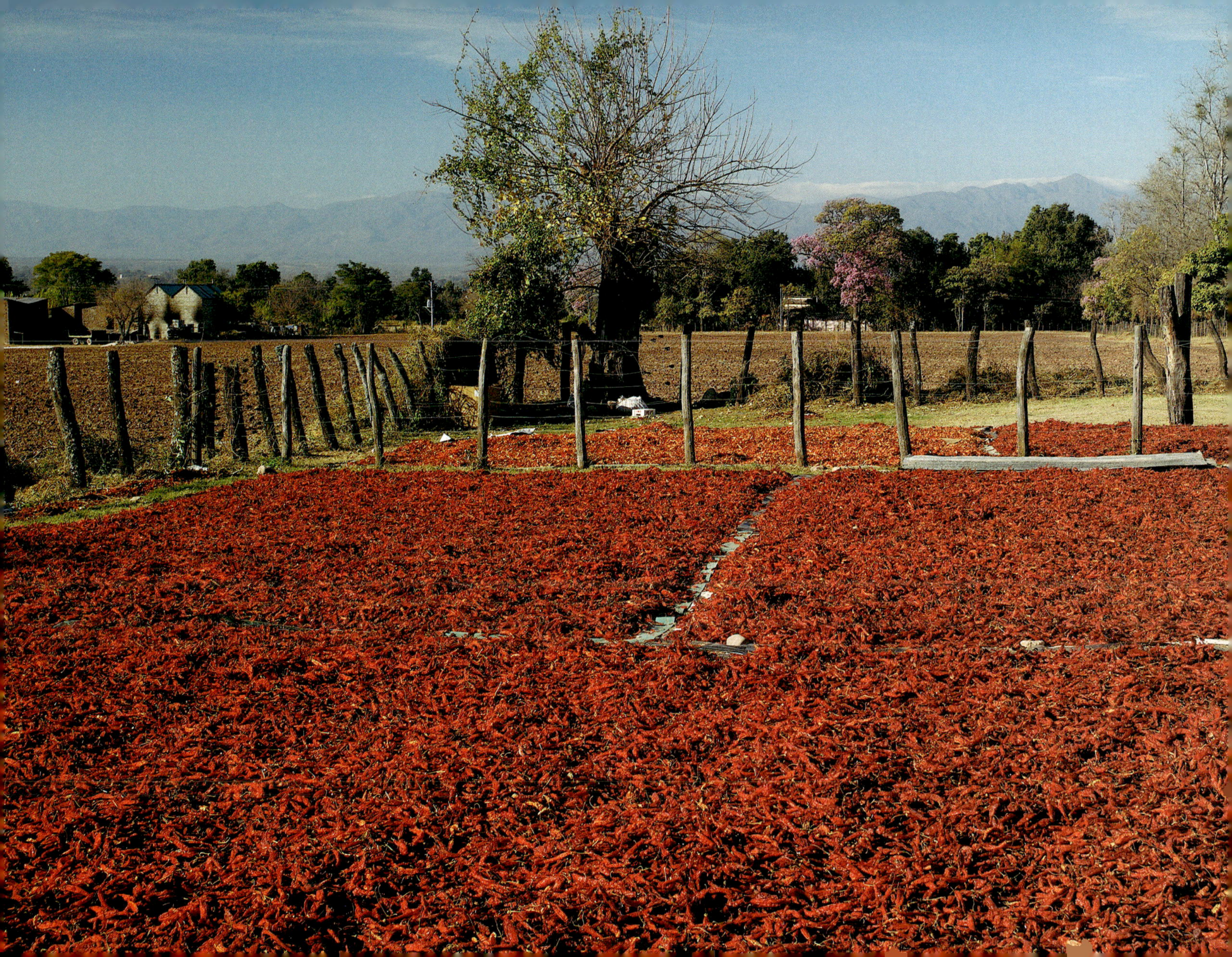

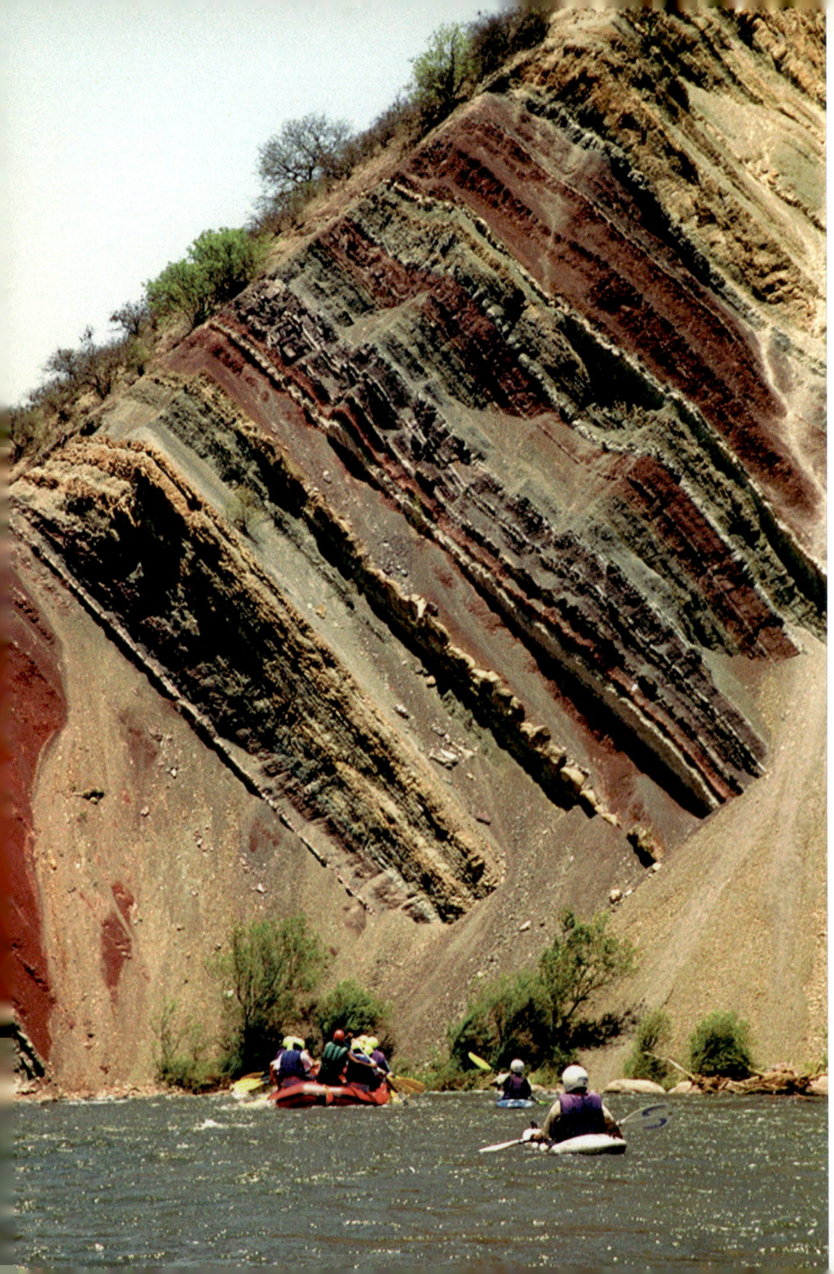

We drive by La Viña, from where one can go on to Guachipas and Pampa Grande, traveling through other mountains with unique scenery. The road cuts across Ampascachi, a farm on the roadside, that as many others of the area has its own village.

From Coronel Moldes we can take route 47, which will take us to the Cabra Corral Dam. This is a hydroelectric dam with a surface near to 11000 hectares. The Salta people enjoy this place fishing, sailing or practicing sports in the water.

Its waters flow south through the Juramento river, where in its rapids one can practice rafting; and in the calm waters slow down to catch ones breath and in the meantime look at the mountain wall on the side of the river where there are footprints of dinosaurs from the Cretaceous Period that have been fossilized there forever.

Rafting, Río Juramento.

Dinosaur footprints.

Sailing under the Cabra Corral Dam bridge.

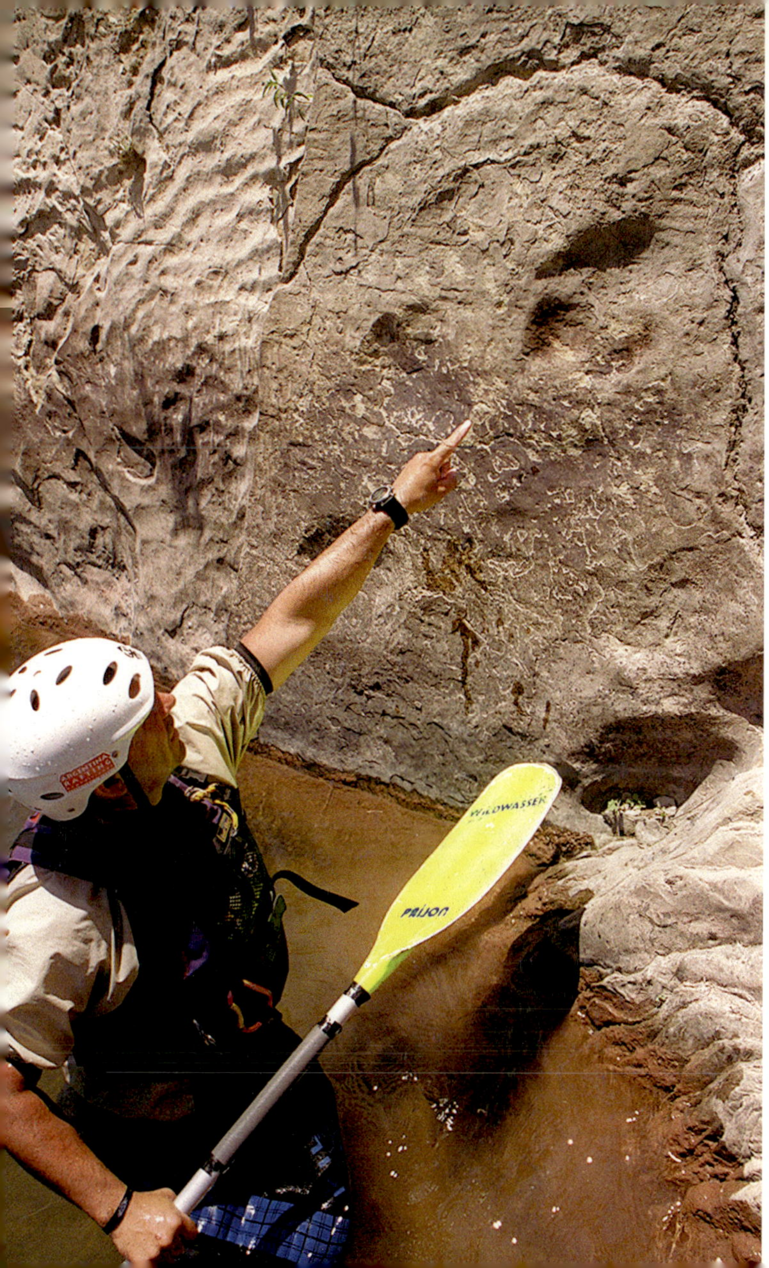

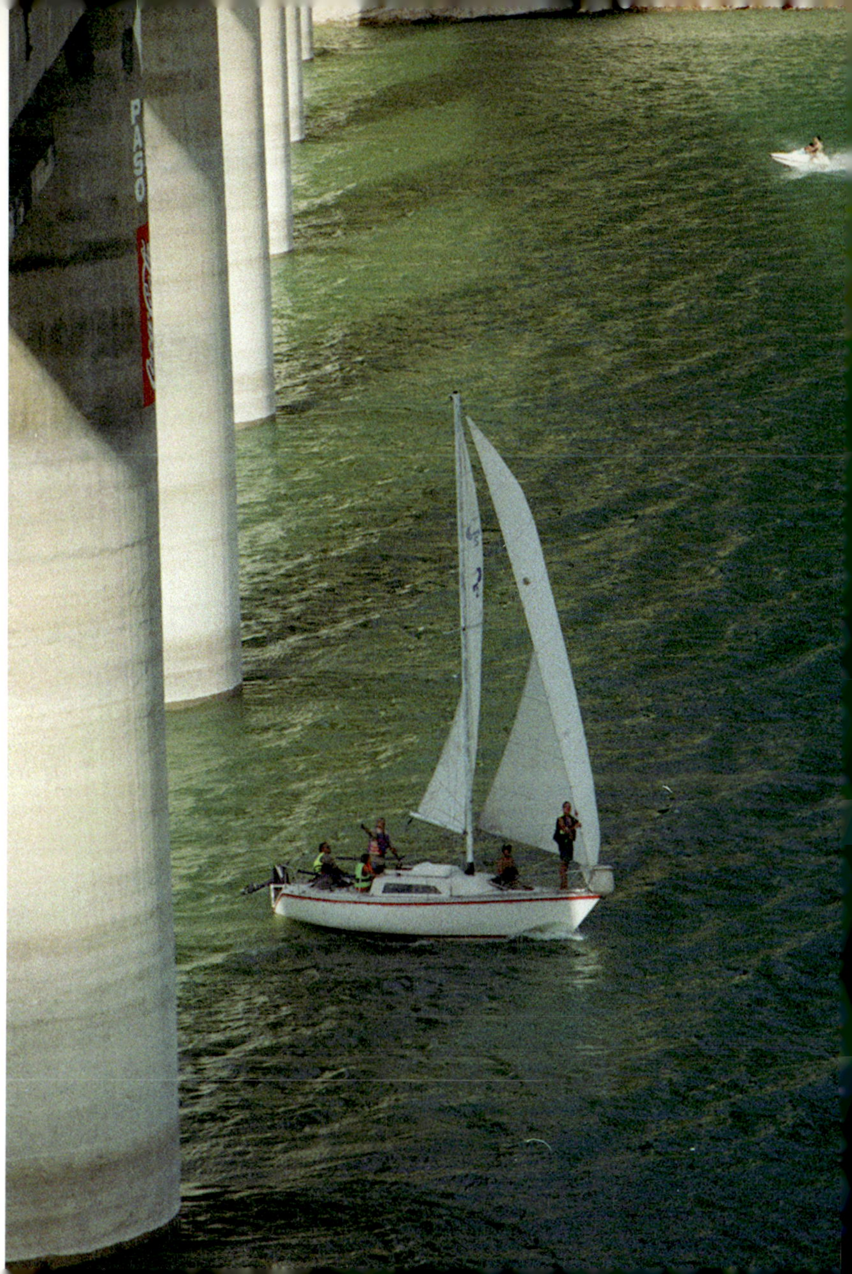
PASO

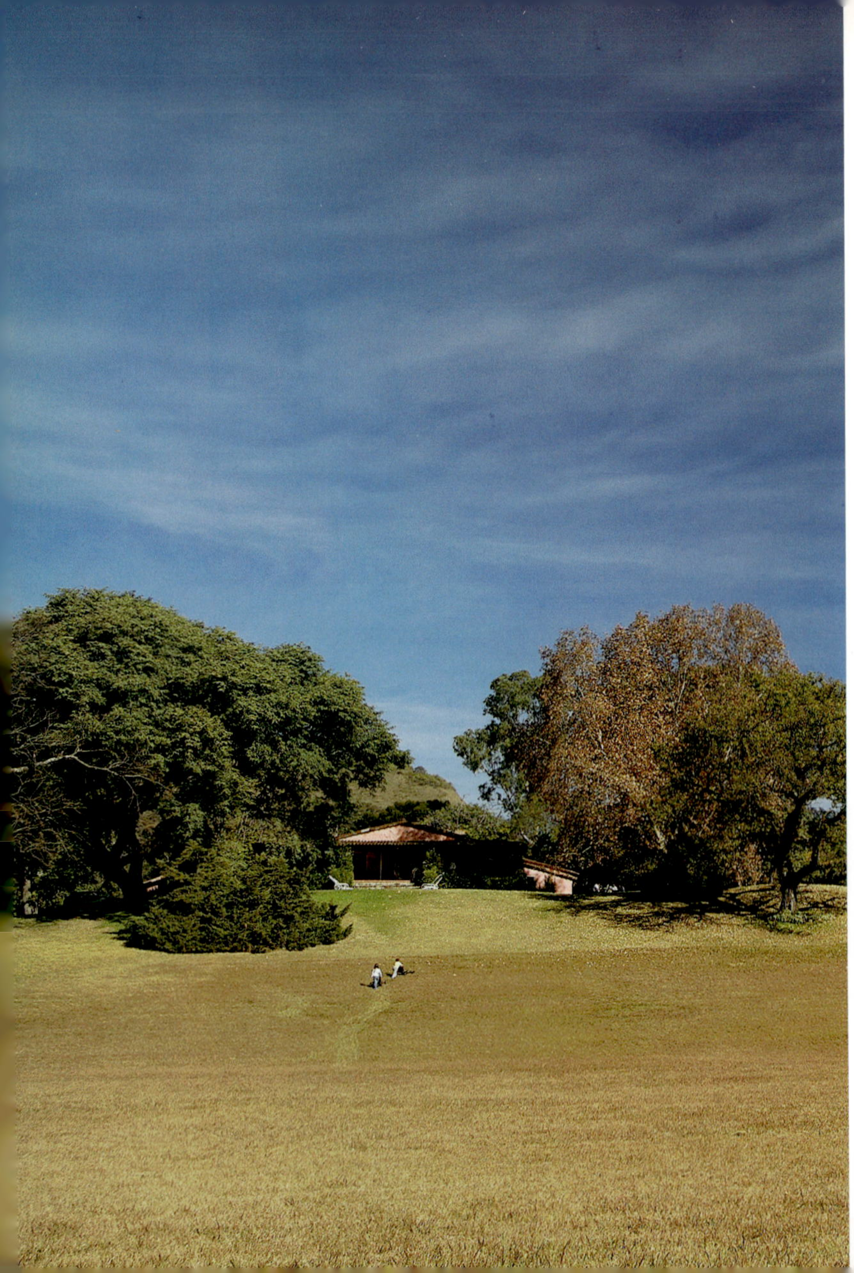

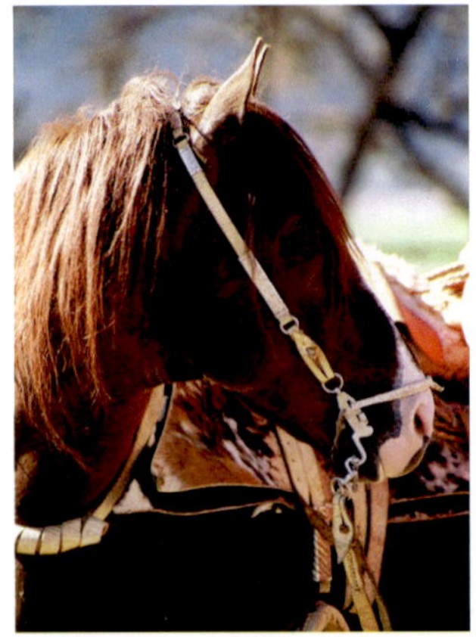

An inseparable part of all these farms is the duo created by the salteño gaucho and his stepping horse, or "caballo de paso". The rider uses leather boots, an embroidered suit, and a wide rimmed hat to protect himself from the northern sun, all together with its distinctive red poncho that made him seem, from a distance, like fire when charging on horse back, that is why during the independence fights against Spanish rule, the gaucho troops under the command of their chief, National Hero Martín Miguel de Güemes, they received the name of the Infernales (those from Hell).

The horse is saddled with the apero, the local saddle, and raw hide guardamontes to protect himself from the thorny under bush when gathering cattle. On party days they adorn themselves with silverware in the reins, whips and leather belt.

The origin of the Peruvian stepping horse goes back to the first Andalusian horses that arrived from Spain to Peru, and from there they came down on the Inca Road to northern Argentina, evolving during more than 300 years to become a unique breed. Its main characteristic is its walking mechanics that gives the rider a feeling of gliding along the road.

Main house at finca Los Los, Chicoana.

Gaucho with Peruvian stepping horse in a Valle de Lerma finca.

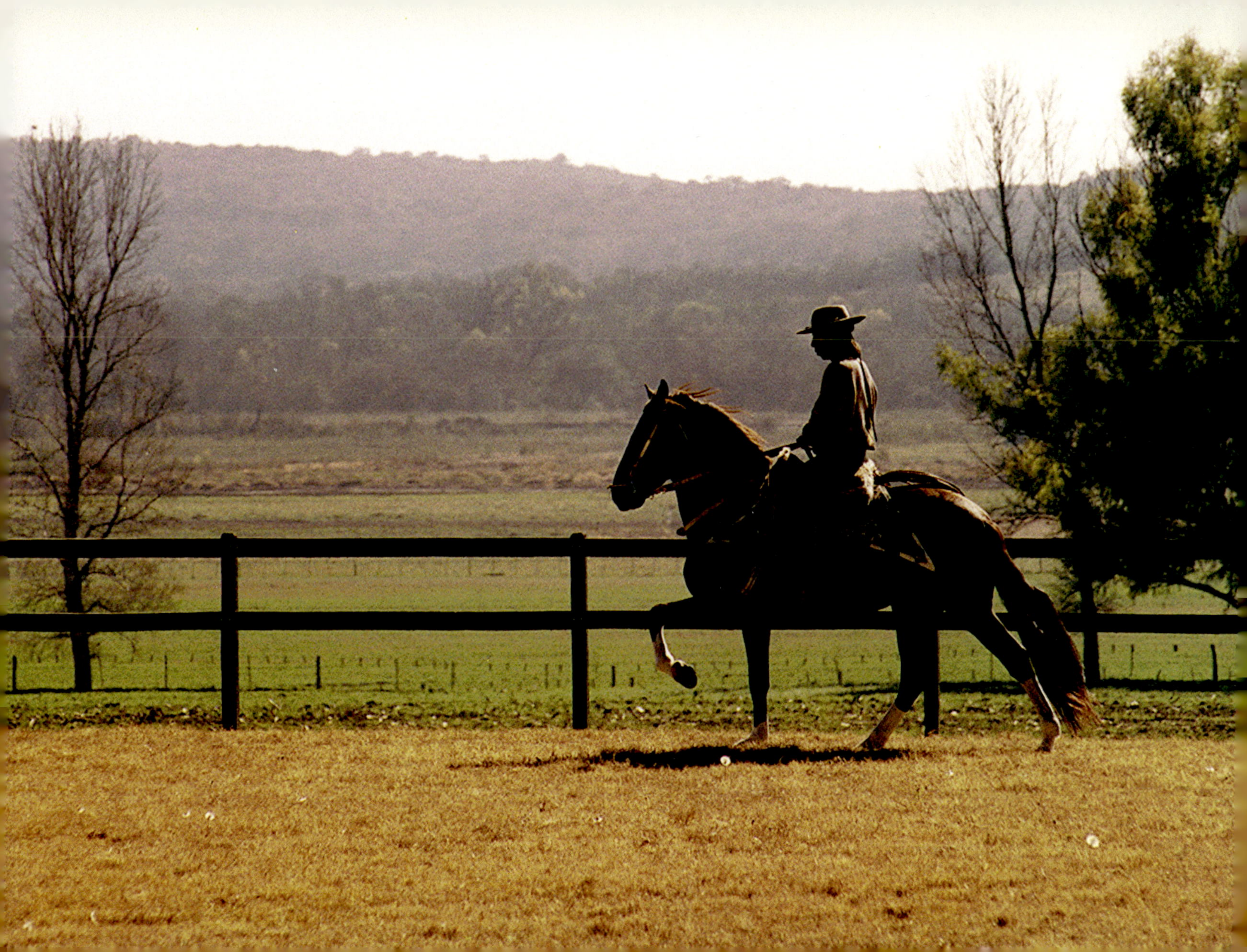

At the end of the day, the city of Salta awaits at he foot of the San Bernardo Hill. Colonial style shows its spirit, since the families of Spanish origin left their seal.

Funded in 1482, it had a strategic location during many years since it was located on the road that joined Peru with the port of Buenos Aires.

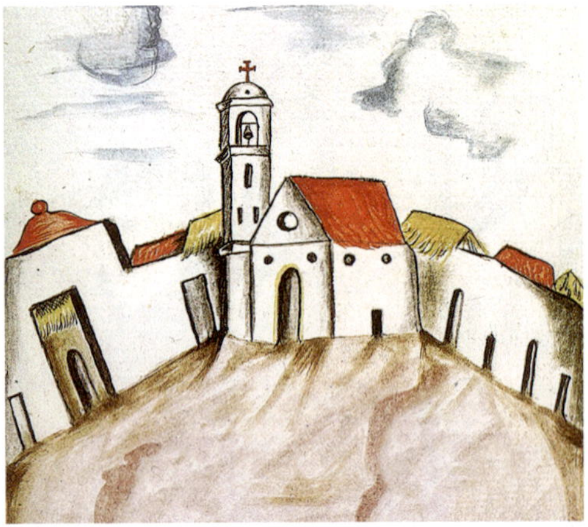

Martínez Compañón (1735–1797), Chapel.

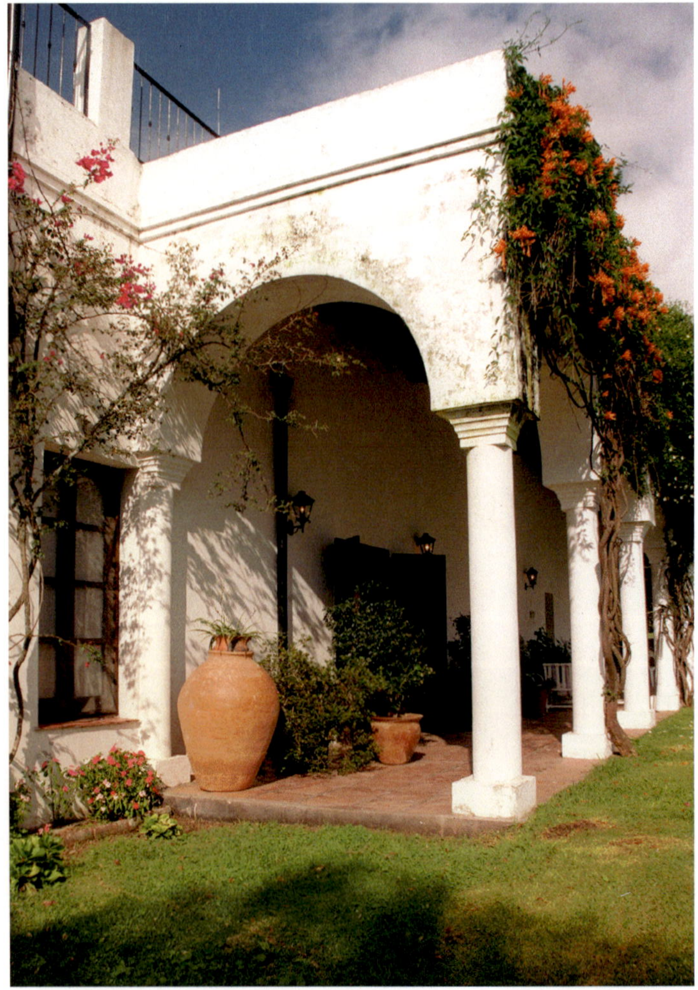

Colonial veranda in the main house of El Manantial del Milagro ,a finca very near Salta.

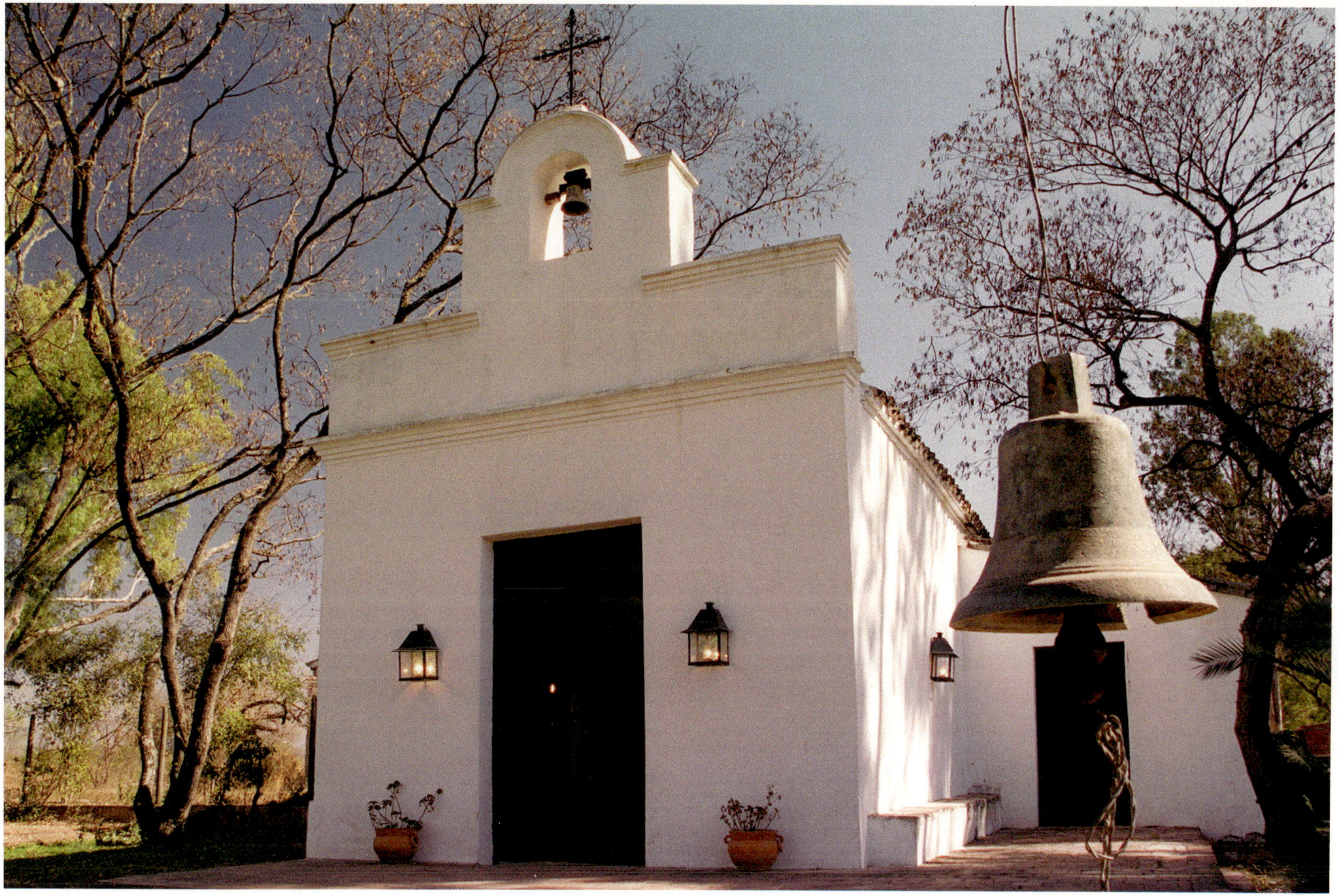

Chapel in a finca.

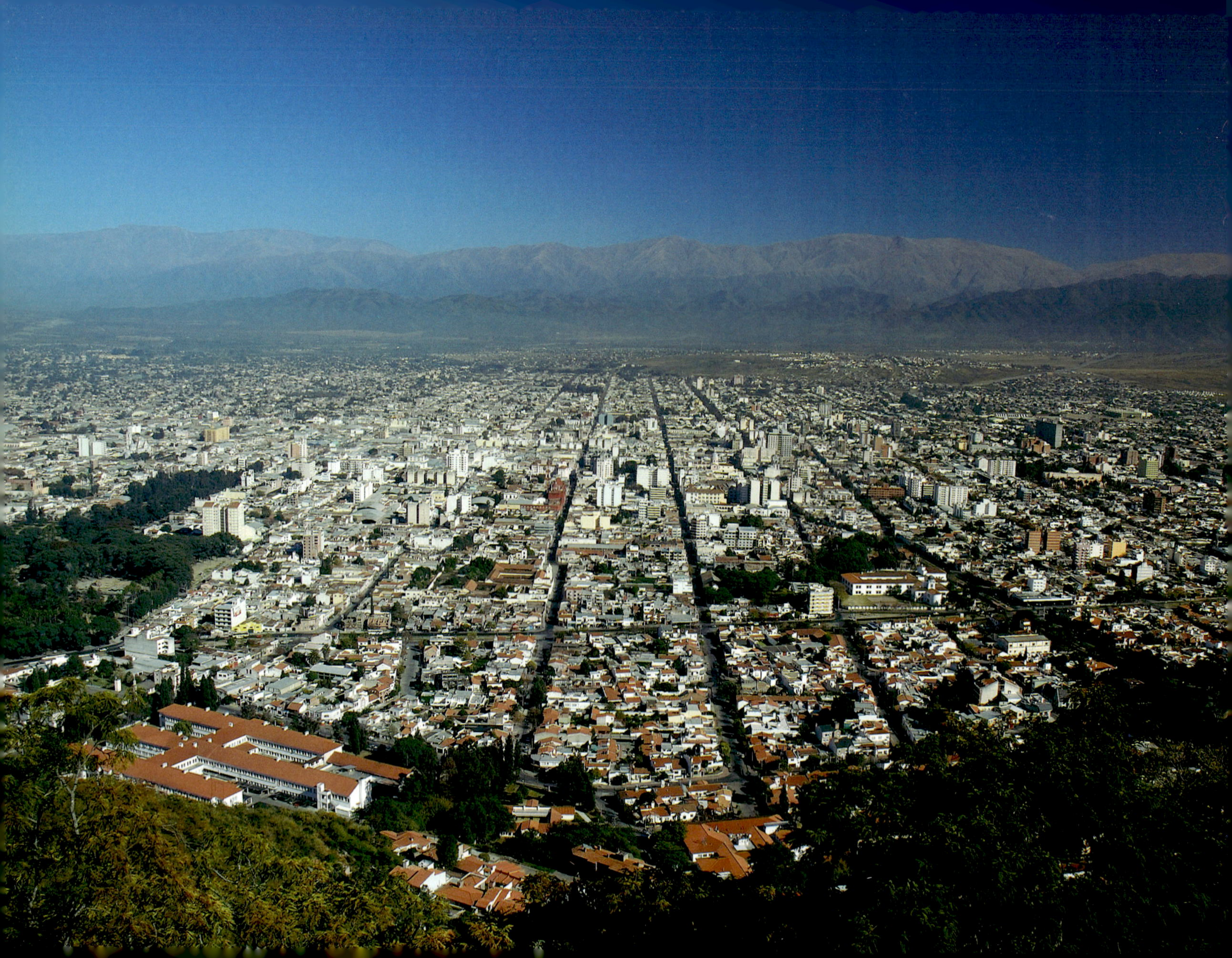

City of Salta and San Lorenzo

The City of Salta is located at the north end of the Valle de Lerma at 1187 m.a.s.l. (3894 ft). Founded by Don Hernando de Lerma in 1582, under the orders of Viceroy Francisco Toledo, it is one of the oldest cities in Argentina. For the most part its architecture is Spanish colonial, but styles changed throughout the years, so there are buildings with a notorious Italian, Moorish or French influence. One only has to walk around with open eyes looking for details. When downtown, looking up we will discover iron and wood Spanish balconies.

Trees line many streets; like the pink lapacho *(Tabebuia avellanedae)* that blooms in September or the jacaranda or tarco, bursting with purple flowers in November, just to name two species.

View of the city of Salta from the San Bernardo Hill. The Andes rise behind.

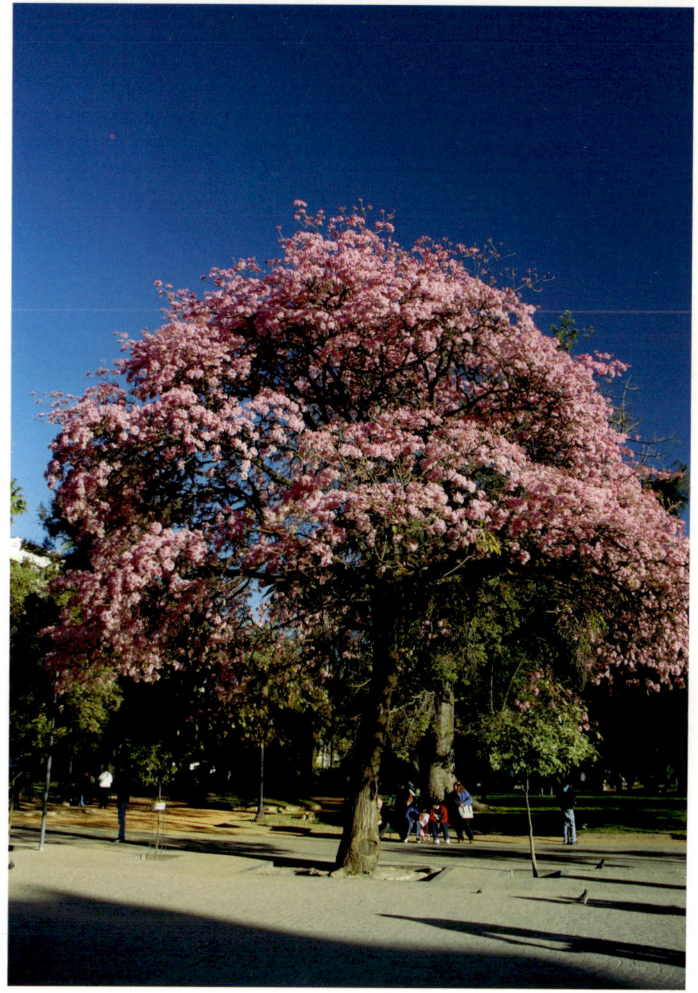

Pink lapacho (Tabebuia avellanedae) in the Plaza 9 de Julio.

Plaza 9 de Julio stands at the center of the city, with palm trees, a gazebo, and the monument to General Arenales, who was governor of Salta and fought in the Independence Wars against Spain.

The plaza's south side faces the Cabildo, or town hall. The original building was built in the late 1500's, and reconstructed later in 1676. It used to have 17 arches above and 19 on the ground floor, and is one of the oldest buildings in the city. Today it houses two Museums; one explores the city's historical past and the other its colonial art. From the balcony, one can get a good view of the Plaza.

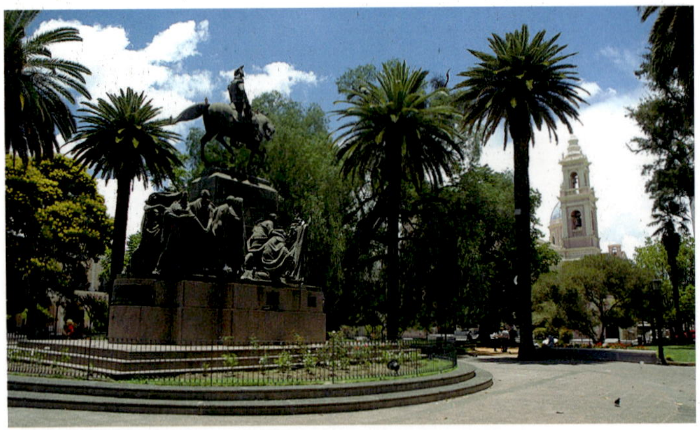

Plaza 9 de Julio. Monument to General Arenales, an Independence hero.

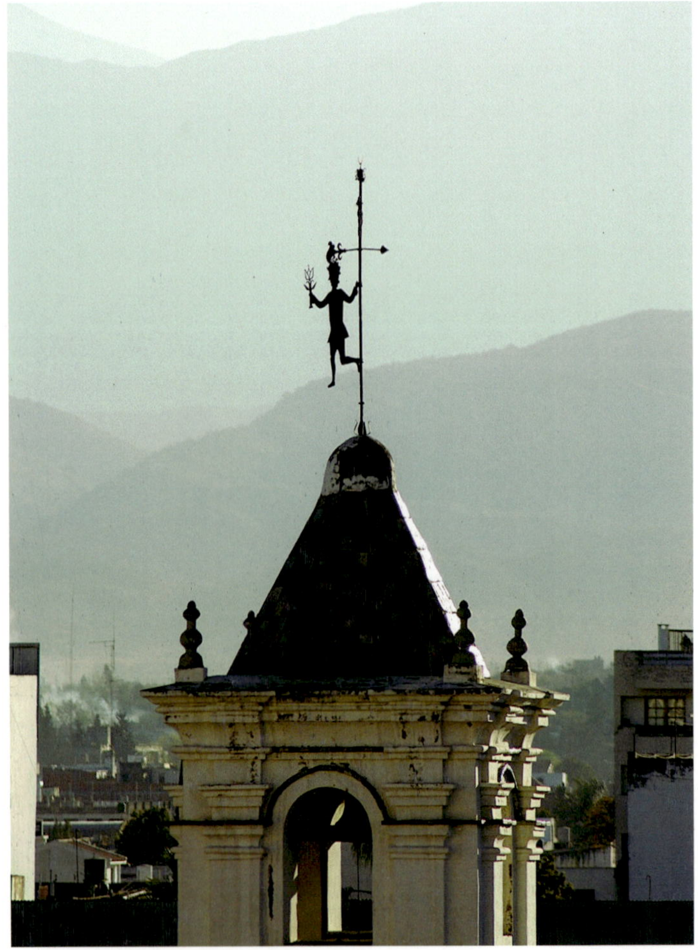

Cast iron weathercock on the top of the Cabildo. The page is popularly known as the "Cabildo's little devil".

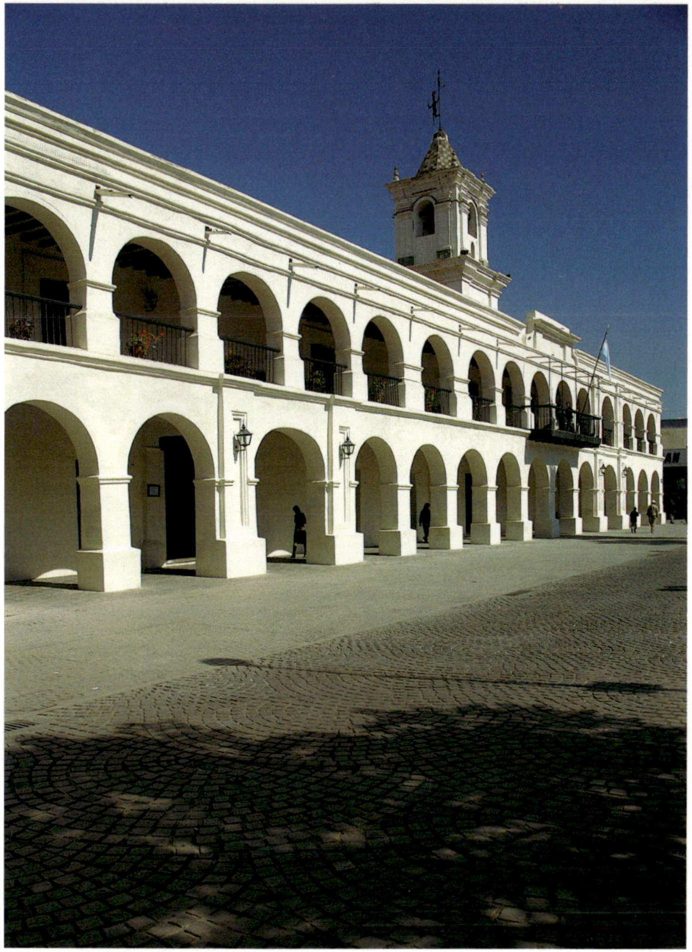

Salta Cabildo. The first building was constructed between 1586 and 1593.

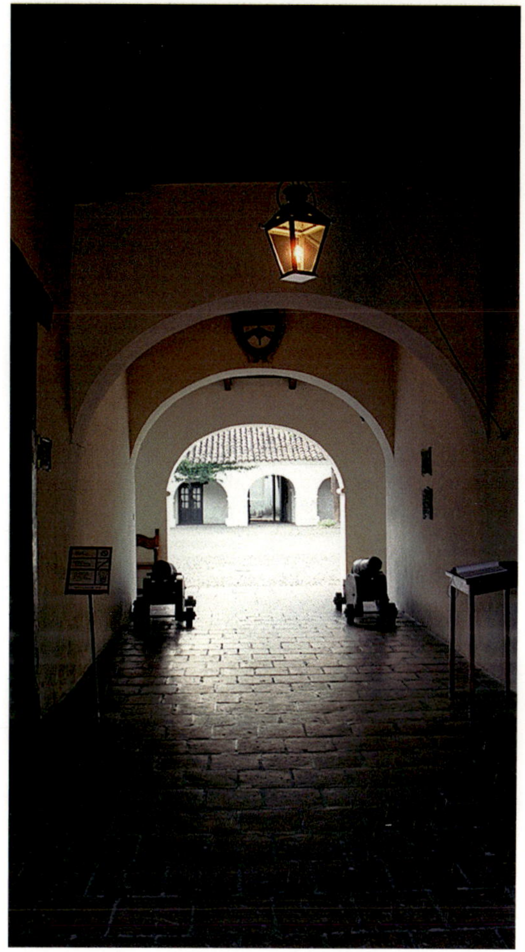

Cabildo entrance. Archway that leads on to the main patio.

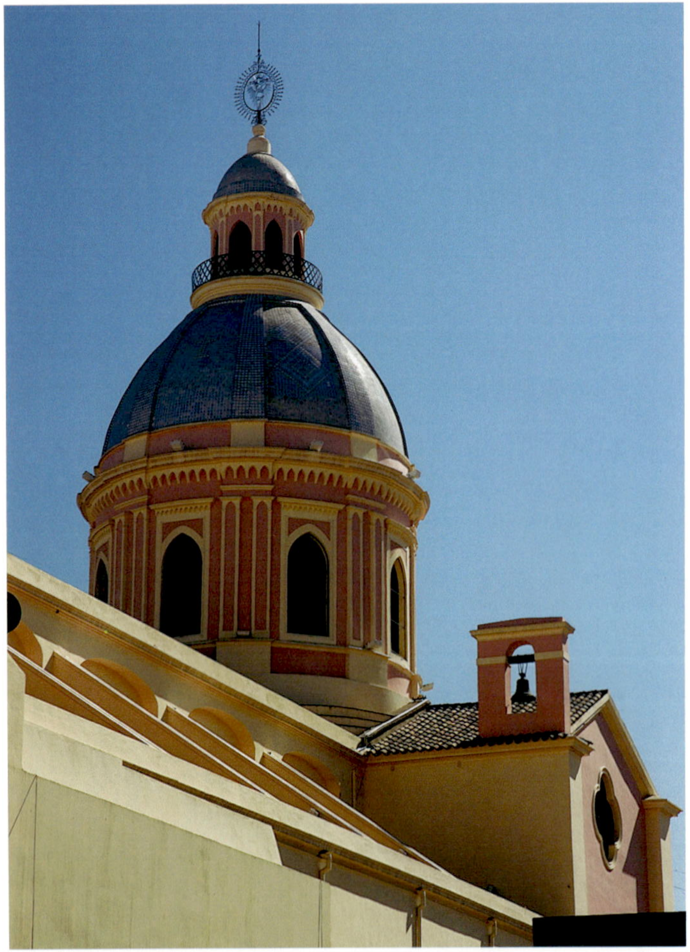

Dome on the Salta Cathedral. A project of Fray Luis Georgi, of the Italian School of Architecture.

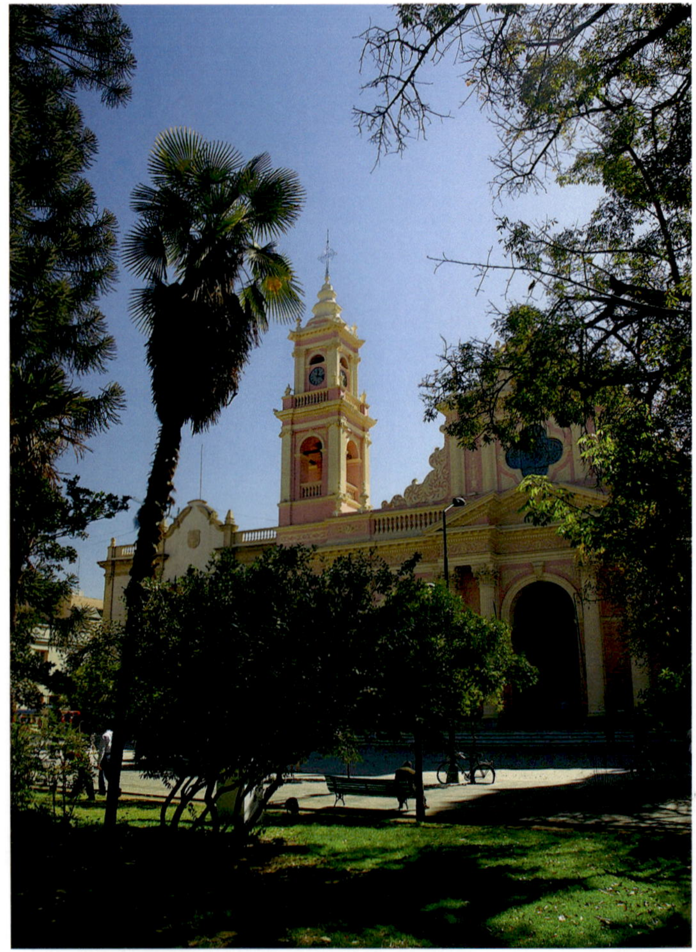

The Cathedral's belfry seen from the main plaza.

The Cathedral is on the north side of the square; the first temple was built just after the city's birth, but was consecrated as a Cathedral later in 1878. Finally near the beginning of the 20th century, all details were finished. Inside we find the images of the Señor and Virgen del Milagro, whom it is said, protect the city since 1692, year when these images were taken out in a procession through the city, after an earthquake. This religious tradition is repeated every 15th of September.

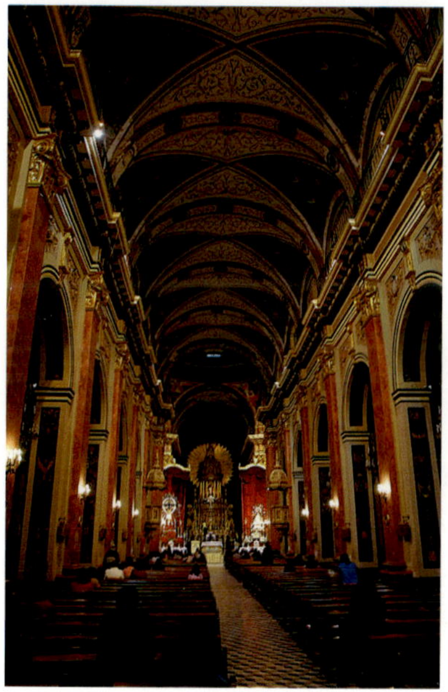

Interior of the Cahtedral. On either side of the altar stand the images of the Señor and Virgen del Milagro.

Señor del Milagro, an image from the second half of he 16th century, sent to this Cathedral from Spain.

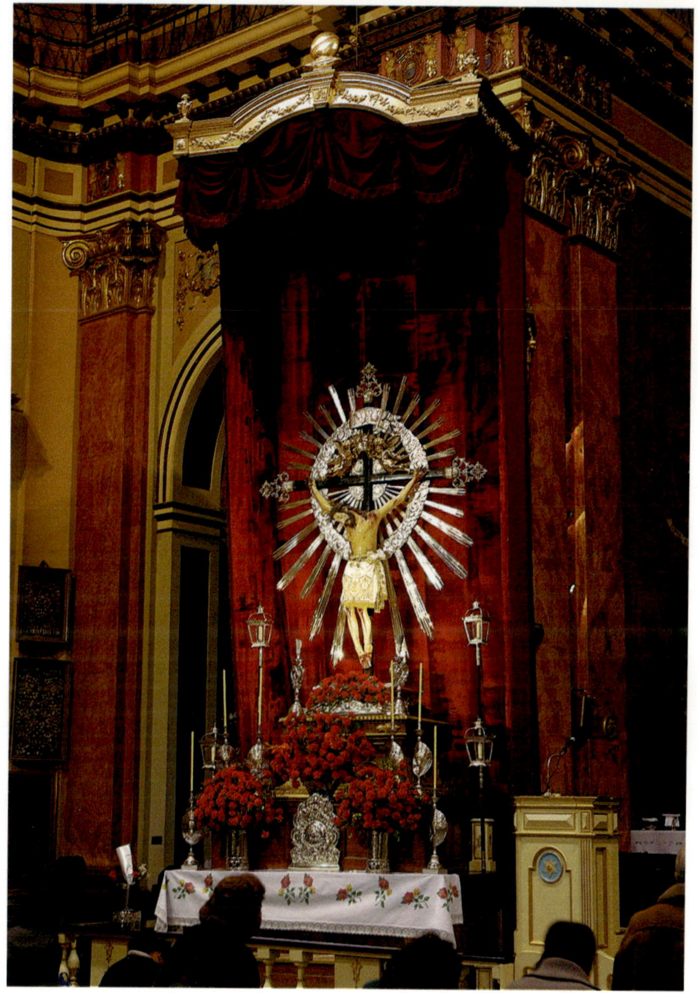

Surrounding the plaza there are arcades under which we find museums, coffee shops, and places to sit down and enjoy an empanada or a tamal.

The MAAM – High Mountain Archeological Museum-takes us 500 years back in time into the Inca culture.

To stroll around this plaza is essential when visiting this city.

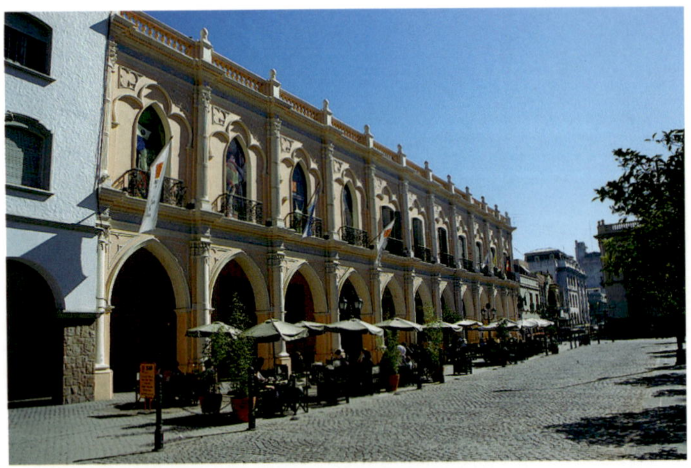

Arches facing the Plaza 9 de Julio. Behind them we find the MAAM (Museum of High Mountain Archeology)

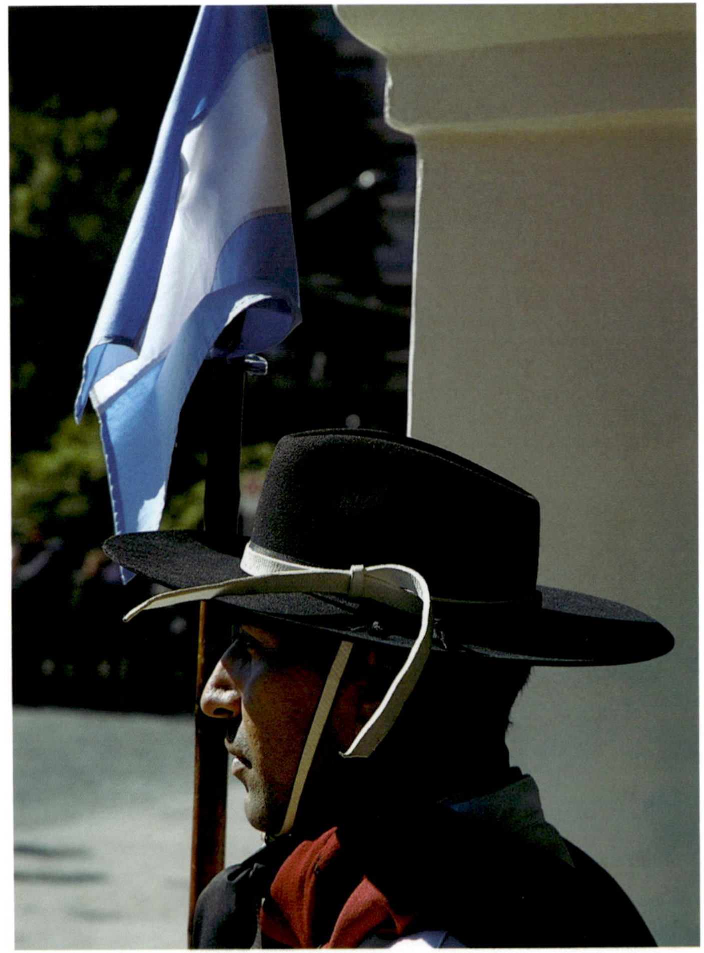

Gaucho during a Change of Guard.

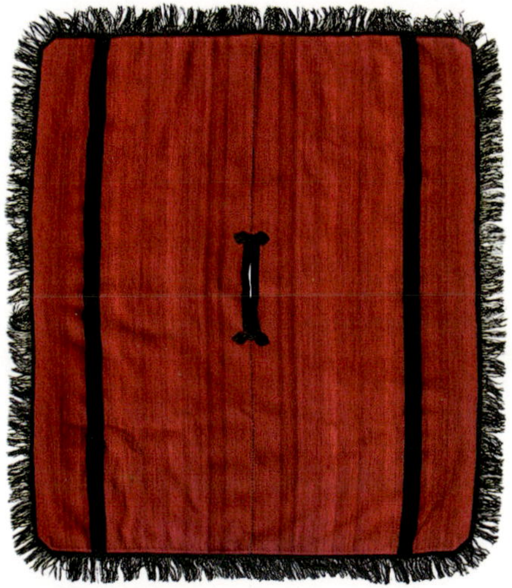

Poncho from Salta, made in Molinos.

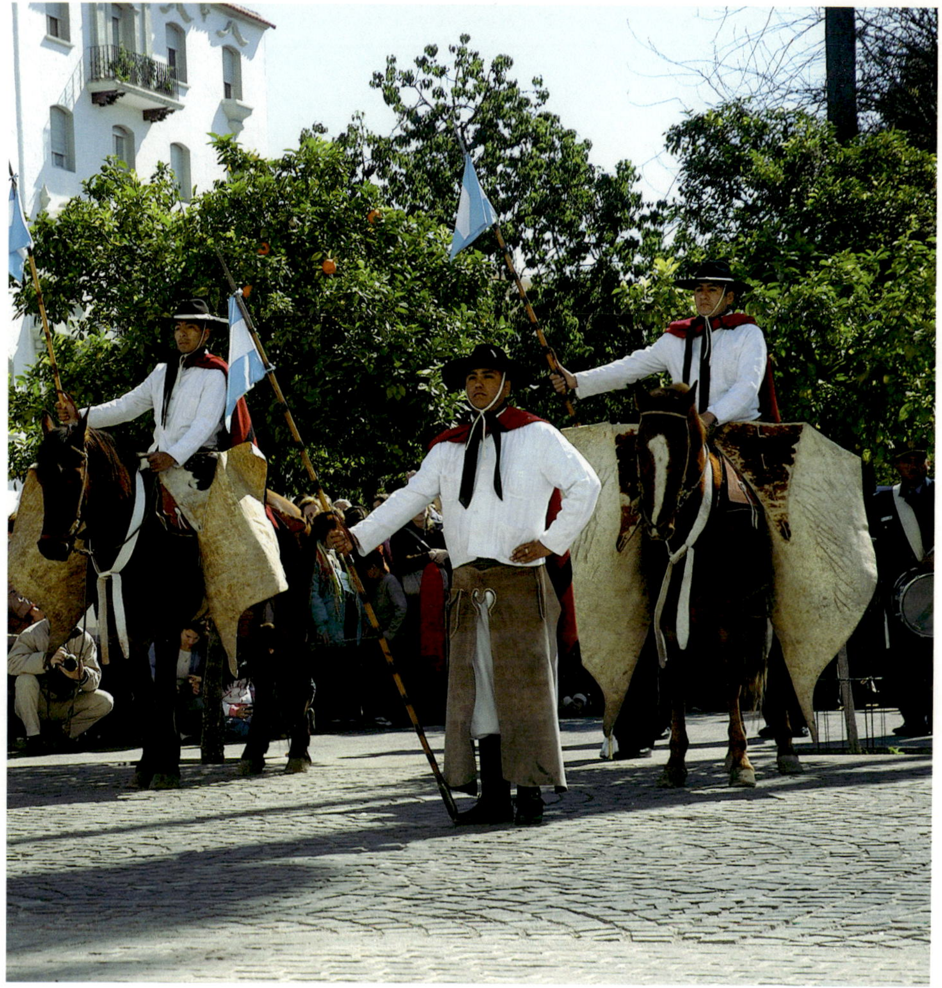

Change of Guard in front of the Cabildo.

Walking down Caseros Street, we pass the Casa de Uriburu, a house built in 1773, a good example of colonial architecture. The imposing Church and Convent of San Francisco rises a few meters ahead. The building we see today is an 18th century reconstruction, directed by Friar Valverde. The tower, designed by Friar Georgi, was inaugurated in 1882 and is considered the highest belfry in South America.

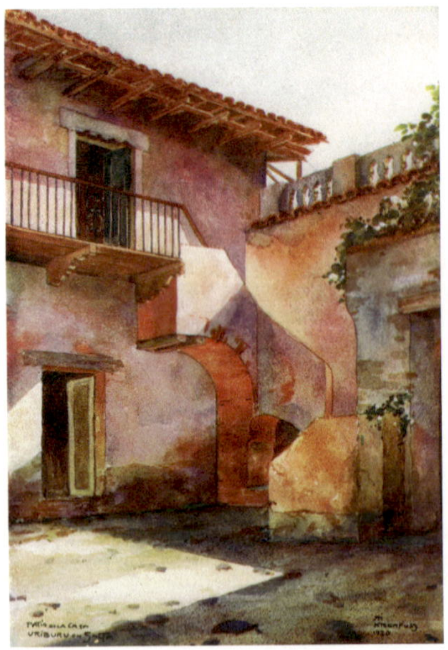

Patio in Uriburu's house, Juan Kronfuss (1872–1944)

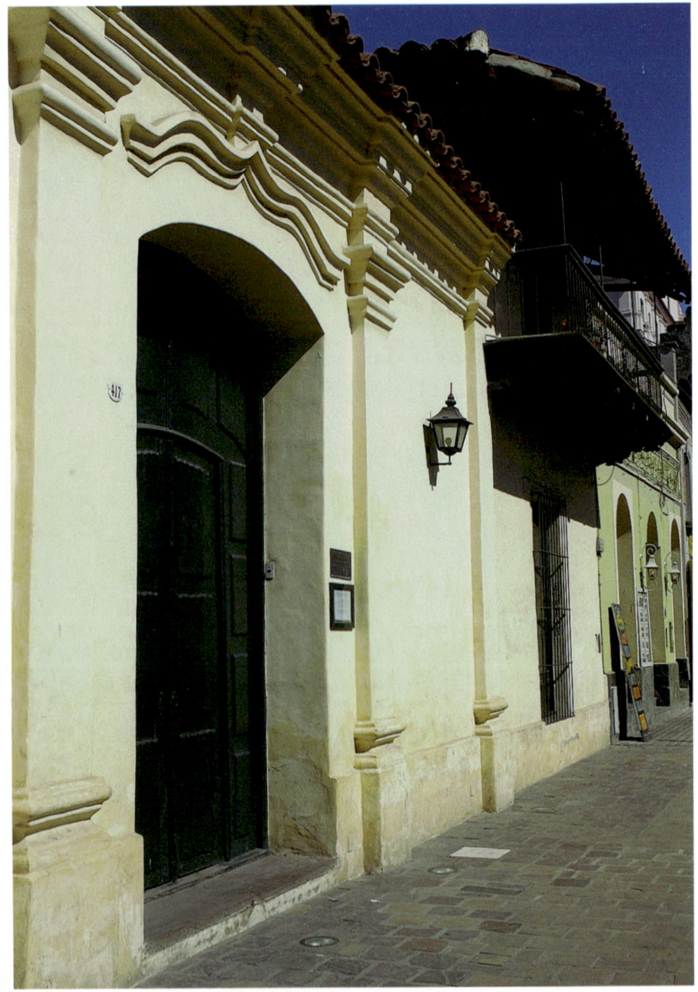

Front of the Casa de Uriburu. Front door and wooden colonial balcony.

San Francisco Church and Convent.
The first church was built just after the city's foundation. The one we see here was desiged by Fray Luis Georgi (photo left) and constructed by Fransico Righetti (1882).

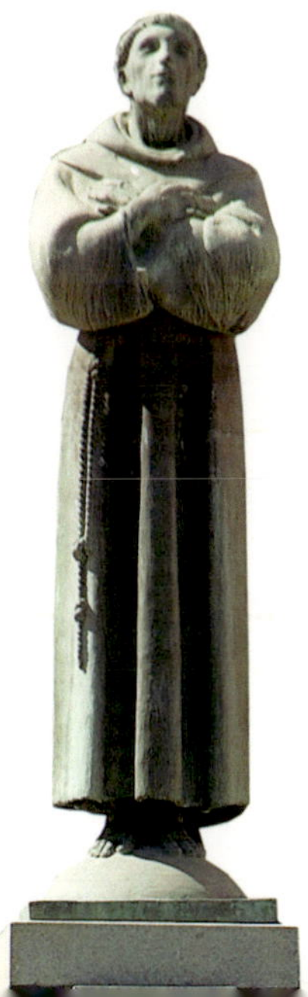

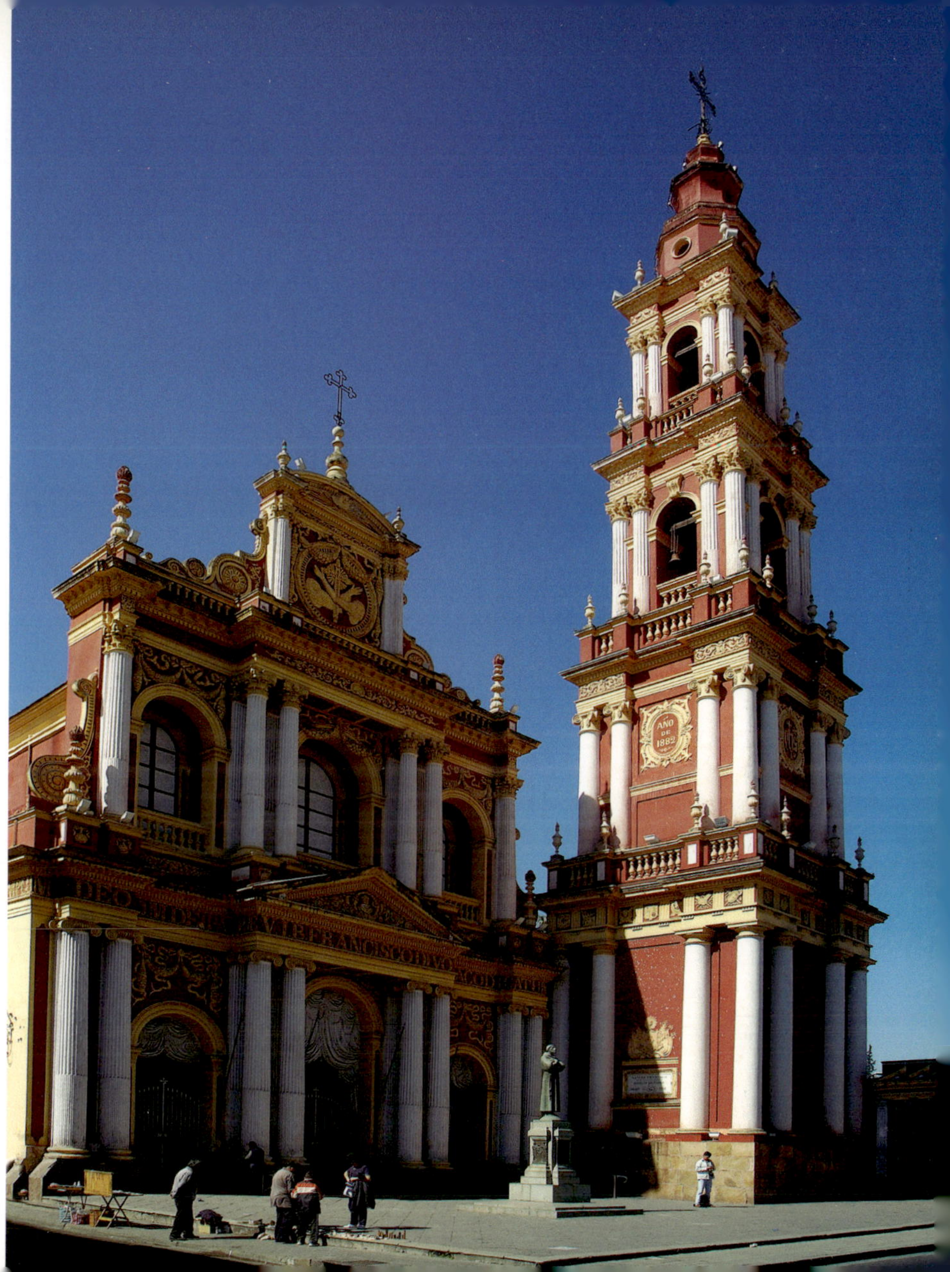

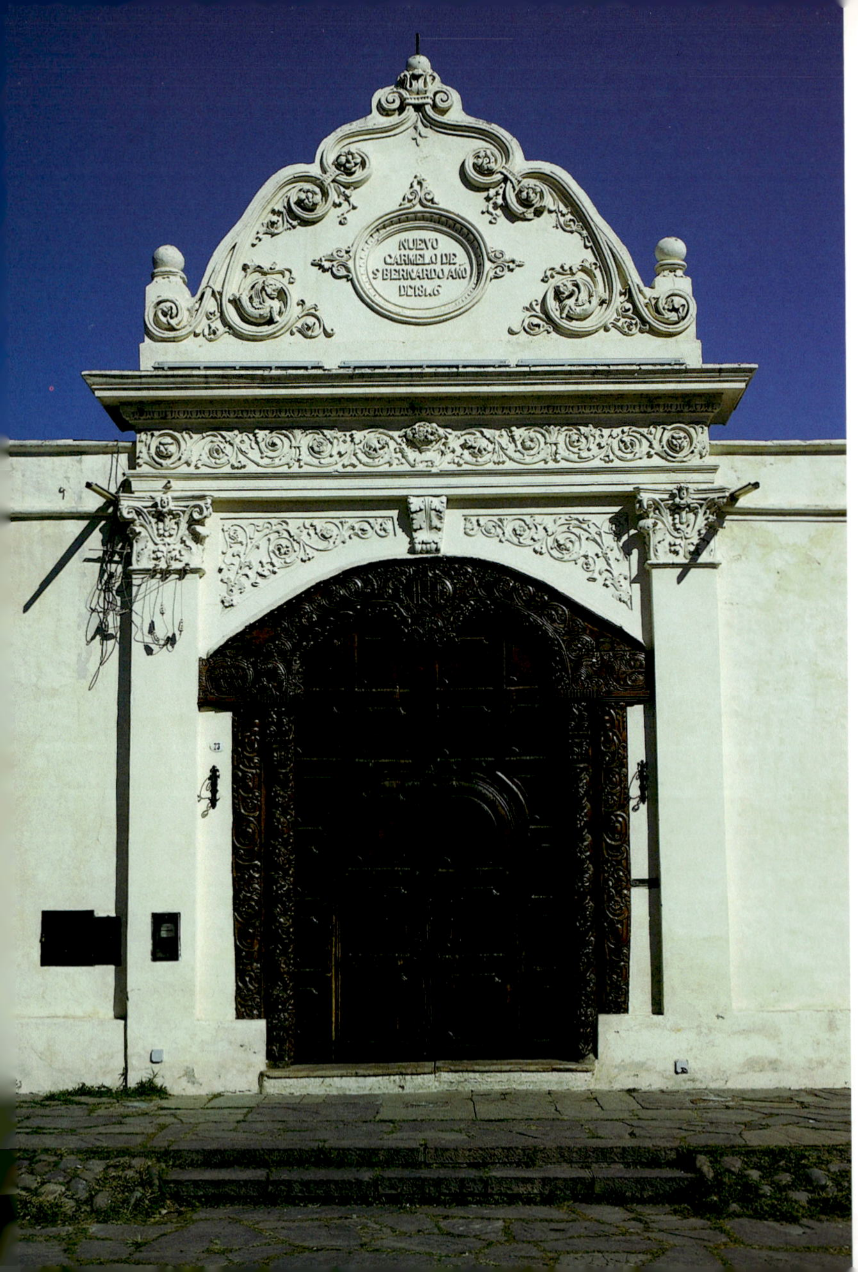

The San Bernardo Convent is one of the most famous postcards of the city. Since early 1800's it is a cloistered convent of the Carmelo Order, whose nuns are called "Carmelitas". Its huge door, made by native artists near 1762, is carved in wood and contrasts with the otherwise stark exterior of the building, originally designed as the city's first hospital.

Carved wood door on the front of the San Bernardo Convent. Dating from 1762, it was offered to the Convent as dowry by a family whose daughter was entering the convent.

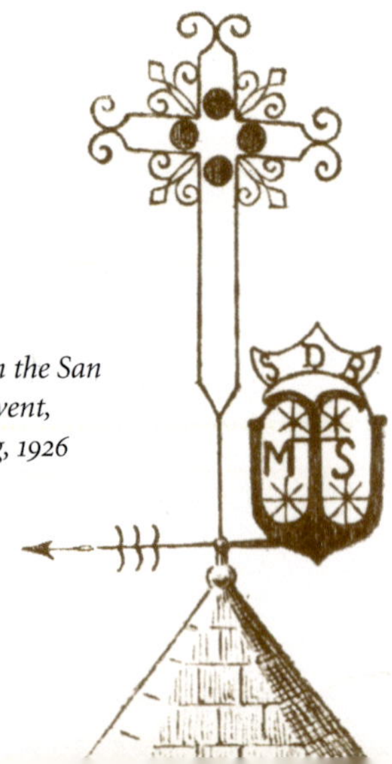

Weathercock in the San Bernardo Convent, Jorge Augspurg, 1926

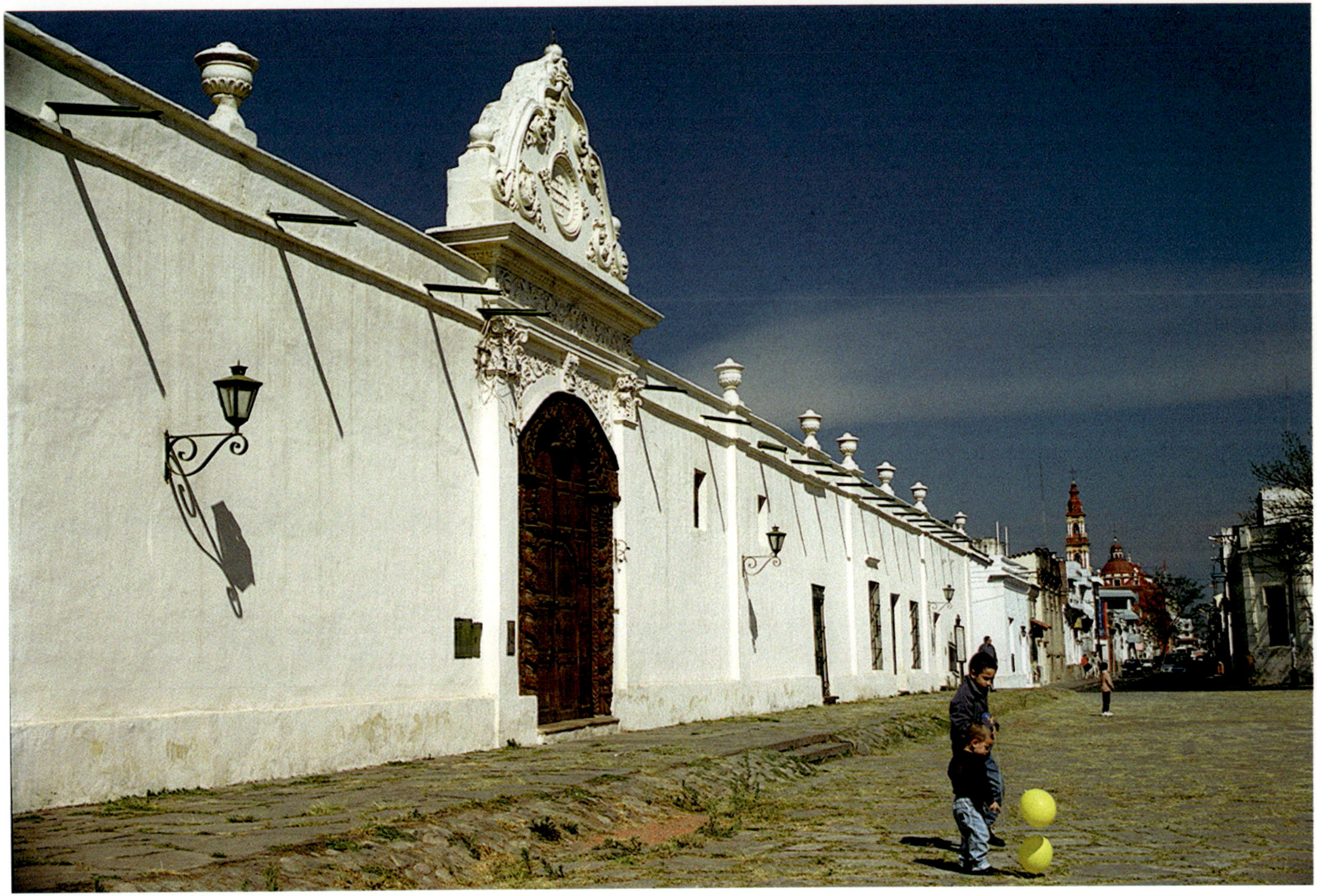

Front of the convent and Caseros Street.

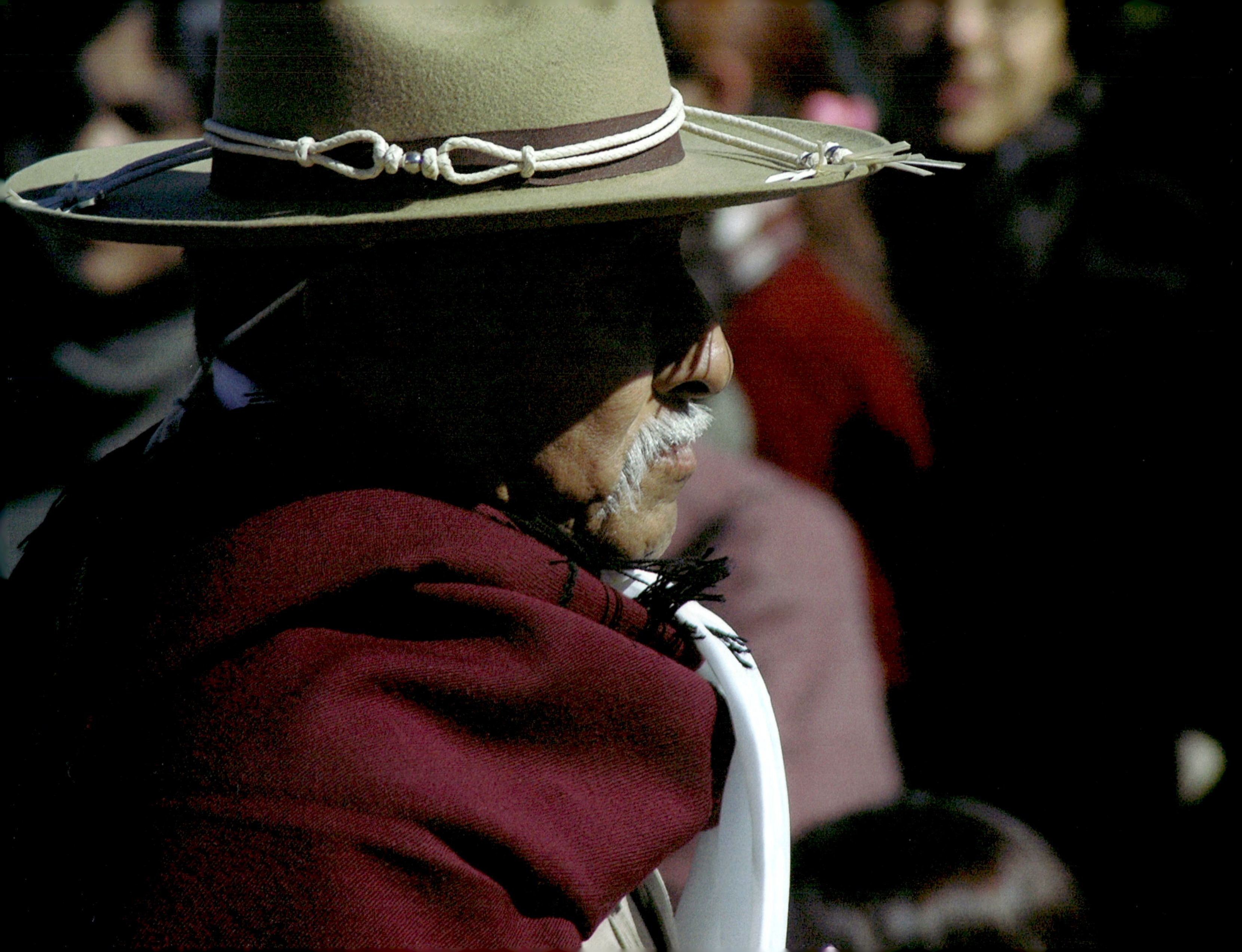

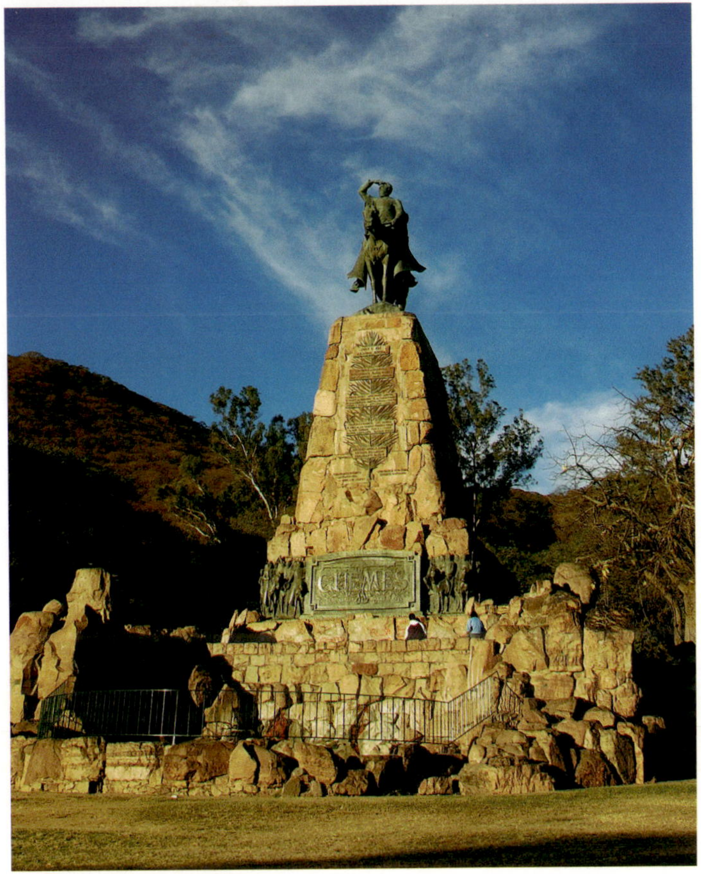

General Martín Miguel de Güemes Monument, at the foot of the San Bernardo Hill. (1961)

A raw hide craft decorates a gaucho hat during a parade held on June 17th to honor the memory of General Güemes. (p. 54)

On weekends, an artisan fair is set up on Balcarce Street, near the train station. And on the same street the old warehouses have turned into coffee shops or restaurants where one can have a drink or a good meal and enjoy a folklore show. To purchase native arts and crafts, one can go to the Mercado Artesanal, set inside a lovely old colonial farm house.

Don Martín Miguel de Güemes, the local gaucho hero that fought in the Wars of Independence, has his monument at the foot of the San Bernardo Hill. The base is made with rocks from that hill; its bronze statue and embossments were made by Victor Gariño.

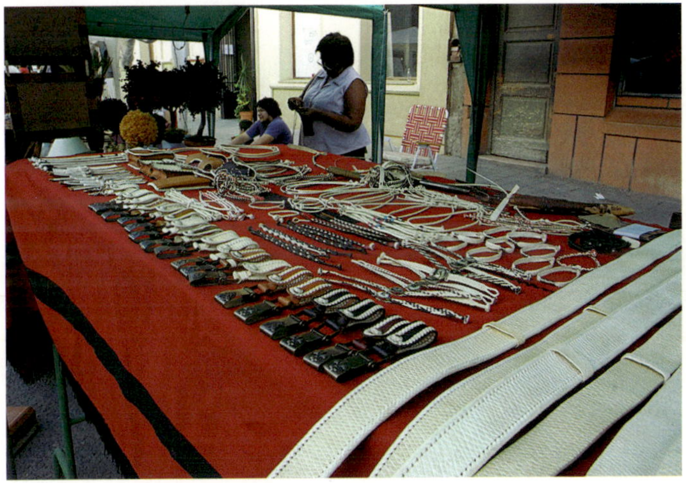

On Sunday's an artisan fare takes place on Balcarce Street, near the train station.

San Lorenzo is only a few minutes away from town. Originally a summer place, today it has become a fashionable residential area where stone colonial houses, all of them with wide verandas, are surrounded by gardens that thrive in this weather. This vegetation is possible here due to the damp microclimate of the village. Its main streets are shaded by seibo trees *(Erithryna sp.)* that are covered with bright red flowers in October .

This is a great starting point for a trek along the many small gorges hidden under huge trees in the surrounding mountains.

There are also many possibilities one can enjoy all year round; like horseback riding, a long bicycle ride, exploring places on a four track or daring to fly with a paraglide.

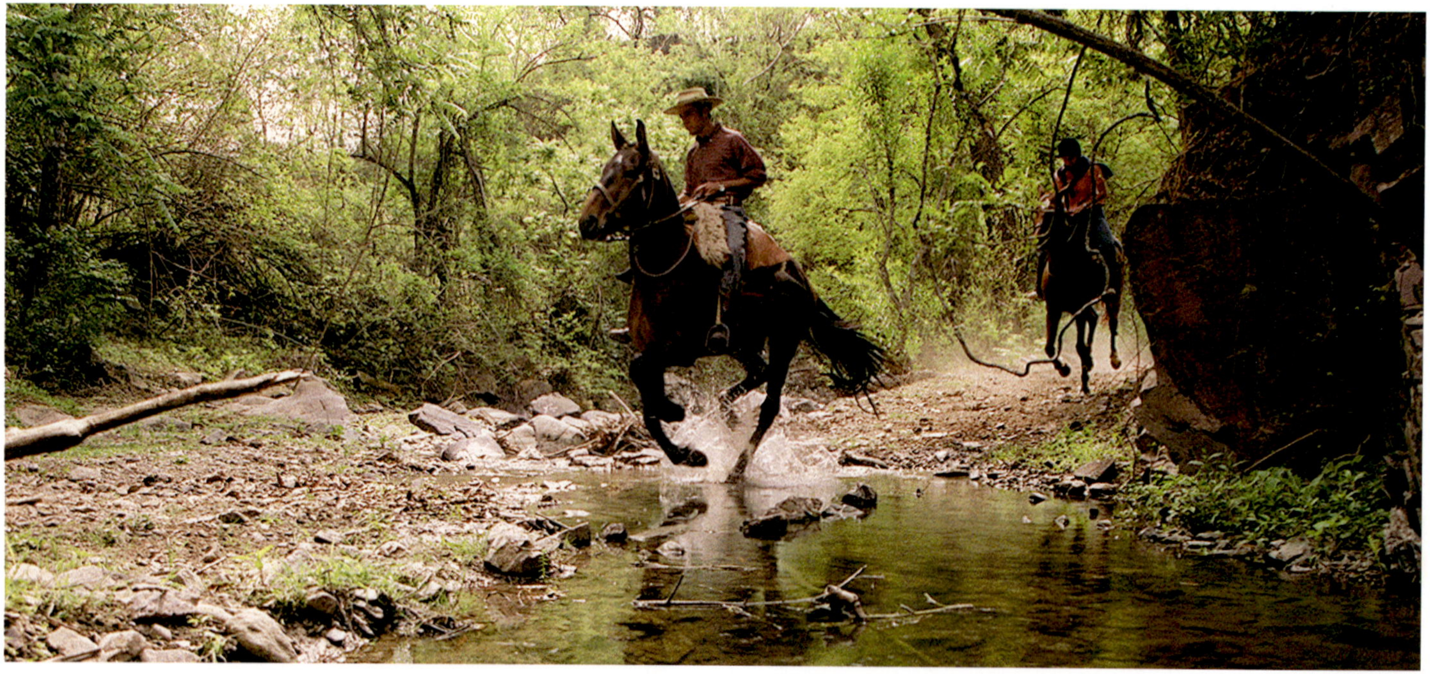

The gorges in San Lorenzo, covered by mountain forest, hide trails to wander on horseback or on foot.

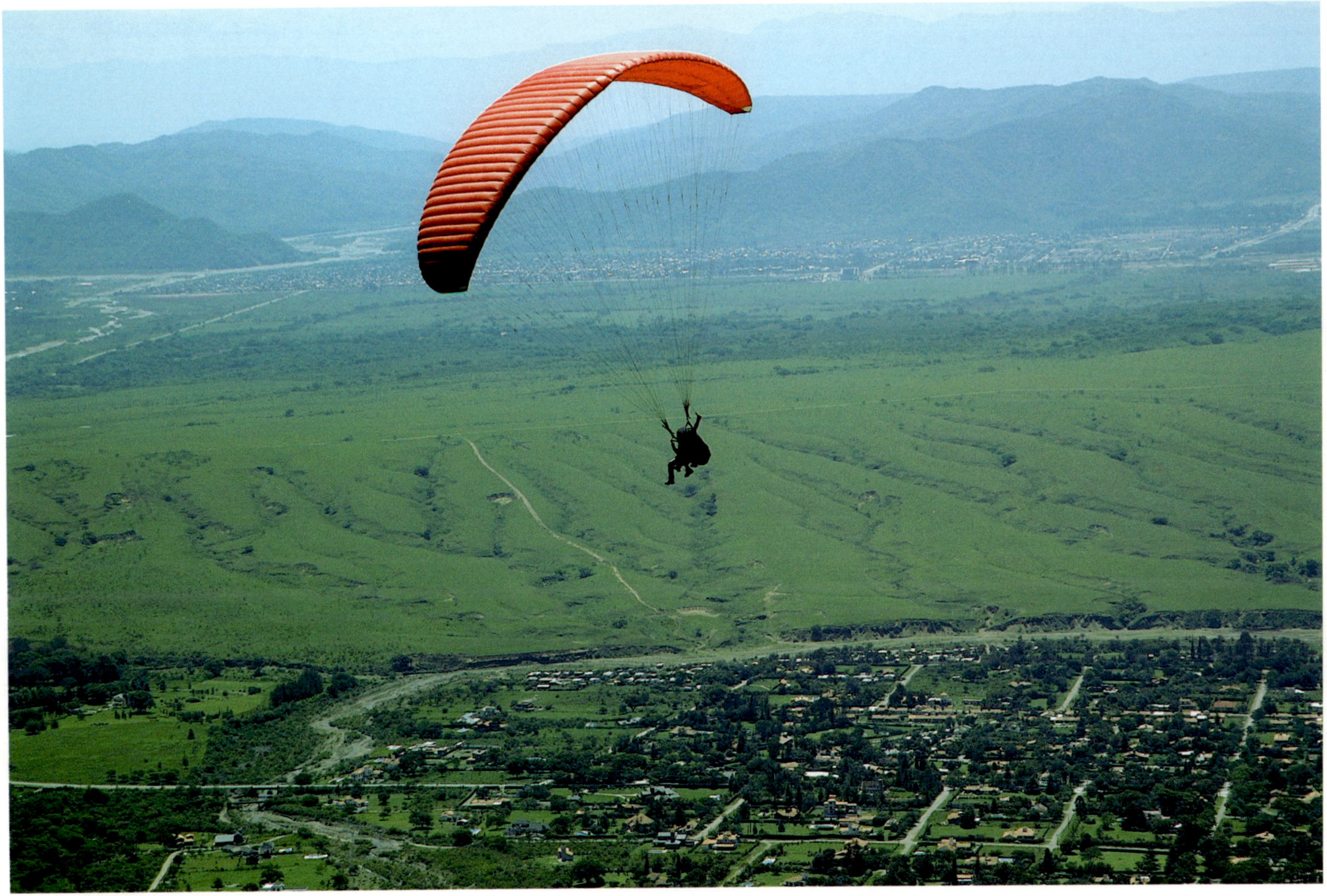

A Paraglide flight, taking off from a hill in San Lorenzo. Below, San Lorenzo and behind the northern suburbs of the city of Salta.

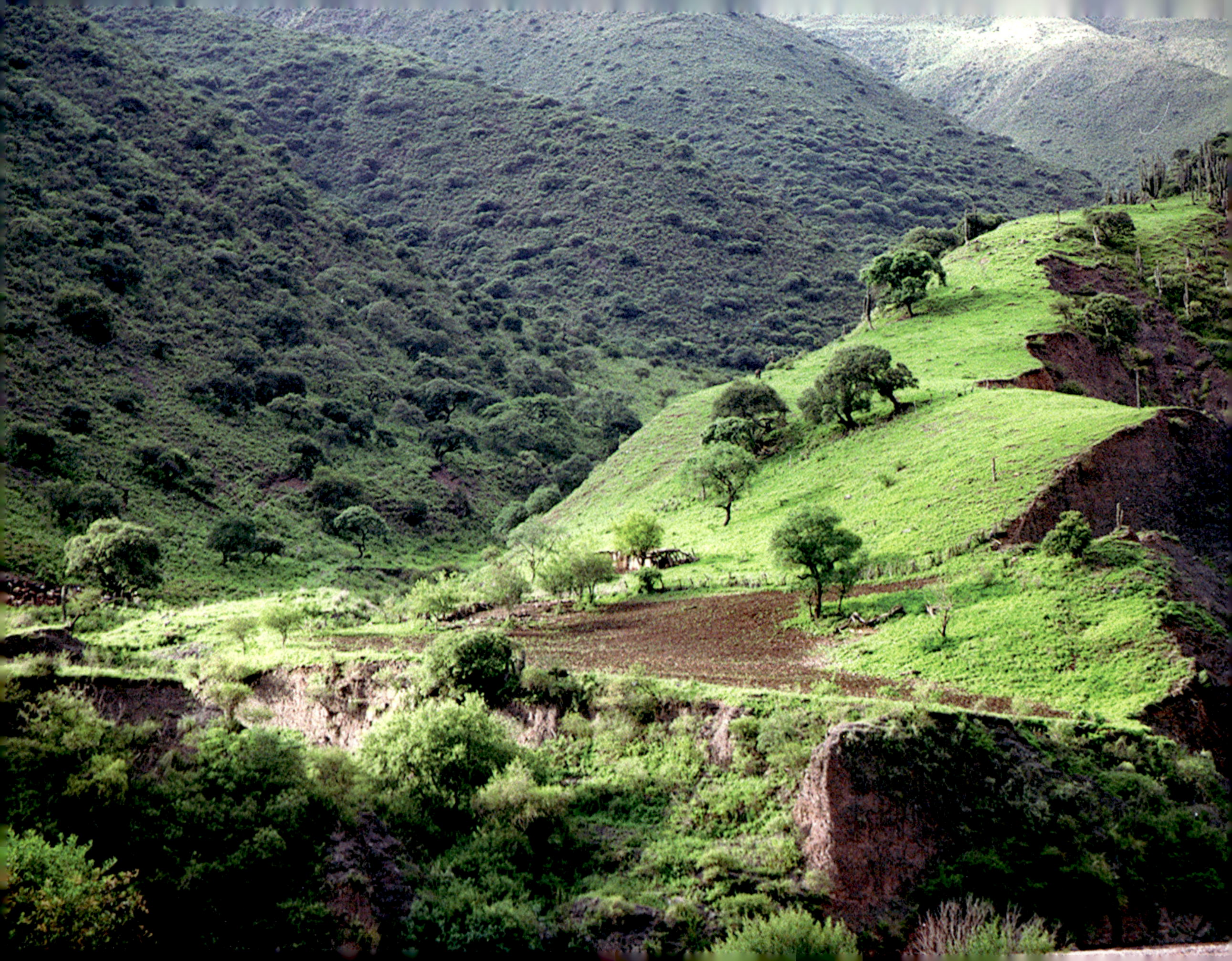

From Salta to Cachi via Cuesta del Obispo. Route 40 to Cafayate.

We head South from Salta, and in the small town of El Carril, set in the midst of the agricultural area of the Valle de Lerma, we turn West on route 33.

After driving across farmlands, colonial houses and tobacco heating barns, the scenery changes and in the area of Los Laureles the road starts twisting under large trees of mountain laurel *(Phoebe porphyria)*, wild walnut *(Junglans australis)*, and cedrelas *(Cedrella sp.)*.

The Quebrada de Escoipe closes in and, after a few kilometres the trees disappear. We pass by San Fernando de Escoipe, where it is usual to see the village children on the roadside selling fresh or dried fruit; or preserves with a smoky taste, since they were prepared over an open fire.

San Fernando de Escoipe. Locals use every bit of flat land to sow their crops. (p. 58)

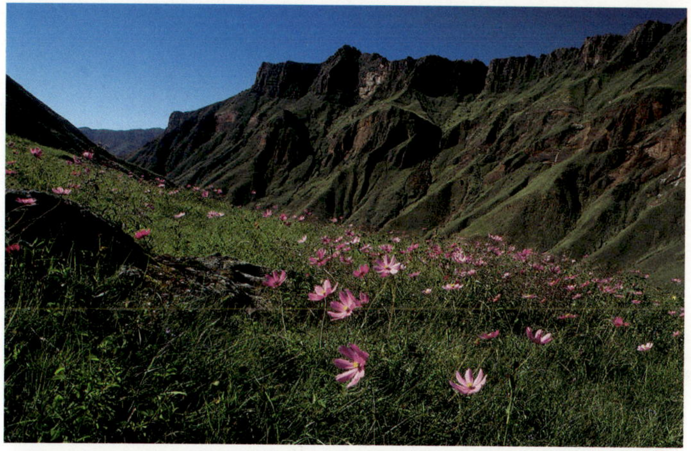

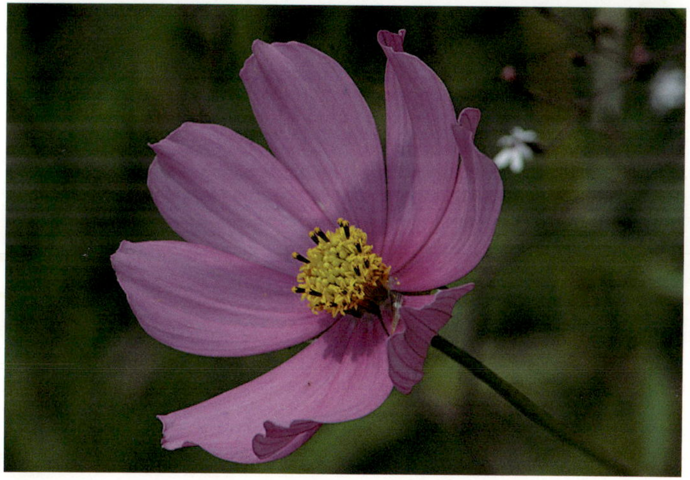

Cuesta del Obispo. Cosmos bloom between February and April.

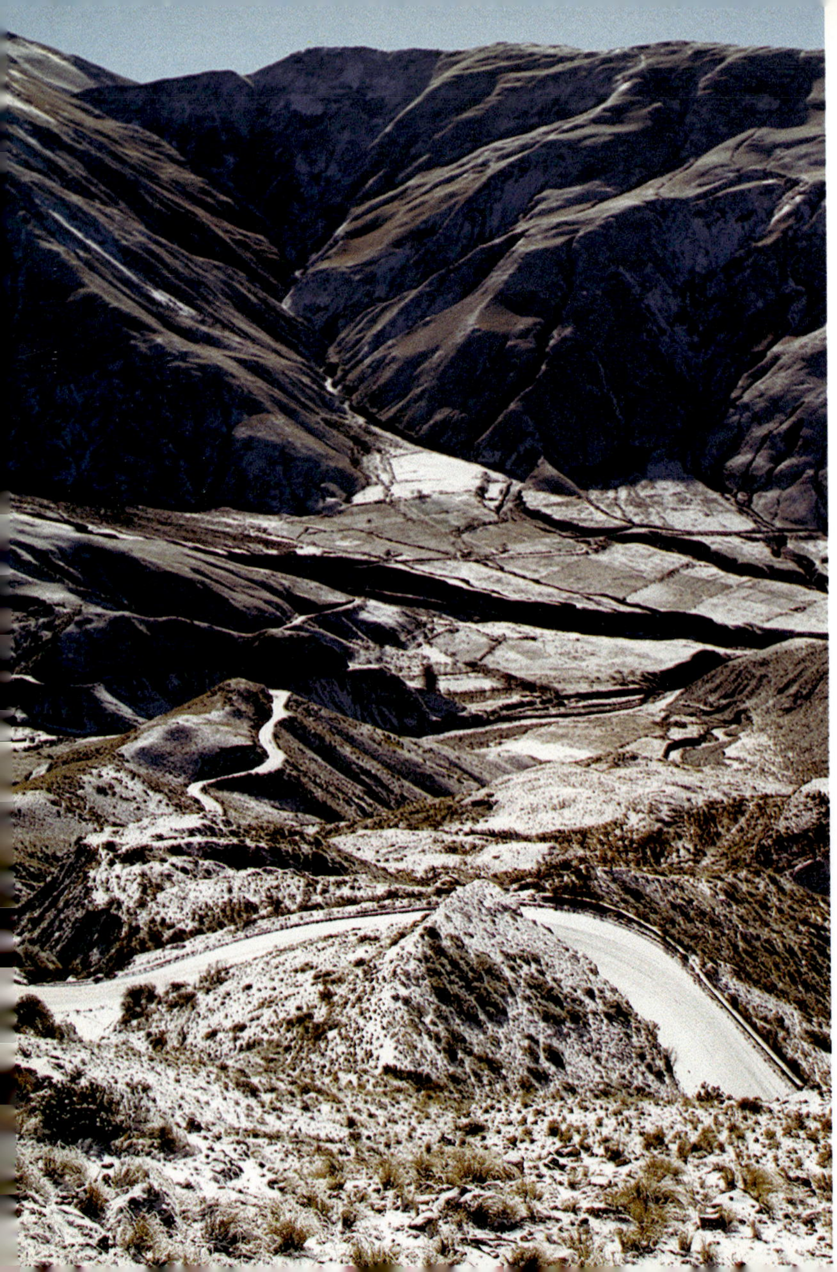

The landscape changes to terracotta coloured soils. We climb up the Cuesta del Obispo, each curve offering a unique view. The road cuts through National Park Los Cardones, and goes by the entrance to the Enchanted Valley, that honours its name.

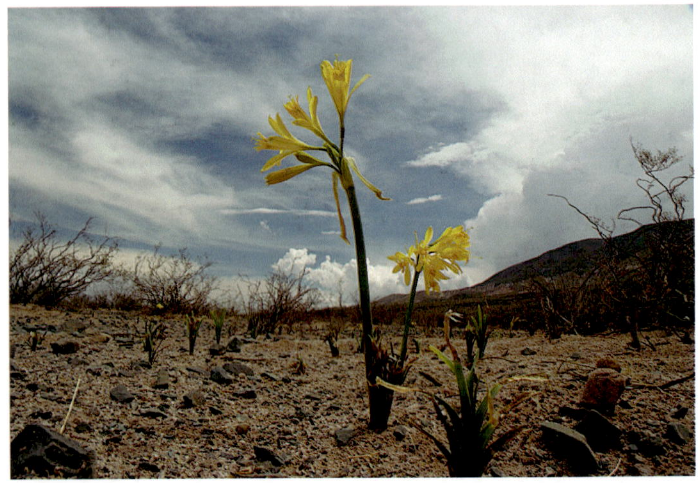

Amancay (Hieronymiella tintinensis). This flower grows in the dry areas of National Park Los Cardones and blooms only after a summer rain.

Cuesta del Obispo with snow.

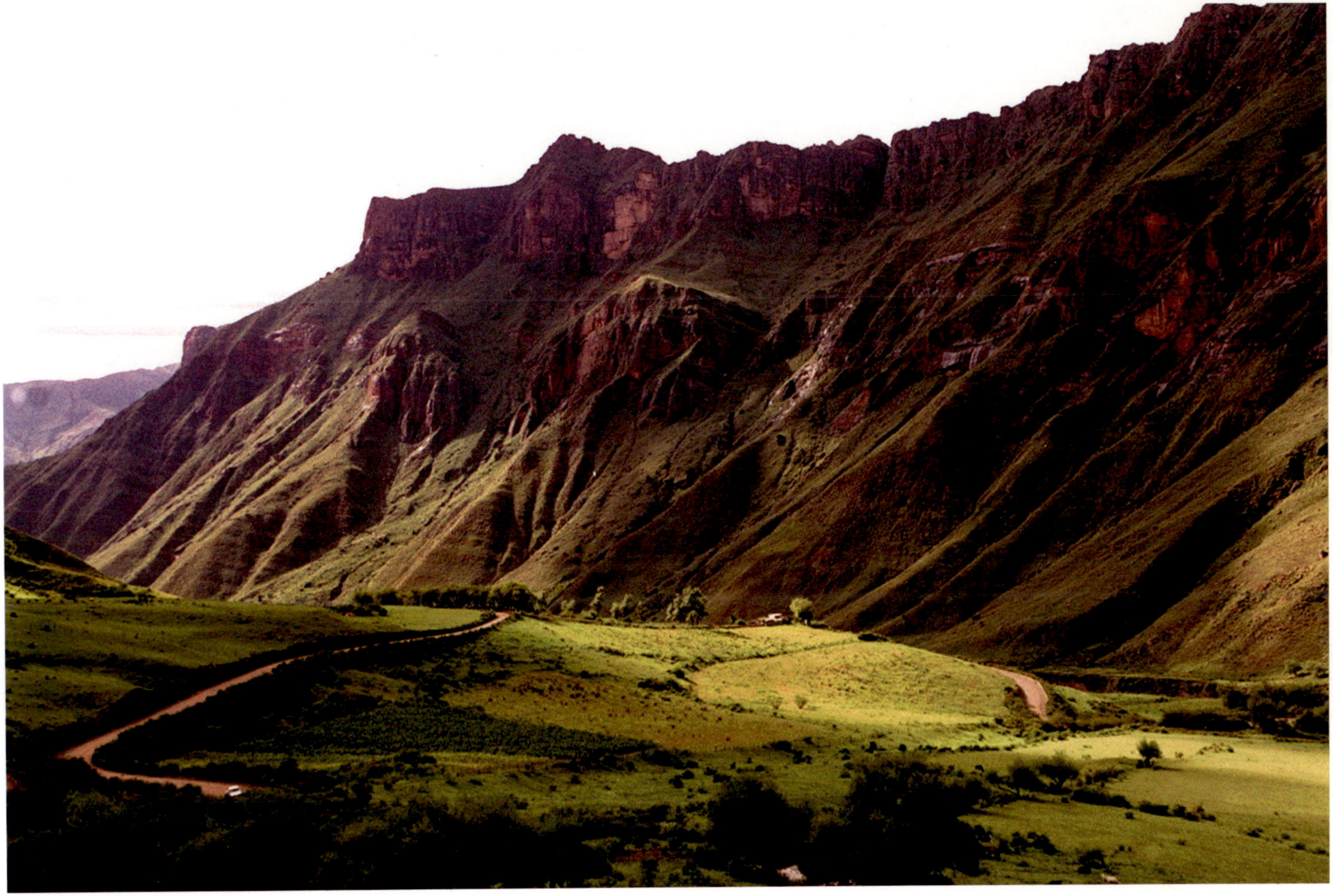

Cuesta del Obispo in summer.

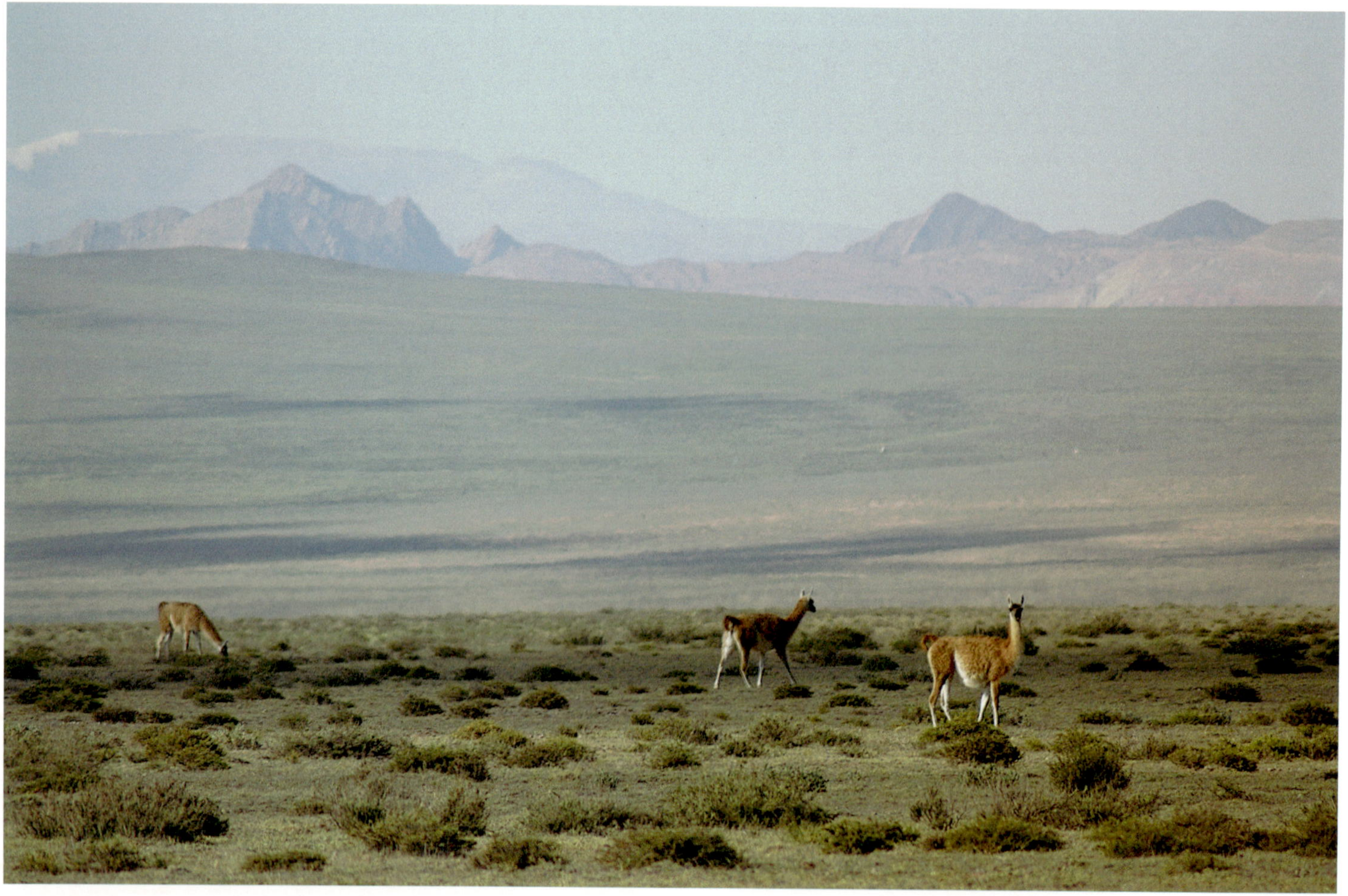

Guanacos (Lama guanicoe) in Cachi Pampa.

A stop at Piedra del Molino, a pass at 3348 m.a.s.l. (10980 ft) is worth it. The road now stretches along a high mountain plateau, called Cachi Pampa, where the guanacos must struggle with wild donkeys for what little grass there is. The clouds usually tumble in here, bringing precious moisture and making this plateau the greenest part of the National Park.

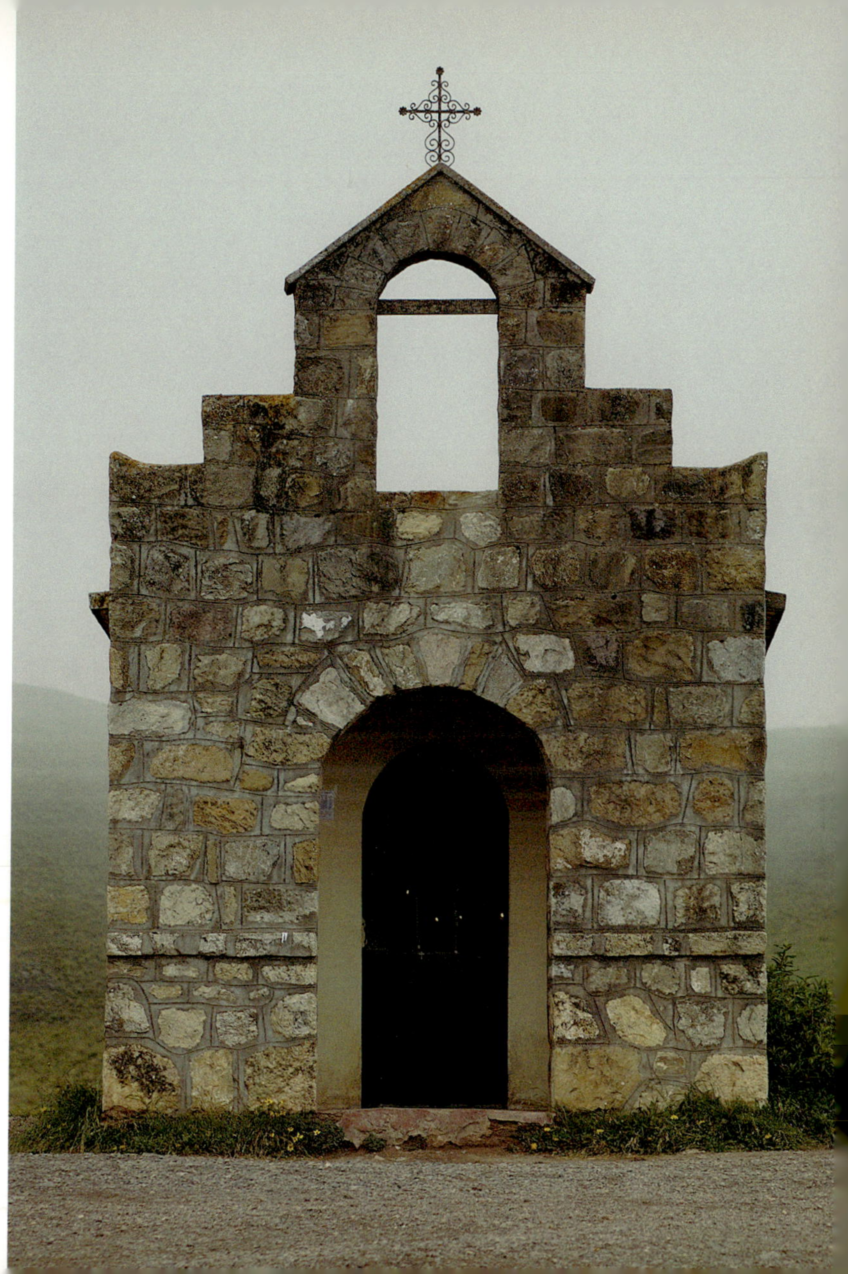

Chapel at Piedra del Molino.

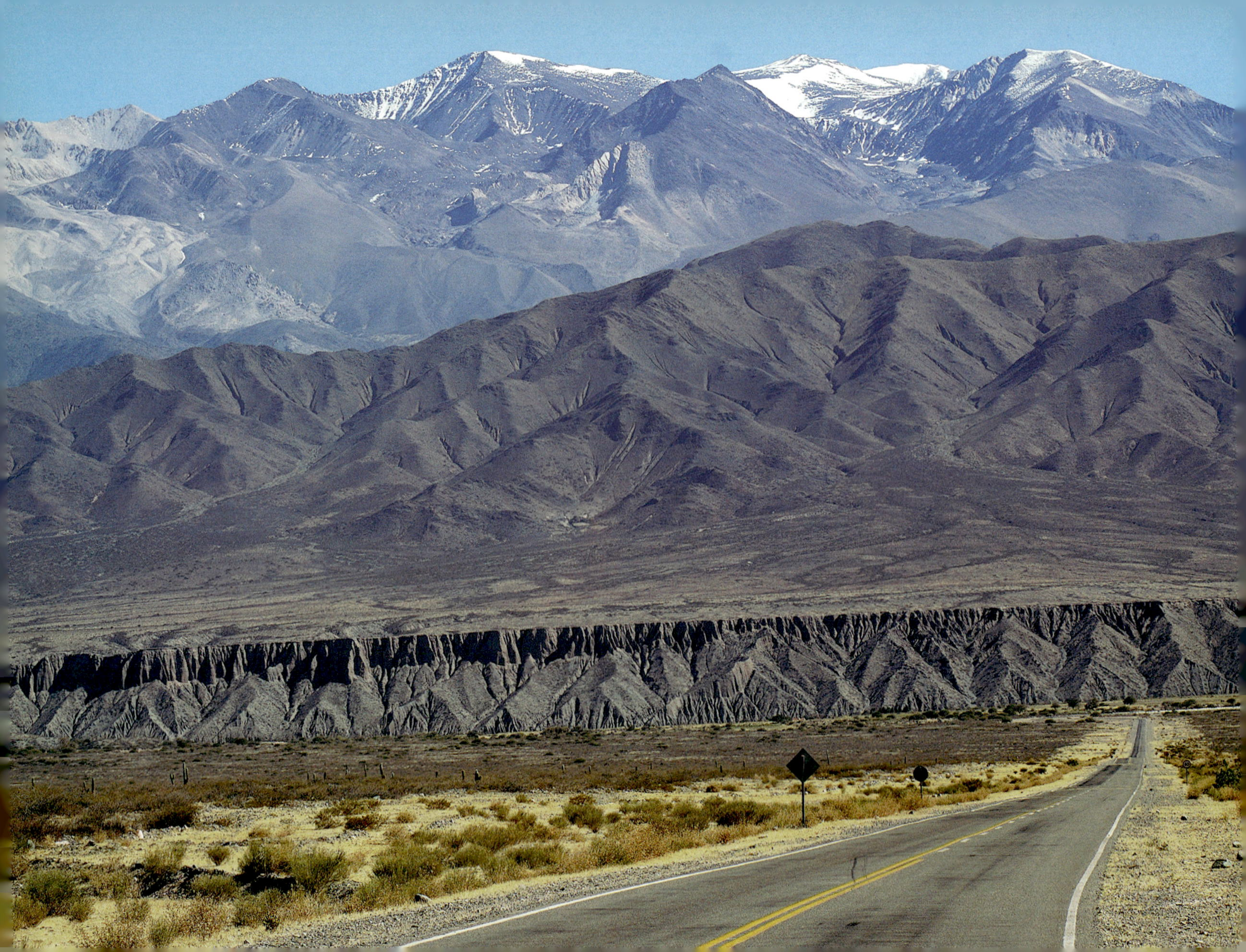

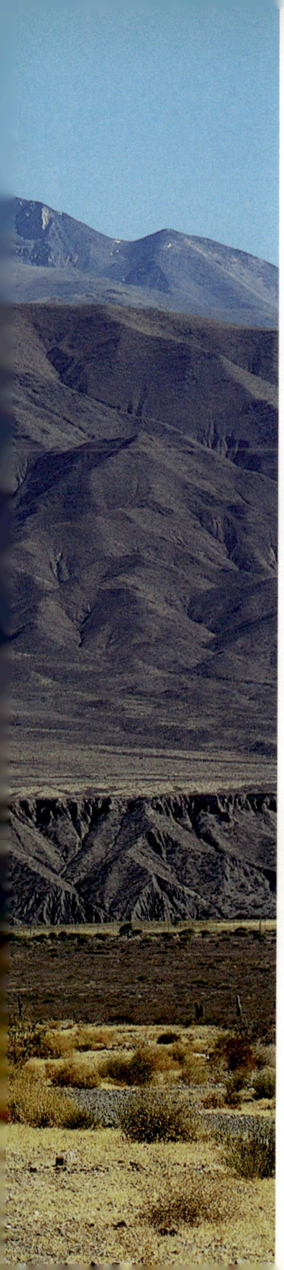

Further ahead, where it is lower and dryer, milliards of cardones *(Trichocereus sp.)* wait for us, like the Andes' sentinels. These amazing cactus plants grow on arid slopes between an altitude of 2000 to 3500 meters (6560 to 11489 ft).

Tin Tin is the name of the only straight stretch of road of the area, and surprises after twisting through the mountains. Below, in front of us, we can see the green fields of alfalfa and maize that grow alongside the Calchaquí River.

The road runs down towards the Calchaquí River; the Cachi Mountain rises behind (6380 m.a.s.l. / 20932 ft).

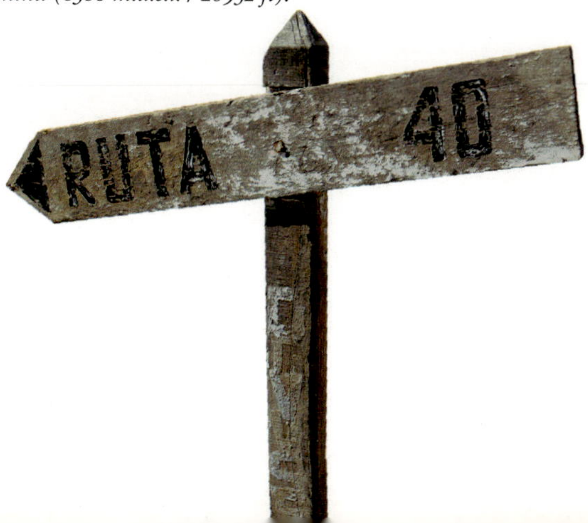

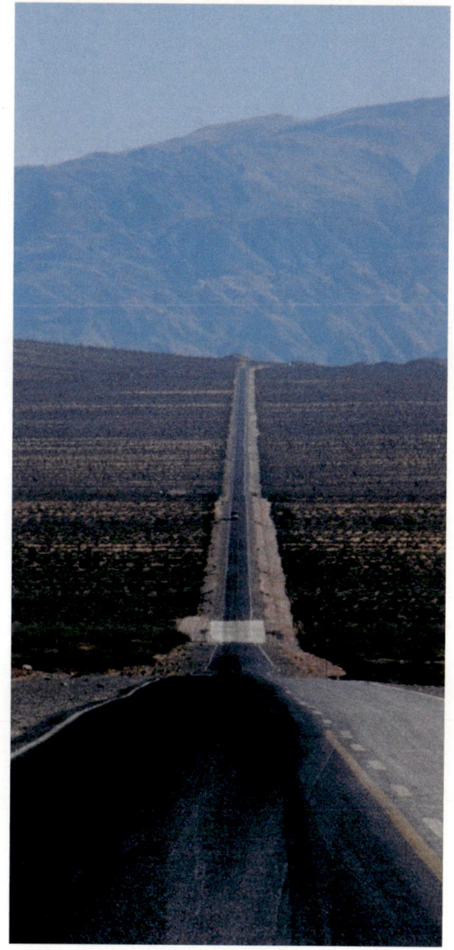

Recta de Tin Tin, built upon an ancient Inca trail.

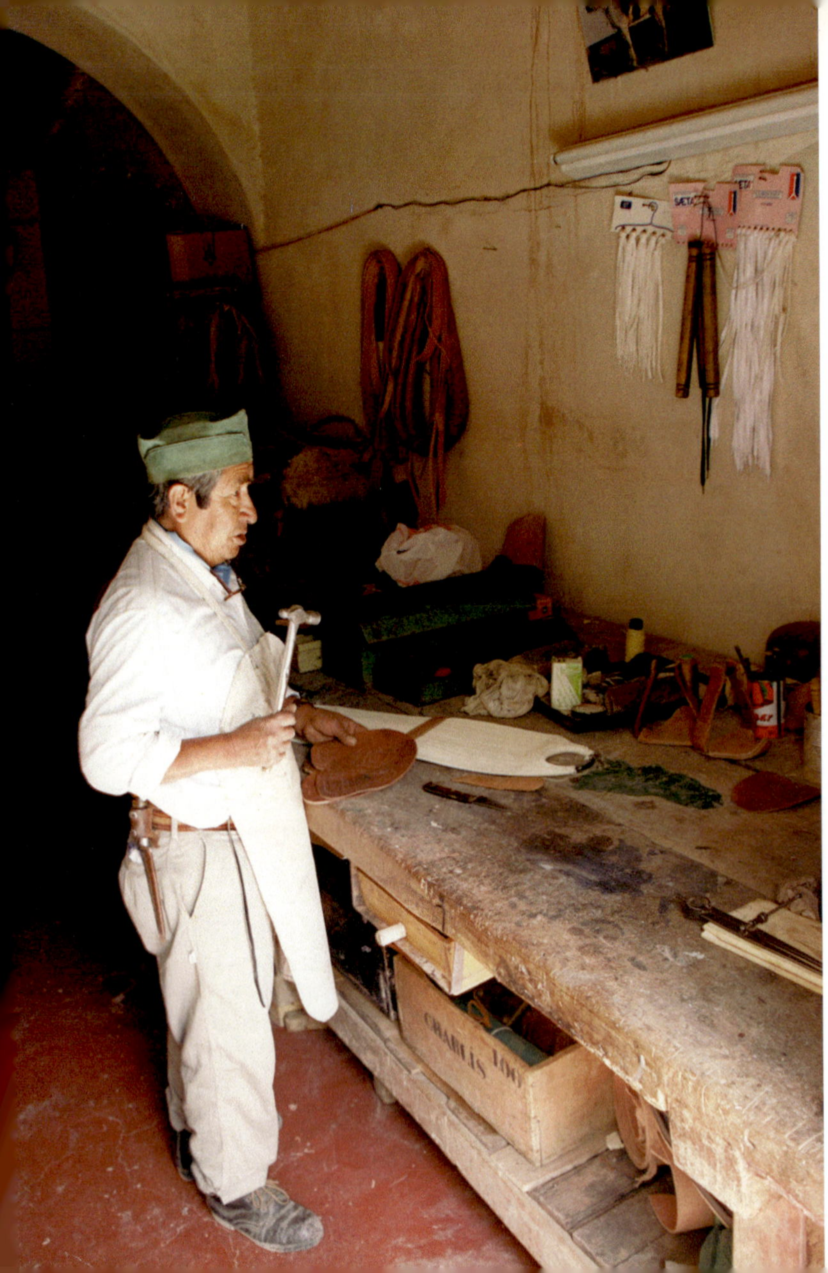

In the village of Payogasta, one gets the feeling of going back in time.

After crossing the river, we are in Cachi, whose name comes from the word for "salt" in Quechua, the tongue of the Inca Empire. It is a town that has preserved its architecture and the main square is surrounded by colonial houses with high sidewalks.

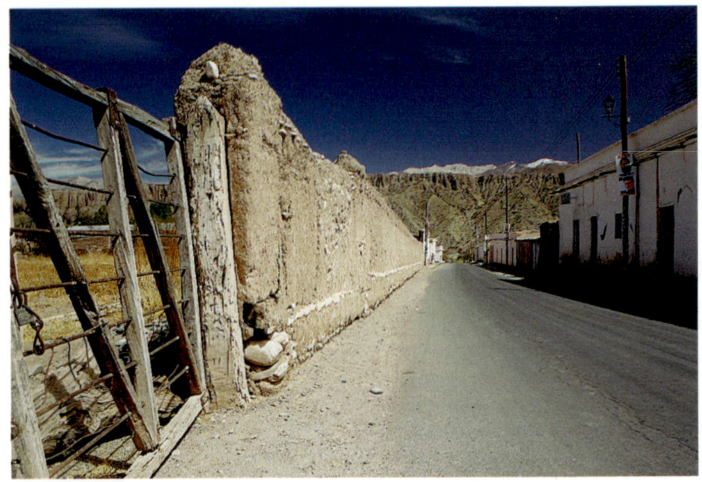

A street in Payogasta.

Saddler in Payogasta.

Cachi. San José Church and the Archeological Museum. (p. 67)

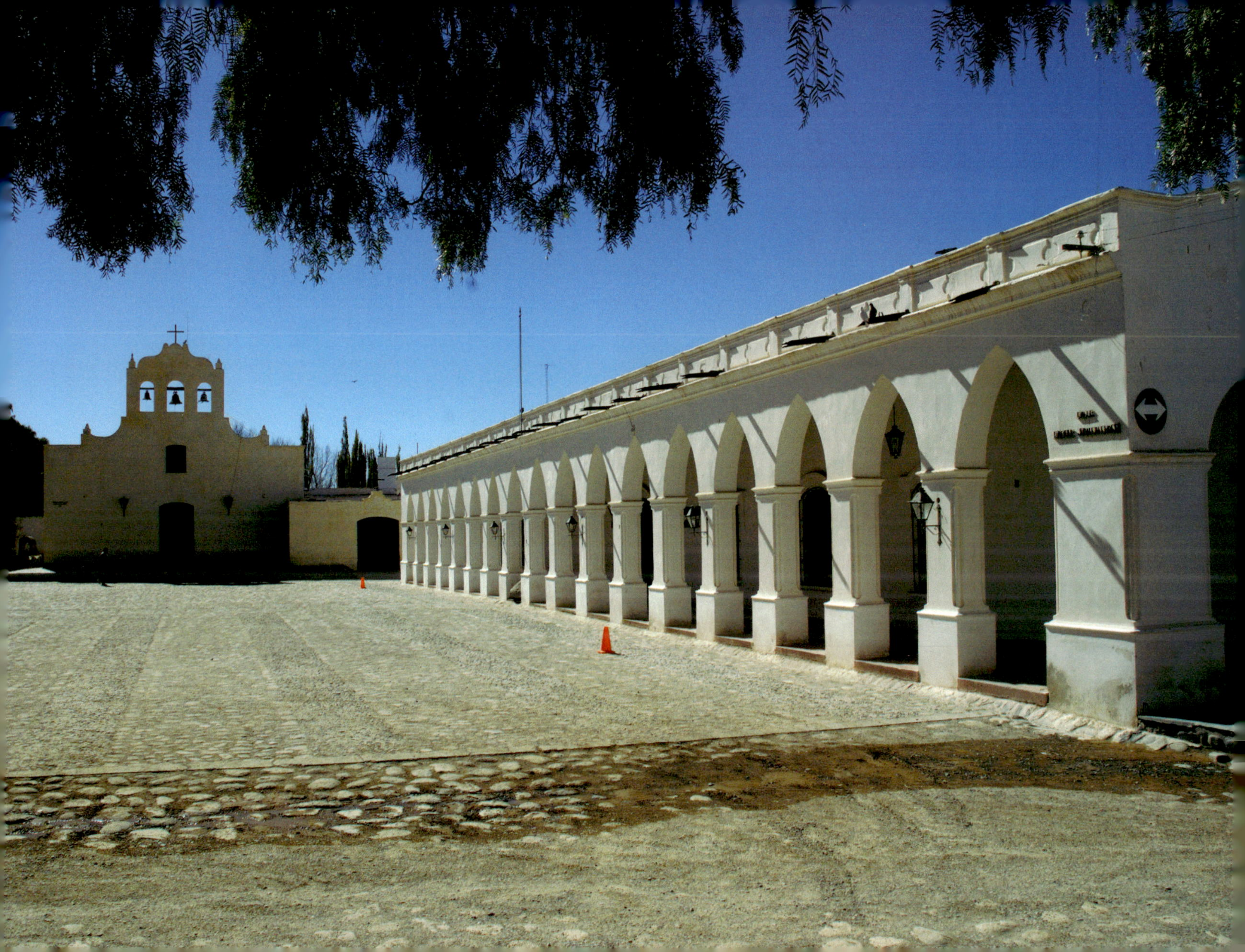

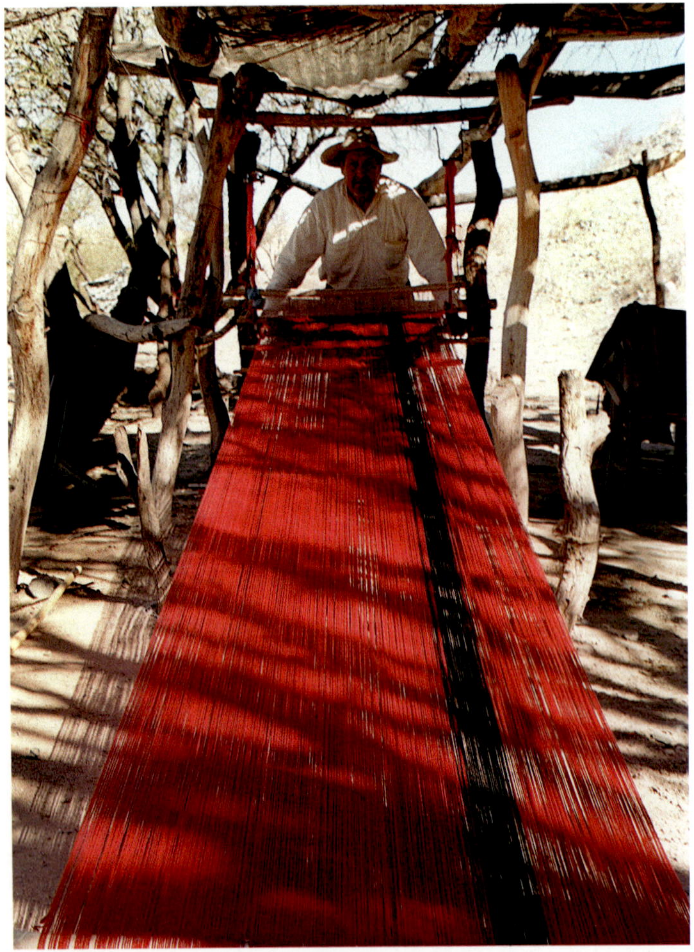

Seclantás. An artisan weaving a poncho in his loom.

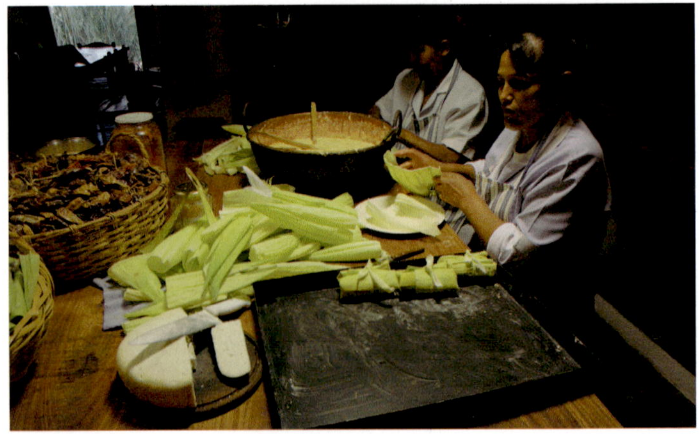

Cooking humitas.

We head along route 40 that reaches down to Patagonia, and will take us now to Cafayate.

It is a dust road that twists and turns, with adobe -mud brick- houses, all dressed up with verandas and columns that support different shaped arches, waiting at every curve. The architecture here is a clear example of the fusion of the Spanish with the Calchaquí cultures. This union is seen in every aspect of daily life: beliefs, music, traditions and religion.

We drive by farms and houses, all of them between the road and the river, creating a green strip that paints this land with life. It is a road to drive along without haste, taking in every detail; discovering the pace of the people of the Valleys, all of them proud of their Calchaquí origin.

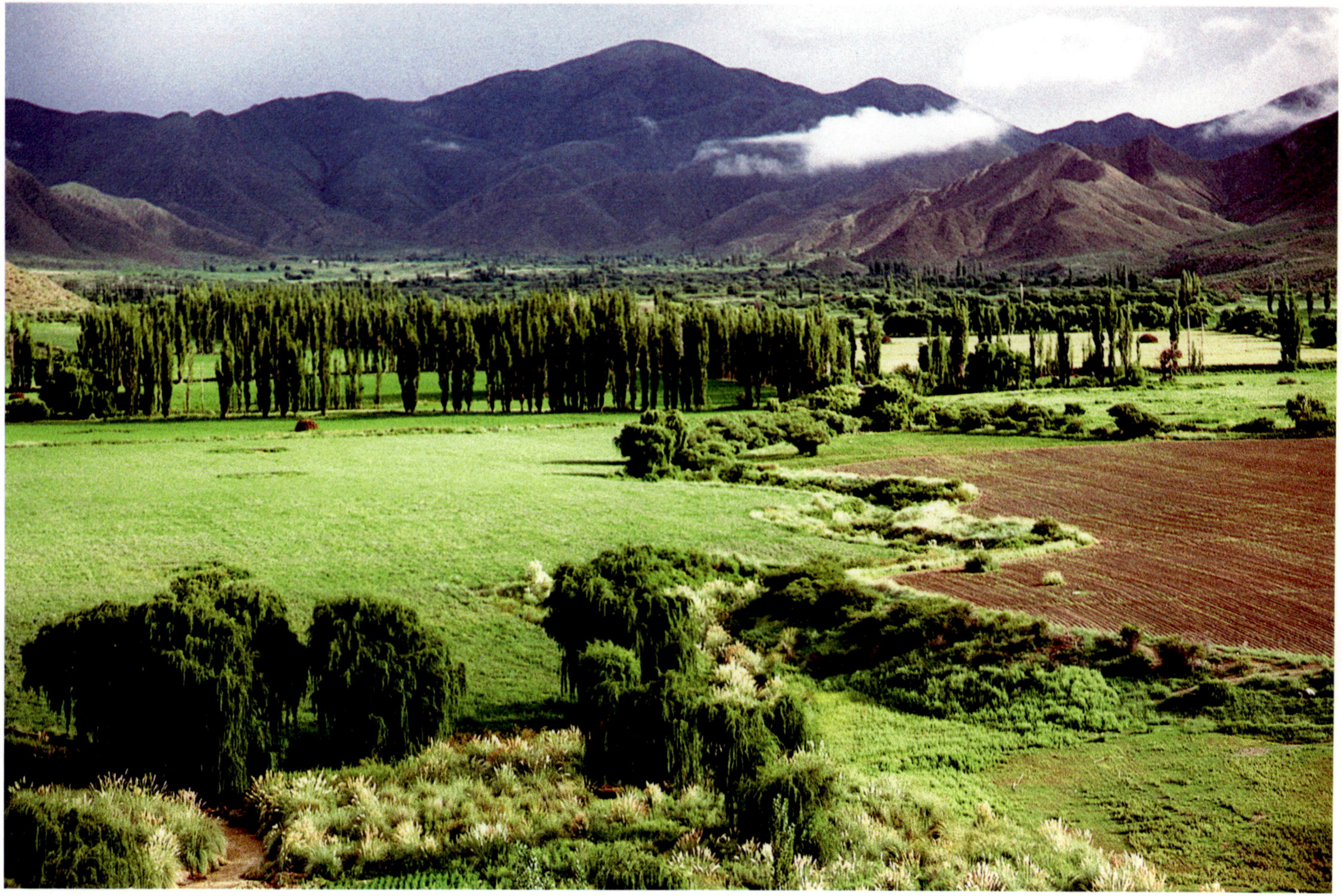

Cachi Adentro. A small protected valley west of Cachi with abundant crops because, being closer to the mountains, it has more water.

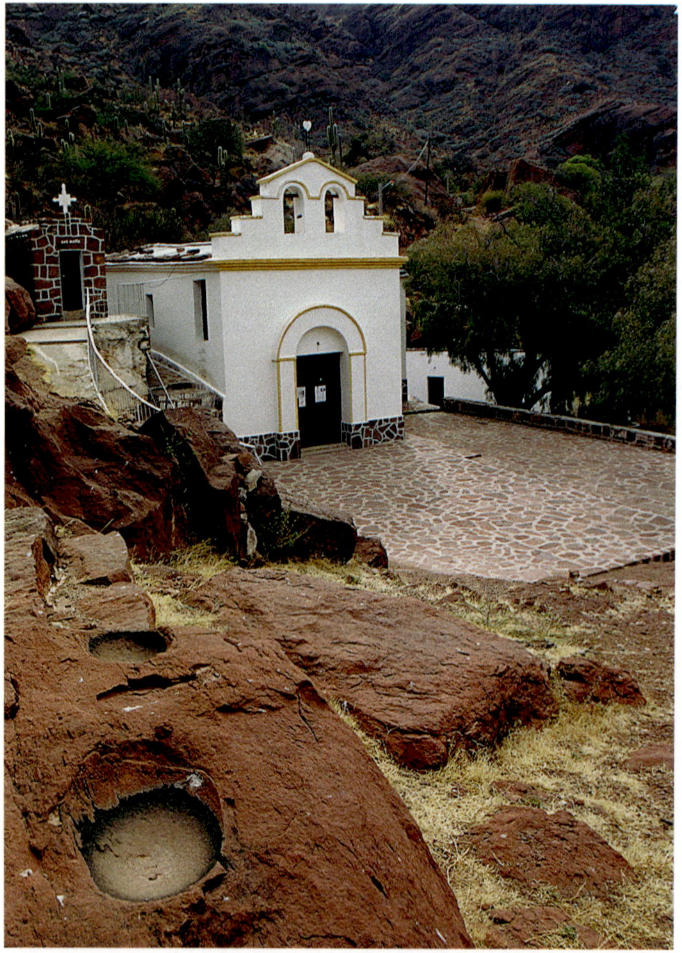

Chapel in the village of Brealito. Below left we see ancient Indian mortars.

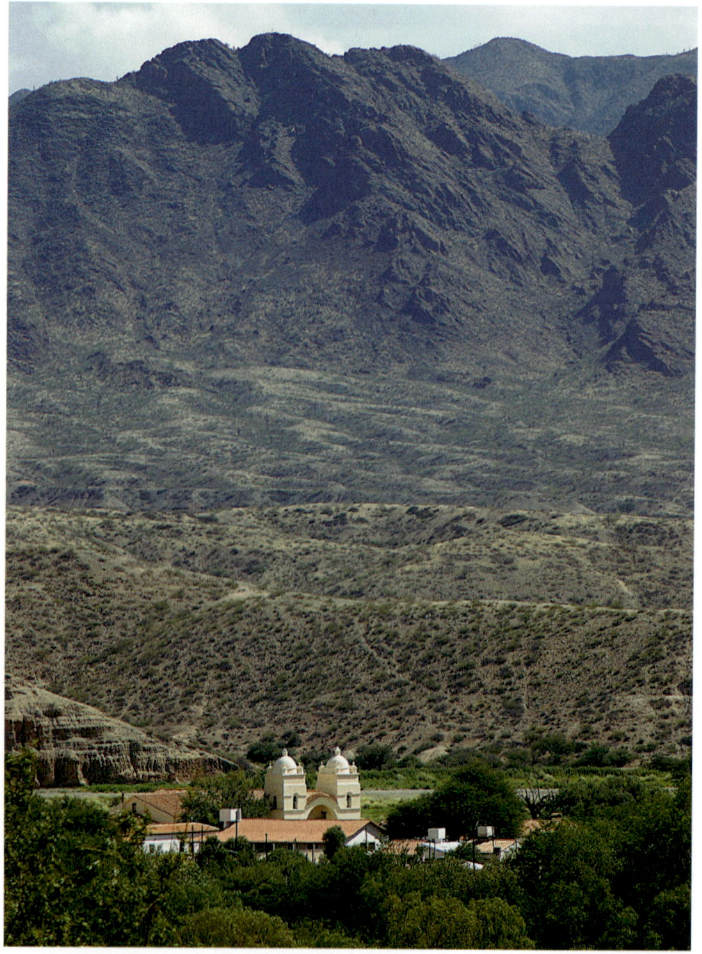

San Pedro Nolasco de Los Molinos' Church.

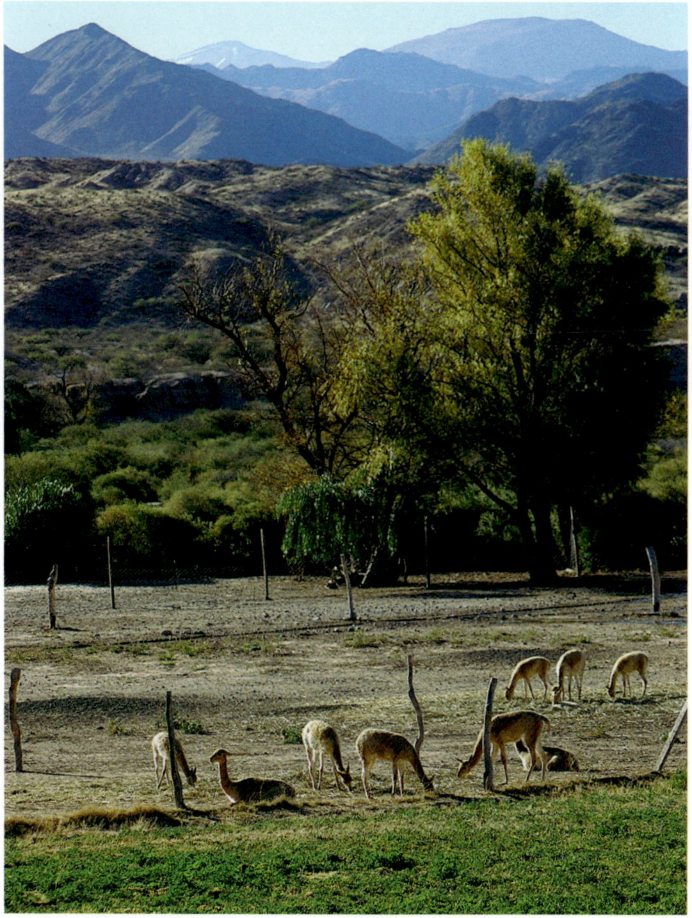

Molinos. Vicuñas successfully bred in captivity. They belong to an artisan coop that sells goods woven with this animal's fine wool.

To reach Seclantás there are two options: to follow route 40, on the West river bank; or to cross the river before, pass through El Colte, a small canyon carved in gray rock, and following from there the Artisans Route, so called because the people work on their looms at the road side.

Molinos comes next, the only village of the area that begun as a Spanish encomienda (land granted by the Spanish King) and was not originally a Calchaquí town. Salta's last royalist governor lived here, Don Nicolás Severo de Isasmendi, who is now buried in the Church. From there we can go on to Colomé, Amaicha and Tacuil; three distinct wineries that have their vineyards in the high mountains, thus producing wines of unique characteristics.

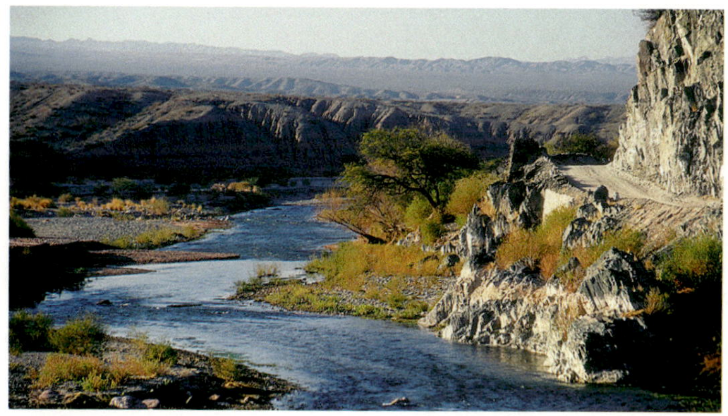

Calchaquí River.

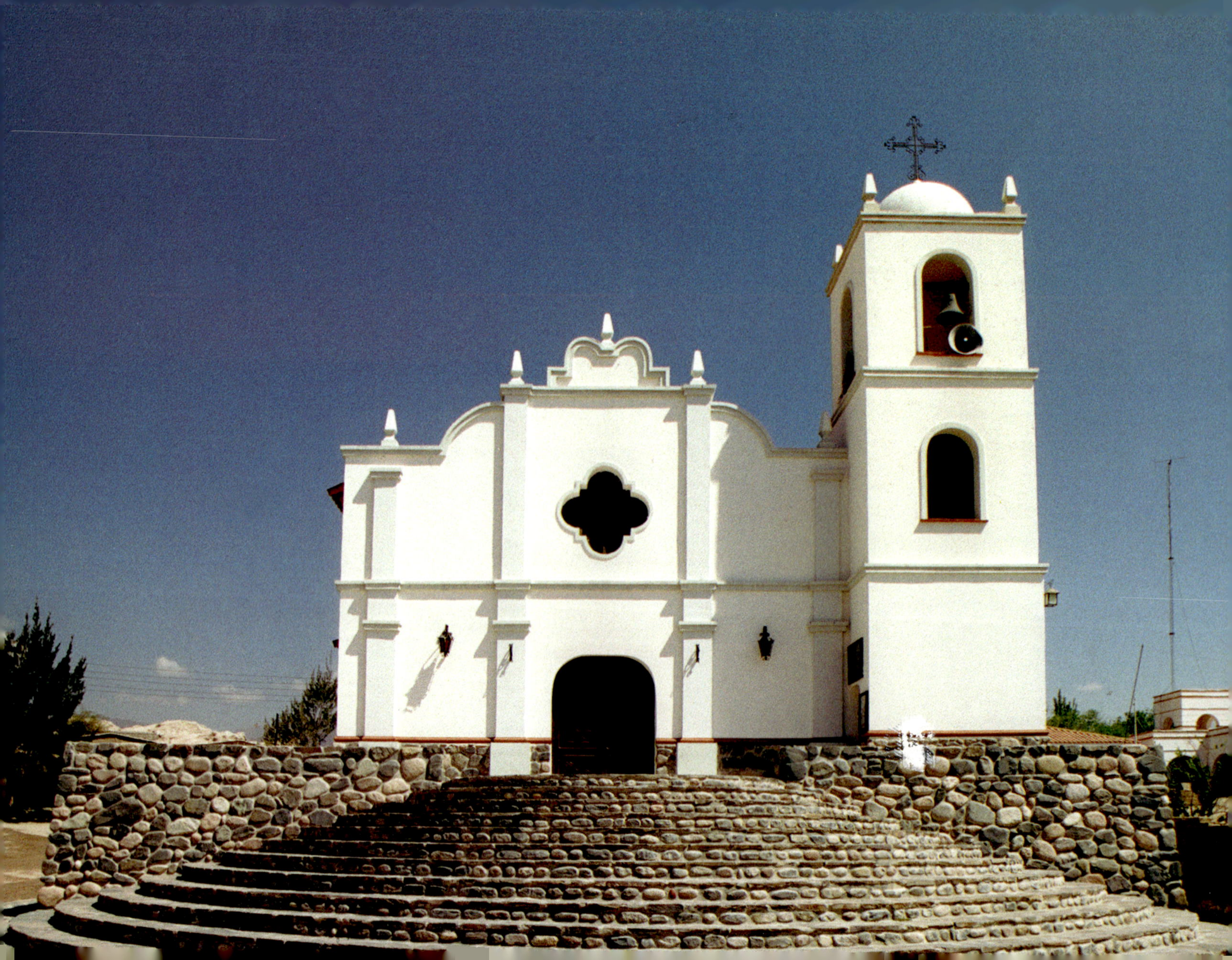

Further along the road, we will find Angastaco, an oasis of vineyards and poplars set amidst a landscape that surprises by its sudden change. Some millions of years ago this was a tropical jungle similar to the one found nowadays in the Paraná River area. The sediments of this prehistoric tropical forest fractured when the Andes range formed. The rest of the work was done, throughout millions of years, by wind and summer rains creating what is known as the Quebrada de las Flechas (Gorge of the Arrowheads), one of the most spectacular places of Argentina's northwest.

As the road rambles along, houses sheltered from the sun by their verandas gaze at passersby. According to the time of the year we choose to make our trip, we will see red peppers drying in the sun, cornfields or green and purple alfalfa meadows swaying in the wind.

Angastaco Church. *(p. 72)*

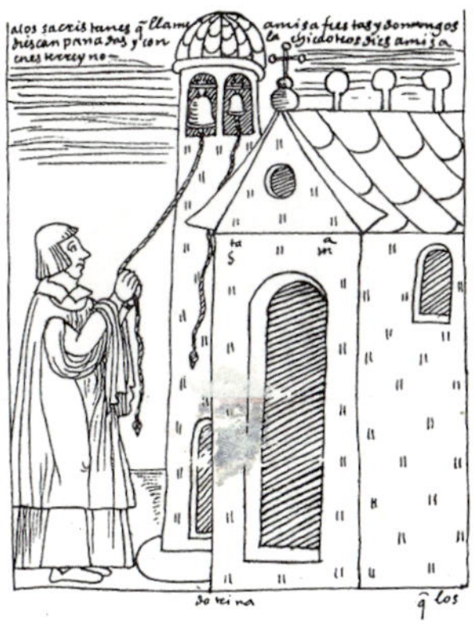

Belfry, Guamán Poma de Ayala, 1587

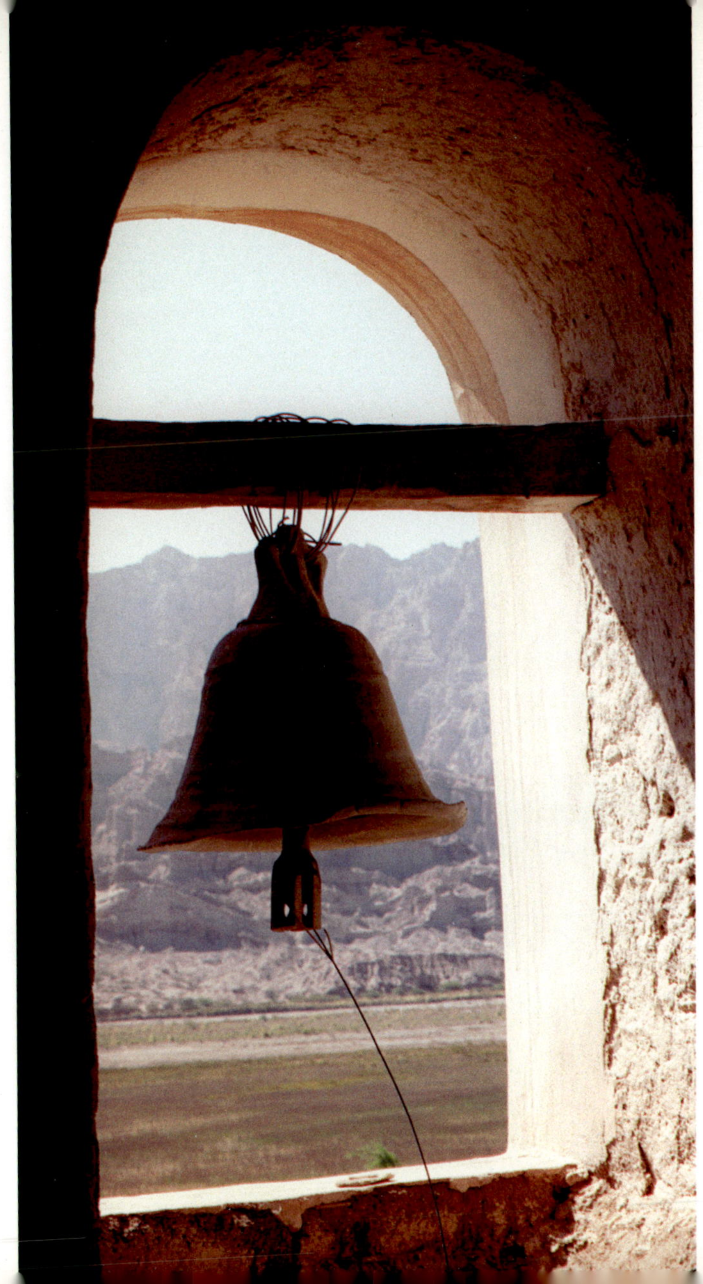

Bell in the chapel of El Carmen.

74

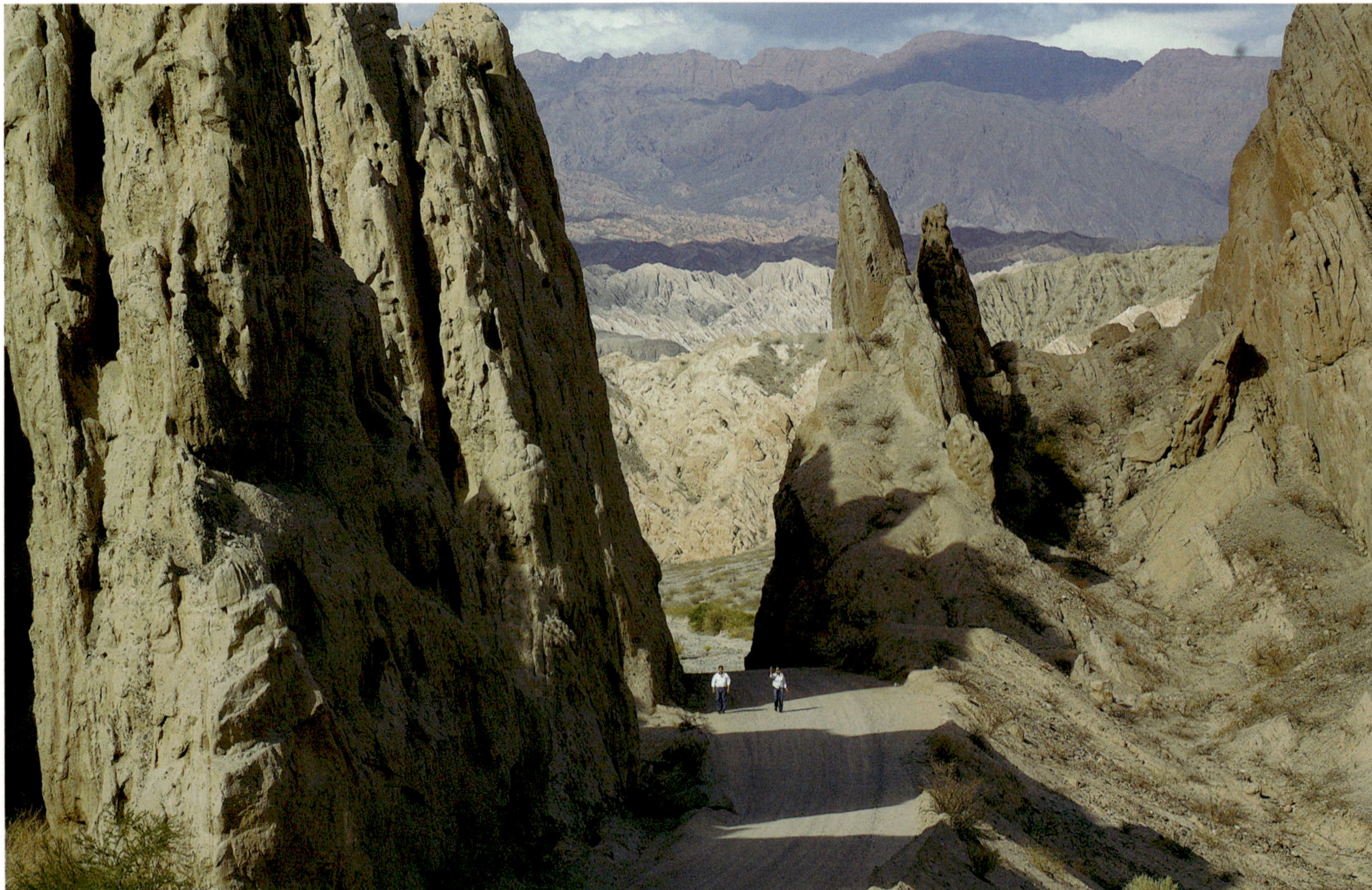

Quebrada de Las Flechas (Gorge of the Arrows).

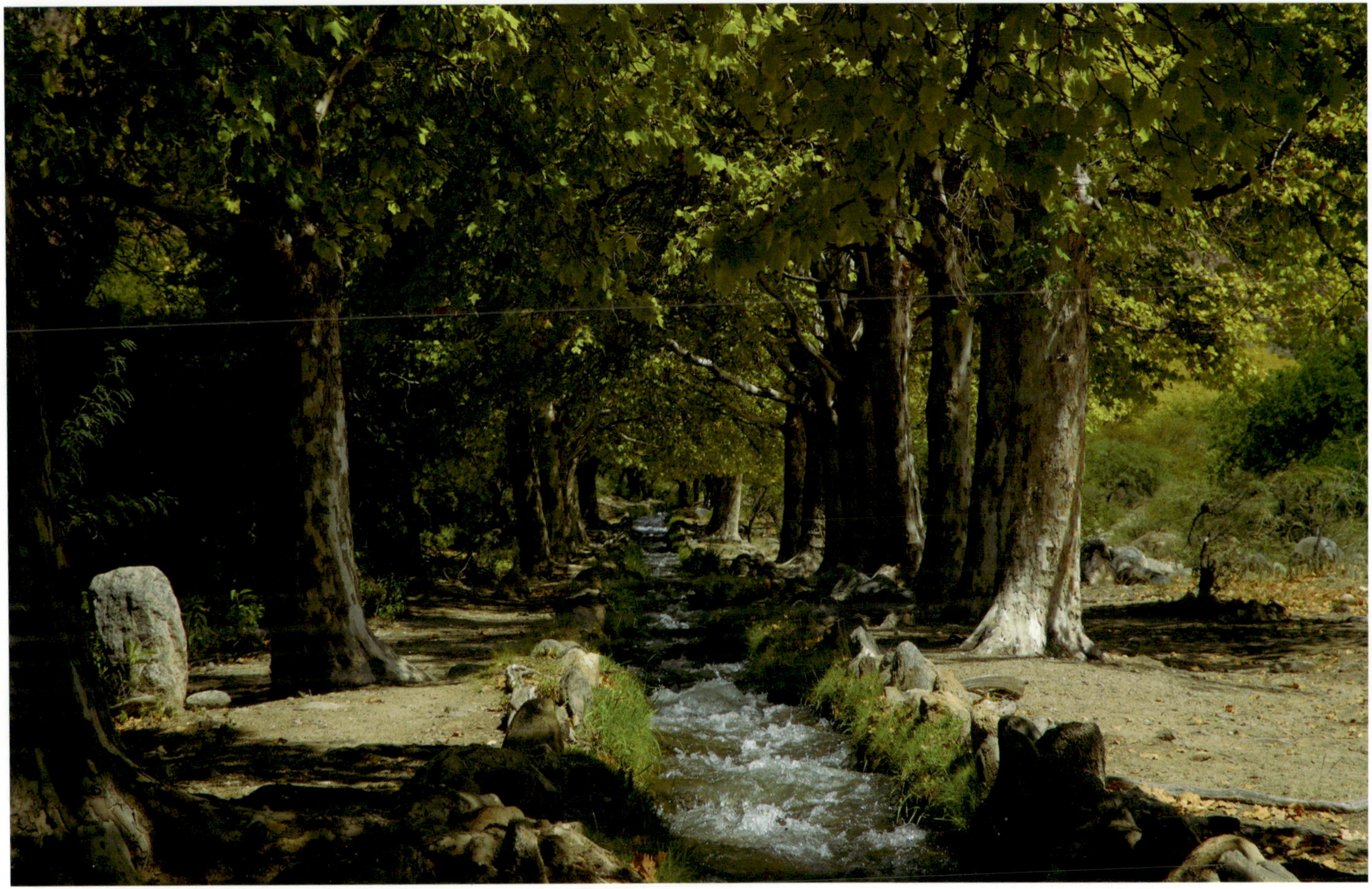

A water canal near Cafayate. The water is taken in the high mountains, and brought down to the valley where it irrigates crops in a semi desert region.

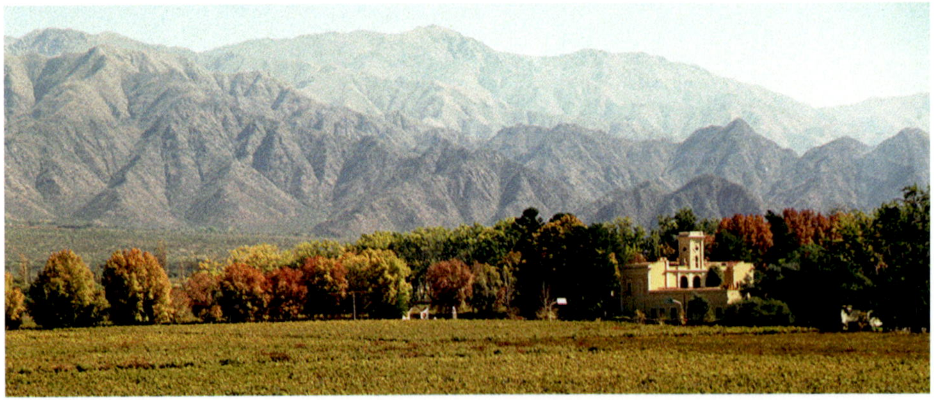

Tacuil, winter. Llamas amongst vienyerds.

Cafayate. Vineyards in El Esteco Winery.

The Valley gets wider, on the West there are mountains of gray Pre Cambrian rocks; they are the Quilmes or Cajón range. The Calchaquí River meanders on the East side, through a wide belt of pure white sand; across it we see red mountains that announce the proximity of the Cafayate Gorge.

We pass through San Carlos, a charming place, whose Church has been rebuilt three times since it was burned down once and again during the Calchaquí Wars. In this town, we can find the clay "quarry" where they make the famous tiles that floor the colonial houses of many farms and wineries.

In Animaná the vineyards grow on both sides of the road, which is now paved and in the widest part of the valley, so it stretches out and the curves disappear.

At last we are driving under old poplar trees; we are in Cafayate, a name that has a touch of wine to it, especially torrontés, a white wine that in this latitude and altitude acquires the taste that makes it recognizable throughout the whole world. The red wines from here, like malbec, cabernet sauvignon, syrah and tannat are appreciated by the most demanding wine connoisseurs.

Cafayate is located at 1660 m.a.s.l. in the heart of the Calchaquí Valleys and has a superb microclimate for vineyards. Due to this, and because it is surrounded by rivers, it is a place chosen by winemakers since the 17th Century.

To visit the different wineries and later sit down at a café on the Plaza to a sip of local wine is a must, to get a flavor of life in this township.

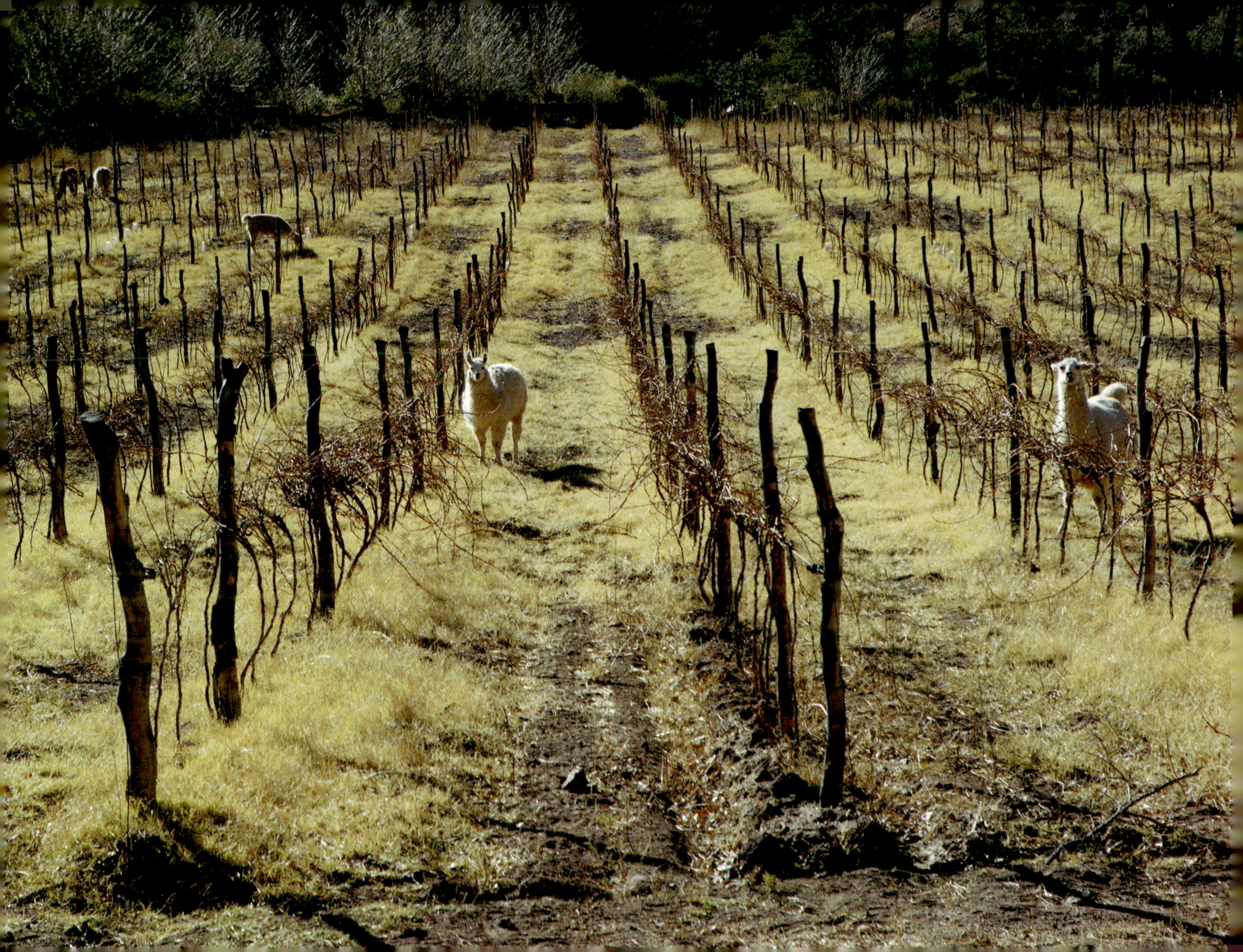

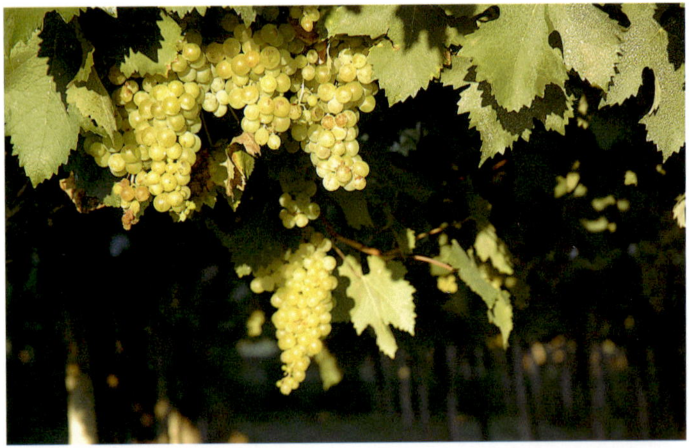

Torrontes grapes. Vintage time.

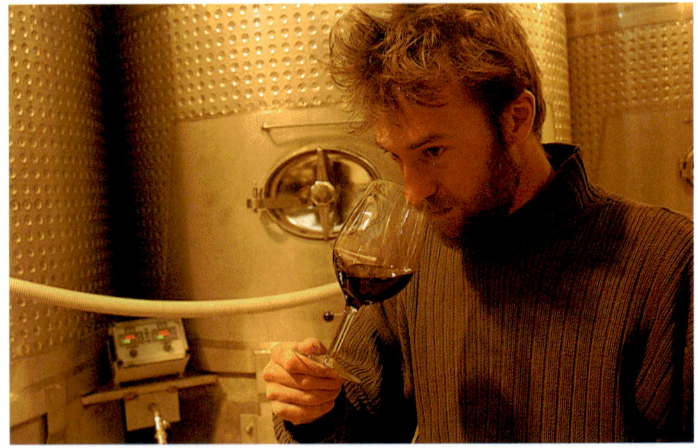

Enologist, Bodega Colomé.

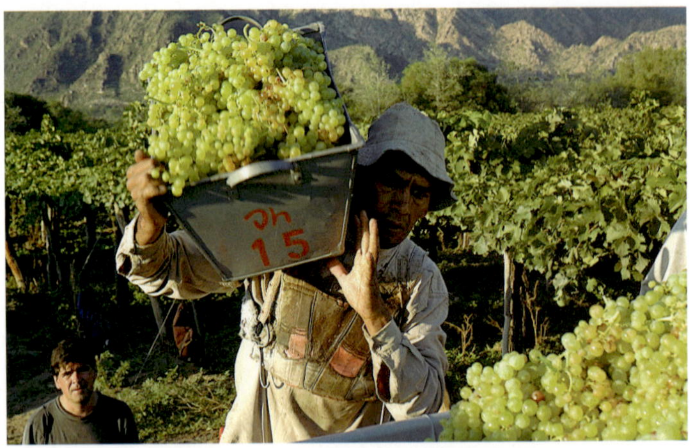

Between February and April the grapes are gathered. Bodega Domingo

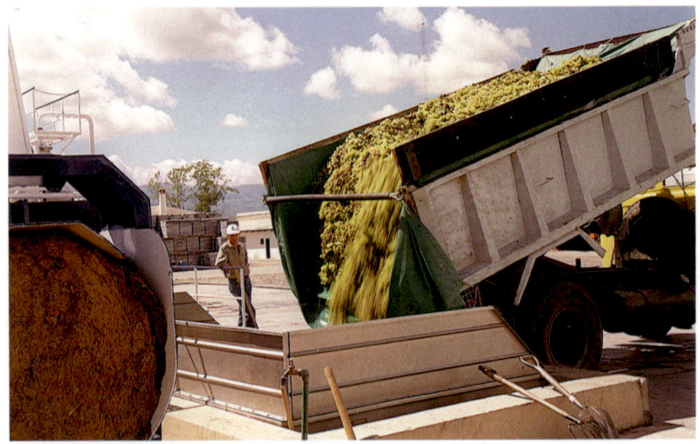

Unloading grapes into the wine press.

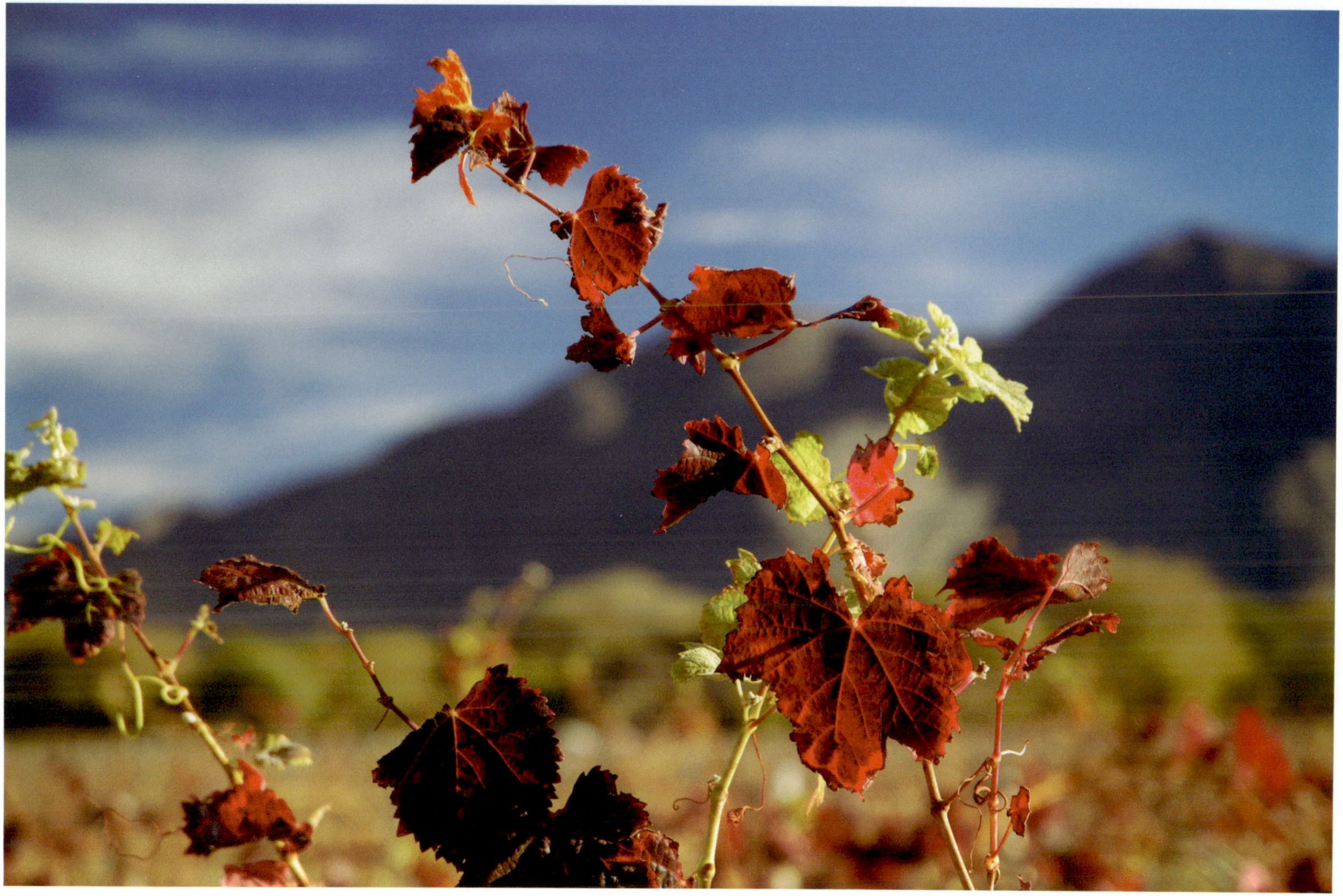

Autumn in the Colomé vineyards.

From Salta to the City of Jujuy via Camino de Cornisa

The Valle de Lerma runs lengthwise in a north-south direction near the center of the province of Salta. If we exit it by its southern end, the driest one, we drive into the Quebrada de las Conchas or Cafayate, which takes us into the Calchaquí Valleys. But now we choose the old road to Jujuy, National Route 9 which will take us out of the valley via its north end. This road is known as the Camino de Cornisa, and will take us through a part of the Mountain Forest or Yungas.

Only a few kilometers out of town the Valley gets narrower. After crossing Vaqueros, a village with vegetable fields and artisans, the road runs next to the Río Caldera in the midst of mountains that are low and covered with vegetation.

After not many curves and on the other side of the river, we see La Caldera, a small town whose main street is built upon the old Inca Trail that joined this area with Cuzco, in Peru. This charming little village dates back to the 16th century and offers an oasis of calm in the midst of the rush of civilization. Its chapel was built by the Jesuits, who preached here from 1615 until they were expelled by Charles III of Spain in 1769.

A part of the Camino de Cornisa (Mountain Road) that joins Salta and Jujuy. Behind, the Andes. *(p. 81)*

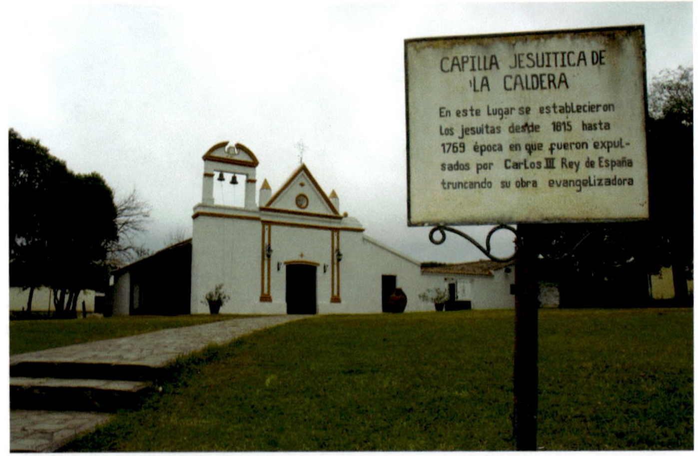

Jesuit Chapel in La Caldera

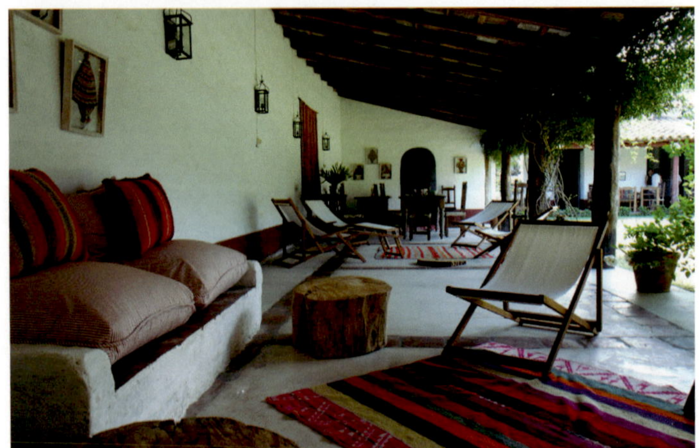

Patio in La Posada de La Caldera, that enchants with its colonial atmosphere.

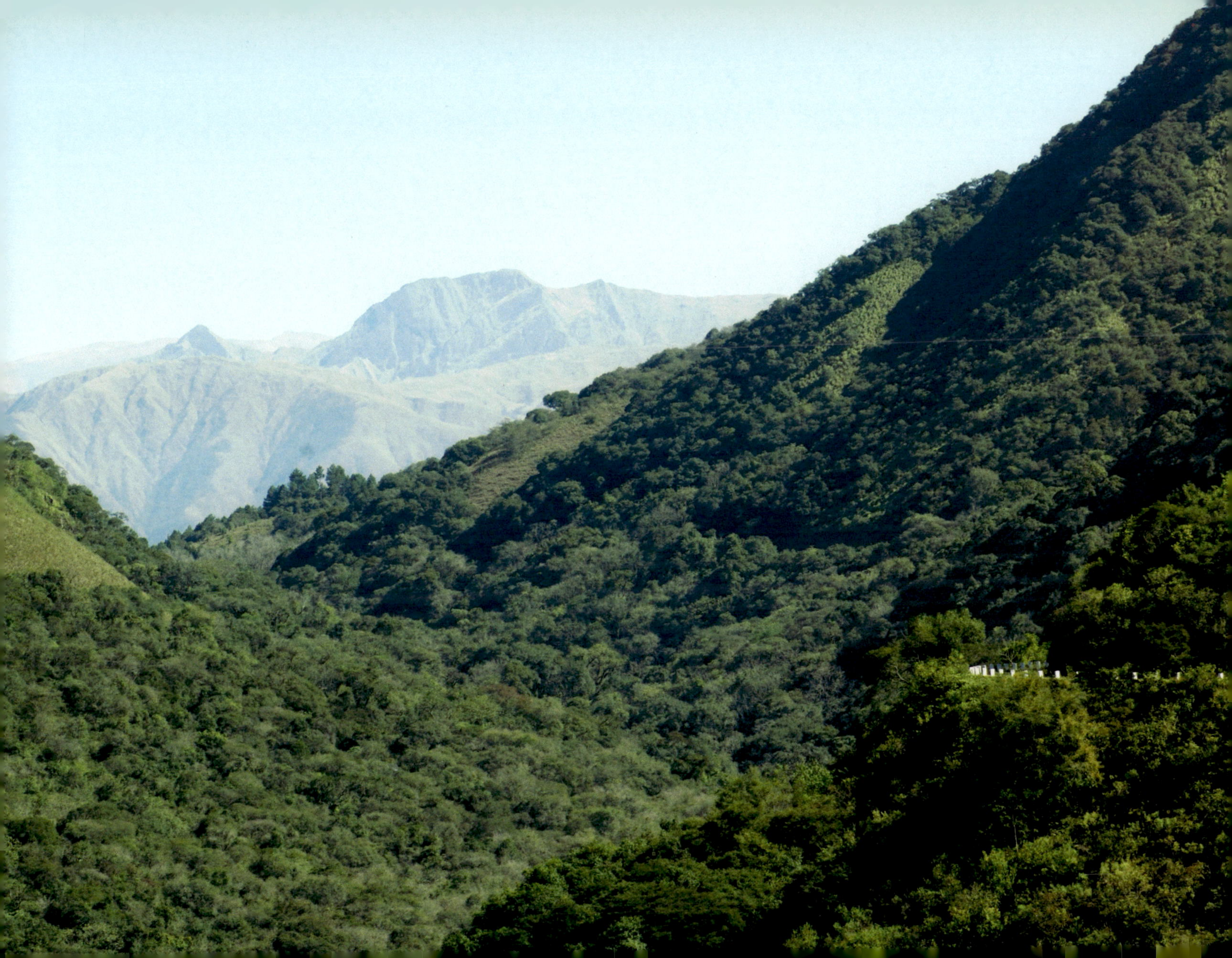

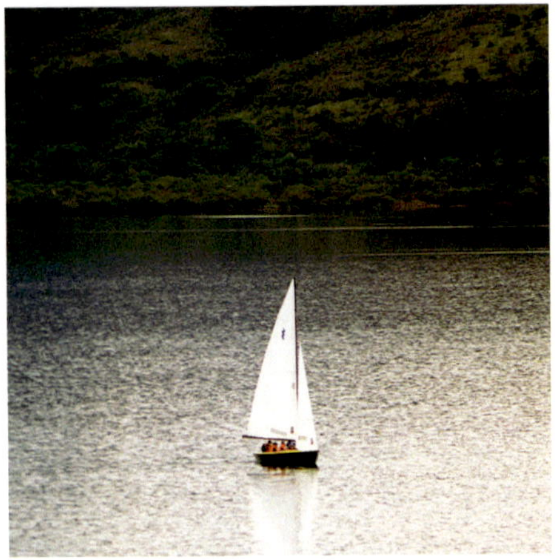

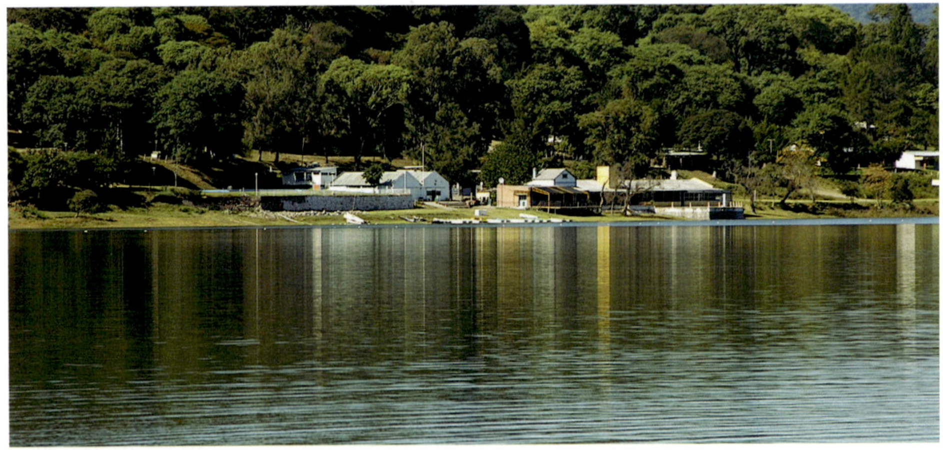

Salta. A sailing boat in the Campo Alegre dam.

Jujuy. La Cienaga dam.

Still going north, we pass by the Campo Alegre Dam, and by pine tree plantations for commercial use.

Soon we are driving along a road that curves around mountains and zigzags under a canopy of leaves that belong to some of these Mountain Forest giants: cedro *(Cedrella sp.)*, laurel del cerro *(Phoebe porphyria)*, palo amarillo o lanza *(Phyllostylon ramnoides)*, tipas *(Tipuana tipu)*, horco molle *(Blepharocalyx gigantea)*; just to name a few of these magnificent trees that cover the steep slopes.

We are crossing a part of the Mountain Forest or Yungas. These are names given to the abundant vegetation that covers the eastern slopes of the different mountain chains in this part of northern Argentina. The vegetation here changes not only in an east–west direction but also according to the altitude above sea level. Up to a height of 500 m.a.s.l. (1640 ft) we find what is called the Transition Forest; lumbering in this area has produced fields suitable for the plantation of crops such as fruit trees, sugar cane, tobacco, maize, and vegetables. Above this, the vegetation turns rich and exuberant, due to a greater rainfall and usually at 900 m.a.s.l. (2950 ft), the mountain sides are covered by clouds, thus increasing humidity. Here the vegetation becomes copious with epiphytes such as bromeliads and orchids that cover whole branches with many climbers that reach up looking for light.

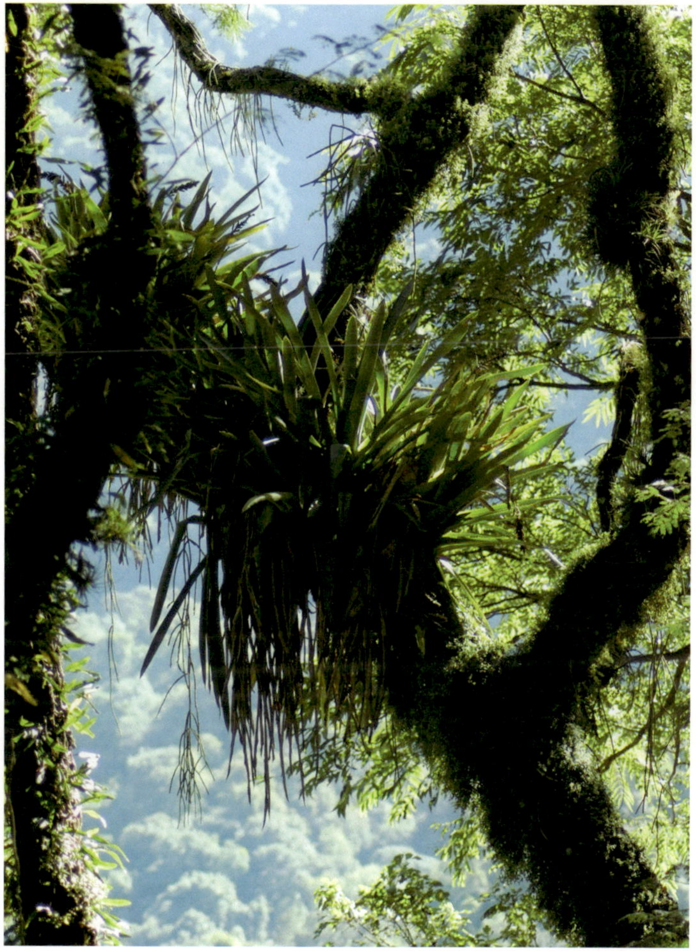

Bromeliads and other epiphytes cover the branches of a tree.

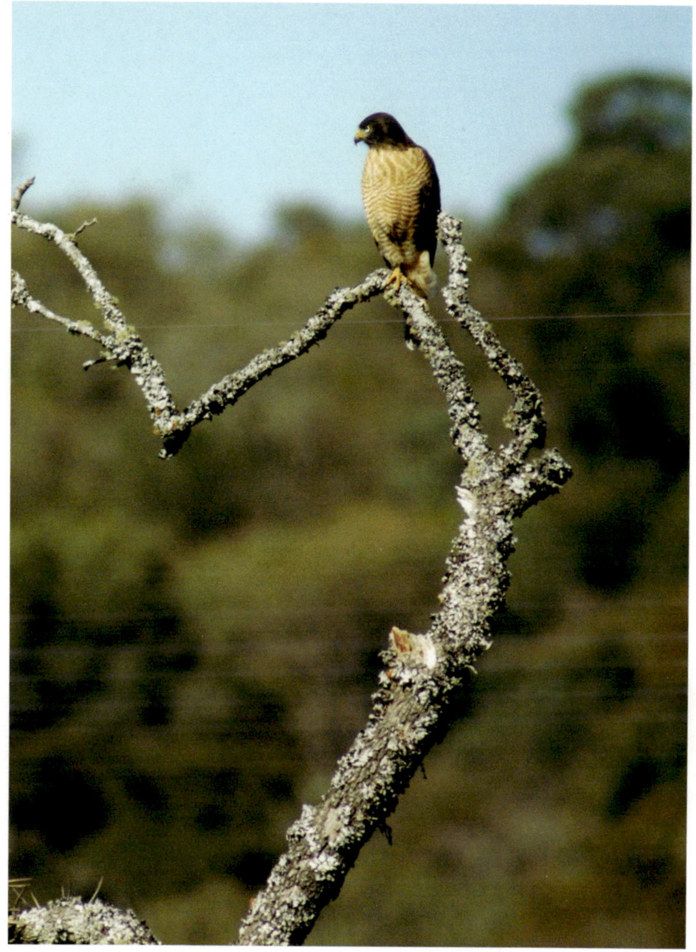

Taguato (Buteo magnirostris)

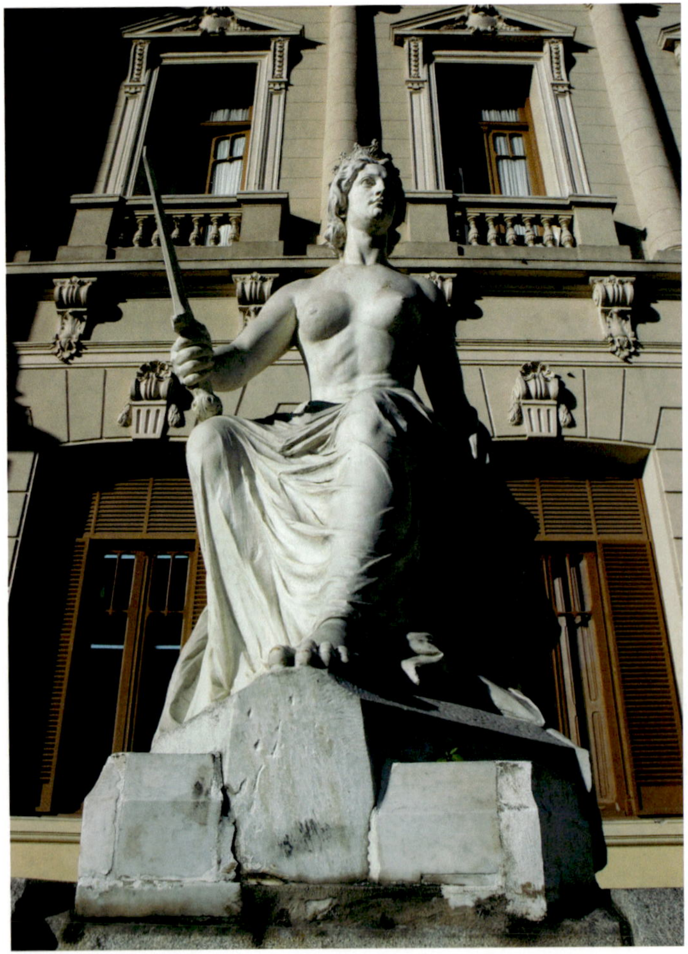

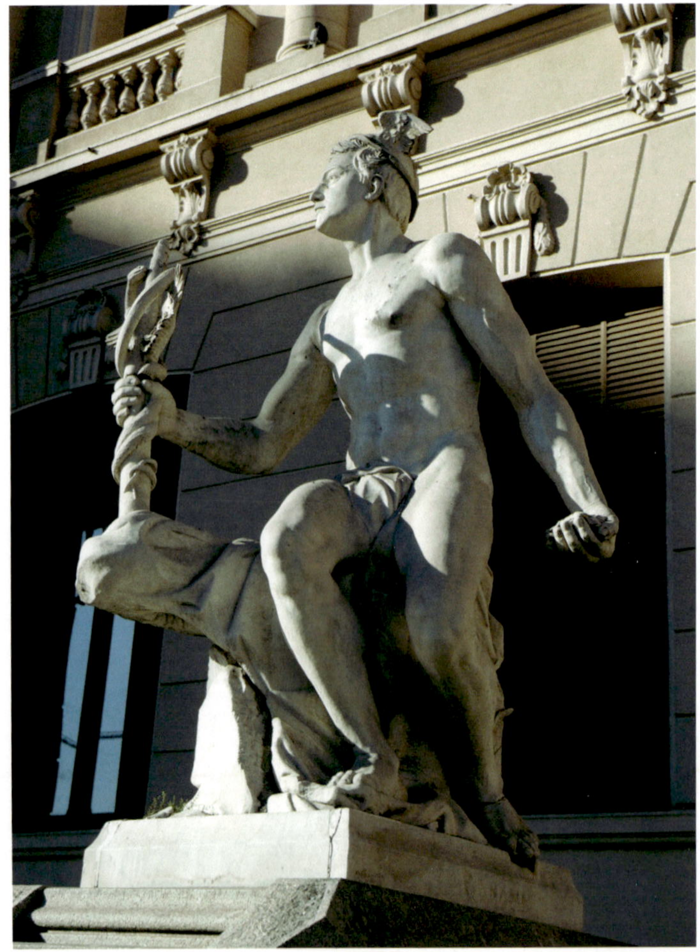

In the city of San Salvador de Jujuy, the Government House is guarded by these sculptures made by Lola Mora.

This exuberance is seen up to 1600 m.a.s.l., with evergreen trees at higher elevations. From there up to a height of 2000 m.a.s.l. the predominant species are alisos *(Alnus jorullensis)* and pinos del cerro *(Podocarpus parlatorei)*.

In this latitude, during the dry season, the underbrush dries up and many trees loose their leaves.

We leave the forest behind when we reach the agricultural area of El Carmen. We travel amongst farms until we reach the city of San Salvador de Jujuy, the capital of the province. Located between the rivers Grande and Xibi Xibi, at 1259 m.a.s.l. (4130 ft), it was founded in 1593 by Francisco de Argañaráz y Murguía, at the orders of Don Juan Ramírez de Velazco; its original name was San Salvador de Velazco in the Valley of Jujuy. Its location became strategic during the Independence wars, so much so, that between the years of 1810 and 1822 the city was invaded eleven times by Spanish troops.

Its architecture shows a contrast between traditional and modern styles. Plaza Belgrano, in the middle of town, is surrounded by the most important buildings.

The Governement house has a baroque style, and holds within its walls the original flag that General Belgrano donated to the citizens of Jujuy after his triumphs in Salta and as a recognition for their sacrifices during the 1812 Exodus and in the Independence Wars.

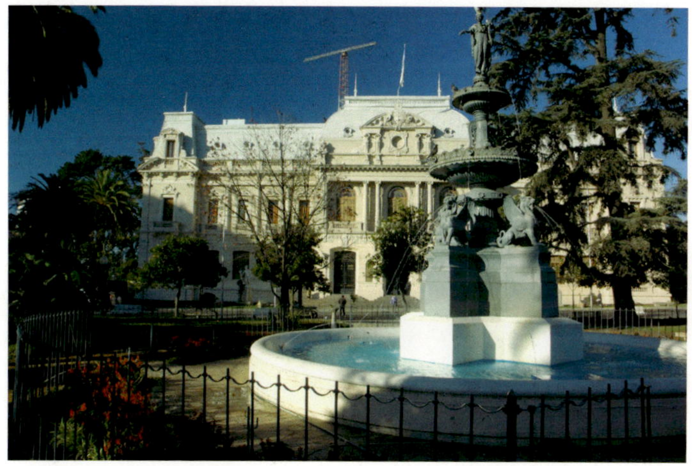

San Salvador de Jujuy, Government House.

The Cathedral, constructed in the early 1600's is also on the Plaza. Its baroque pulpit is famous, carved in wood and highlighted with gold leaf. It is one of the best pieces of its kind in America.

In front of the Plaza we find the Cabildo, the colonial town hall. Today this building houses the Police Headquarters. A couple of blocks away the San Francisco Church is guarded by beautiful ironwork (rejas), and near it the old house where General Lavalle was shot in 1841 is now the Provincial Historical Museum.

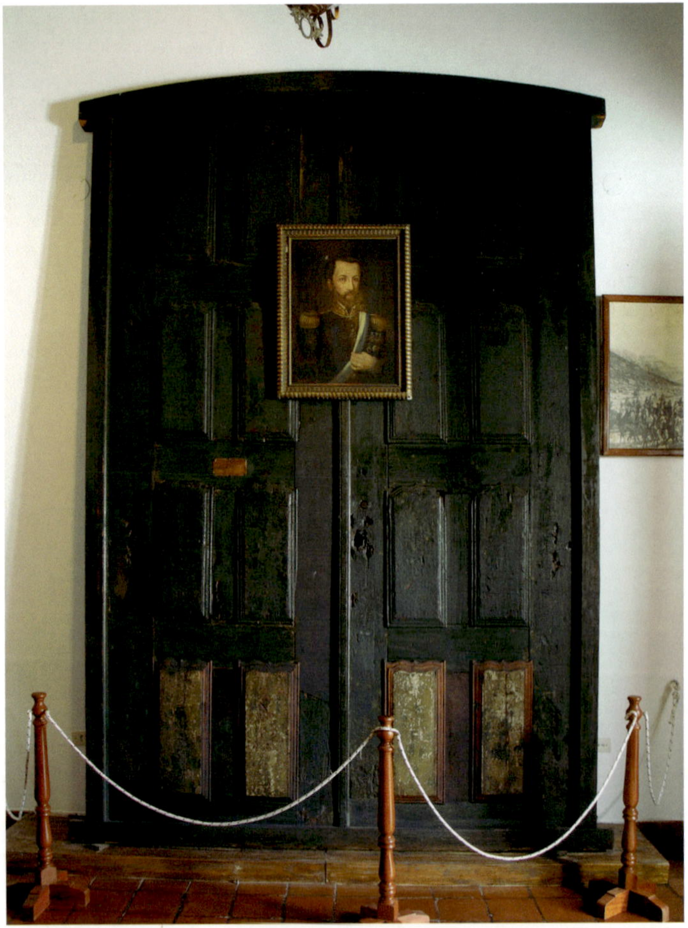

Provincial Historical Museum. Through this door, General Juan Galo Lavalle was shot in 1841.

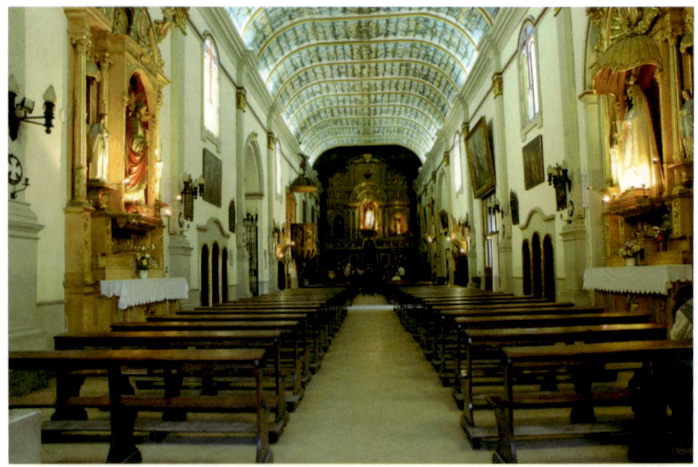

Interior of the San Salvador de Jujuy Cathedral.

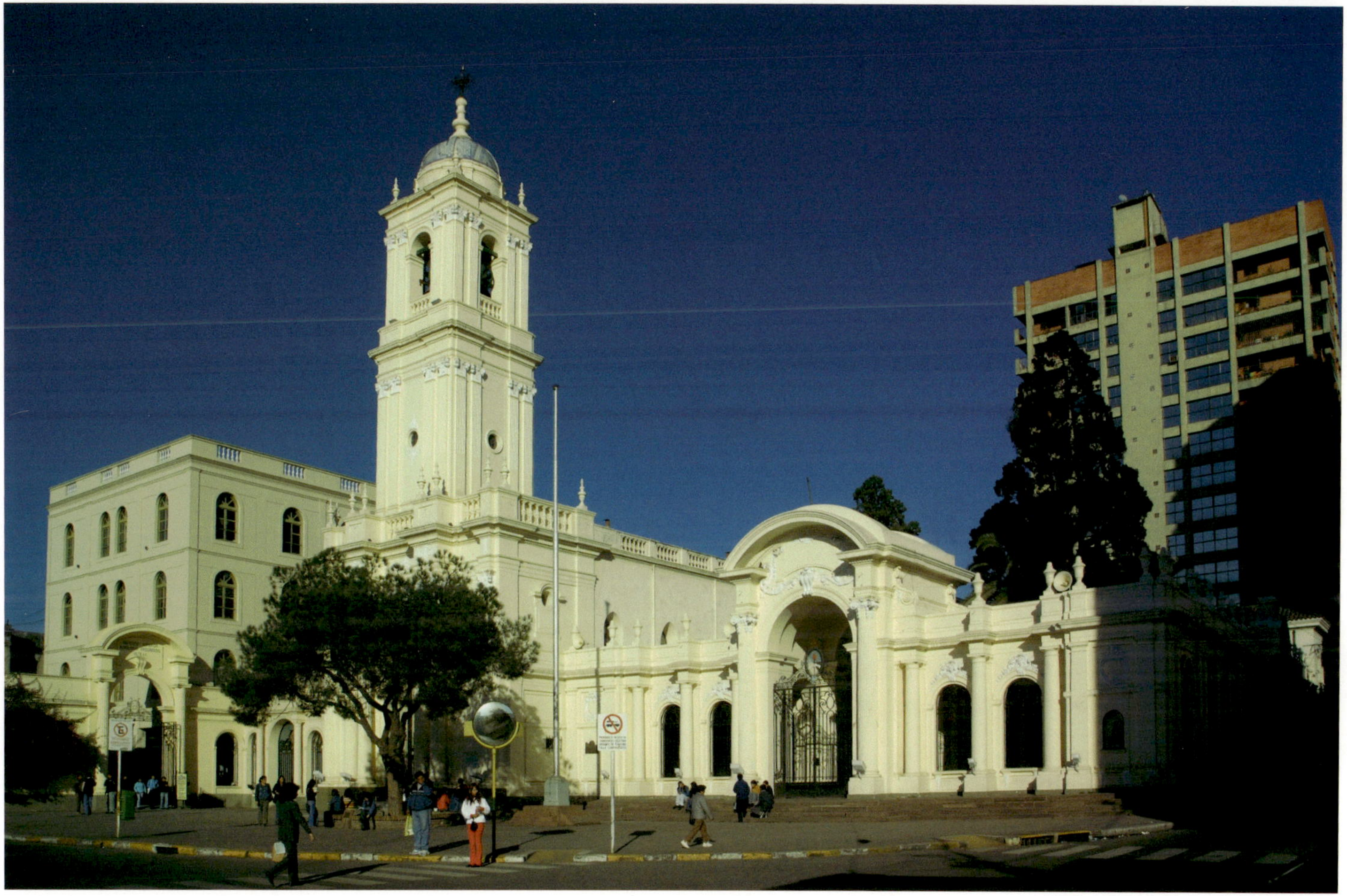

Cathedral of San Salvador de Jujuy. This neoclassical church was built in the early 1600's.

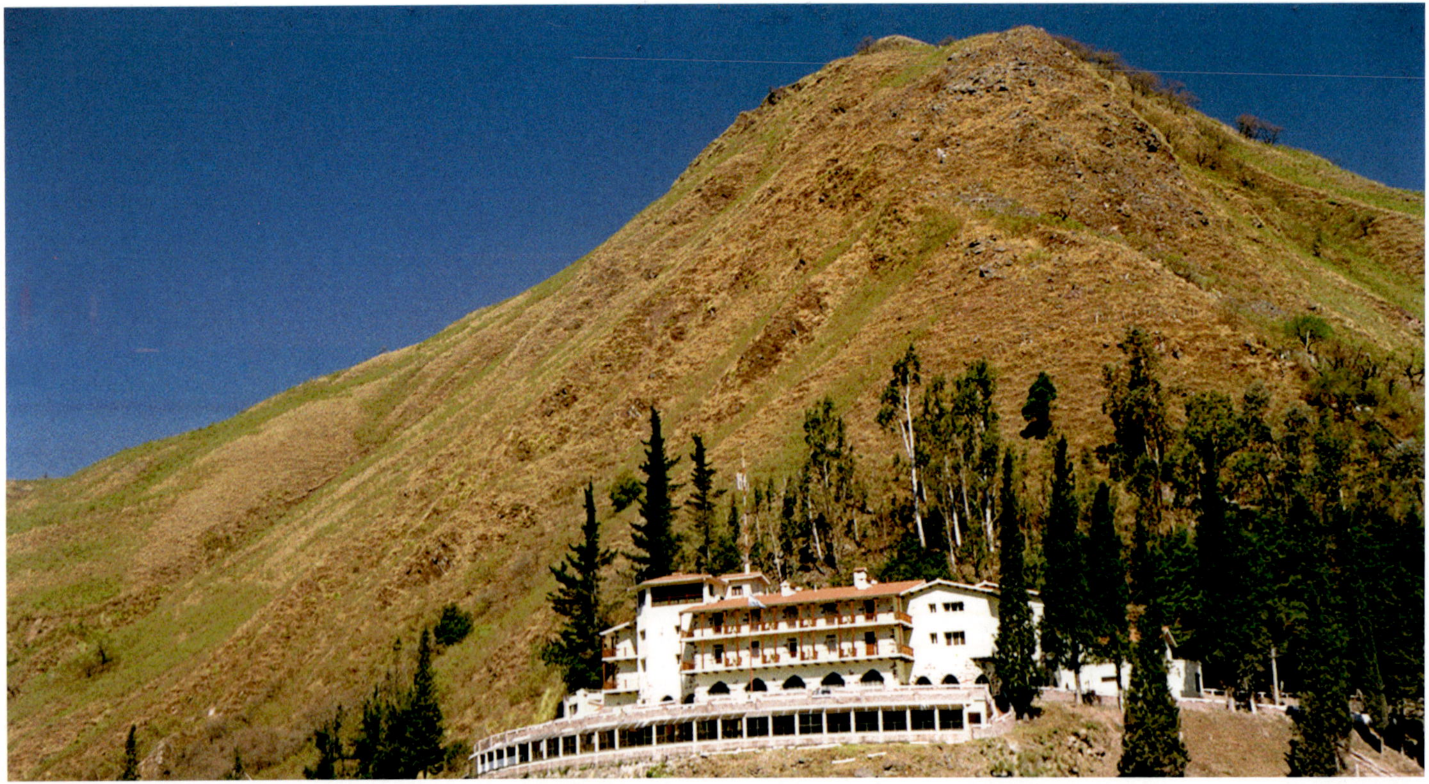

Termas de Reyes Hotel, located north of the city of Jujuy. Its thermal waters were used by the Inca Chiefs, hence the name given to this place by the Spaniards.

Once out of the city, to the north we pass through the villages of Lozano, Tiraxi and Termas de Reyes, all set in green landscape that invites us to enjoy nature. Or we can go up to the Yala lagoons that are fed from the snow capped Andean peaks. They create their own microclimate, and are surrounded by trees and ferns. Then, we carry on to the north where the road climbs and the valley narrows. We are already on our way towards the Quebrada de Humahuaca.

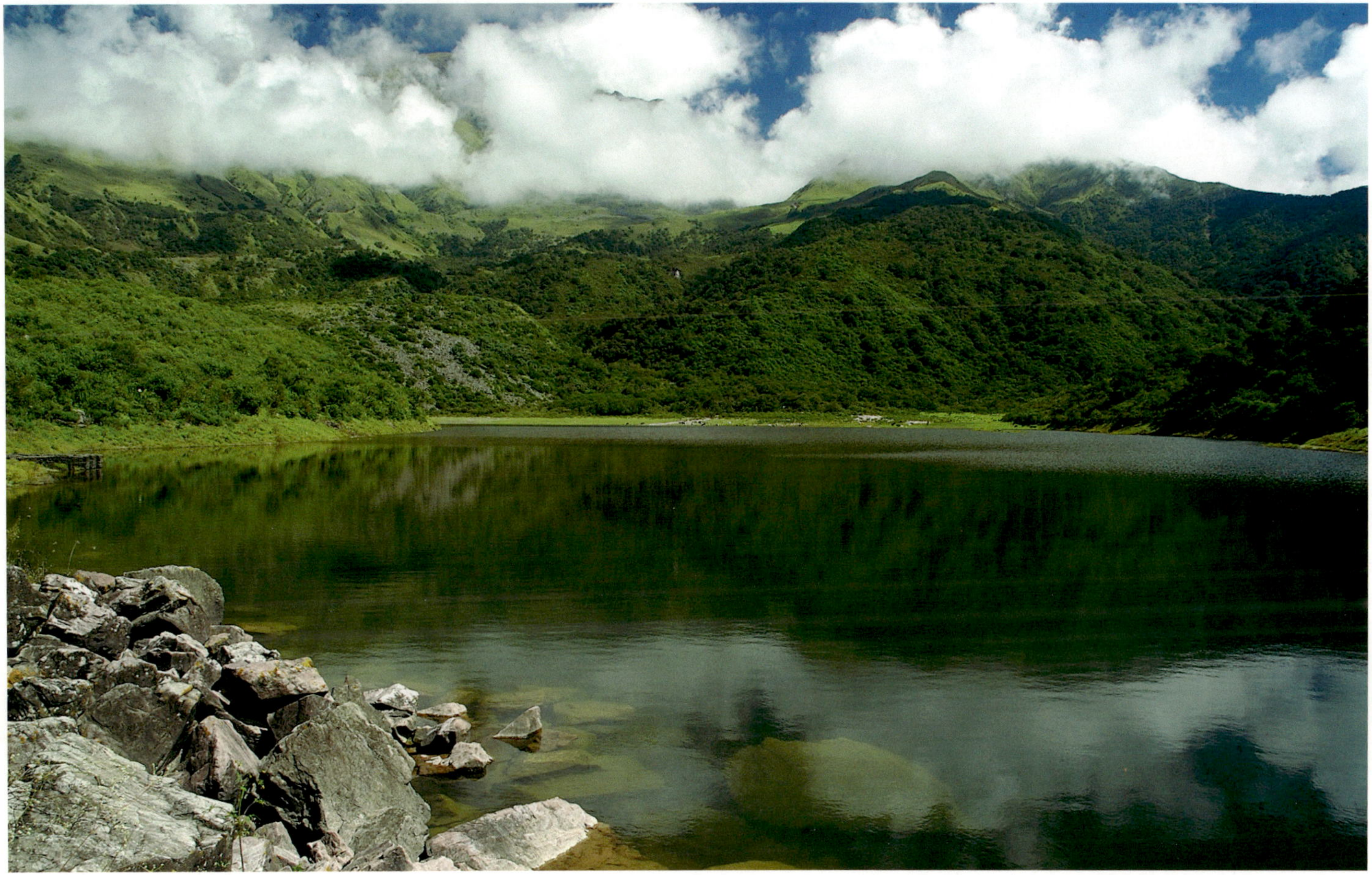

One of the Yala lagoons.

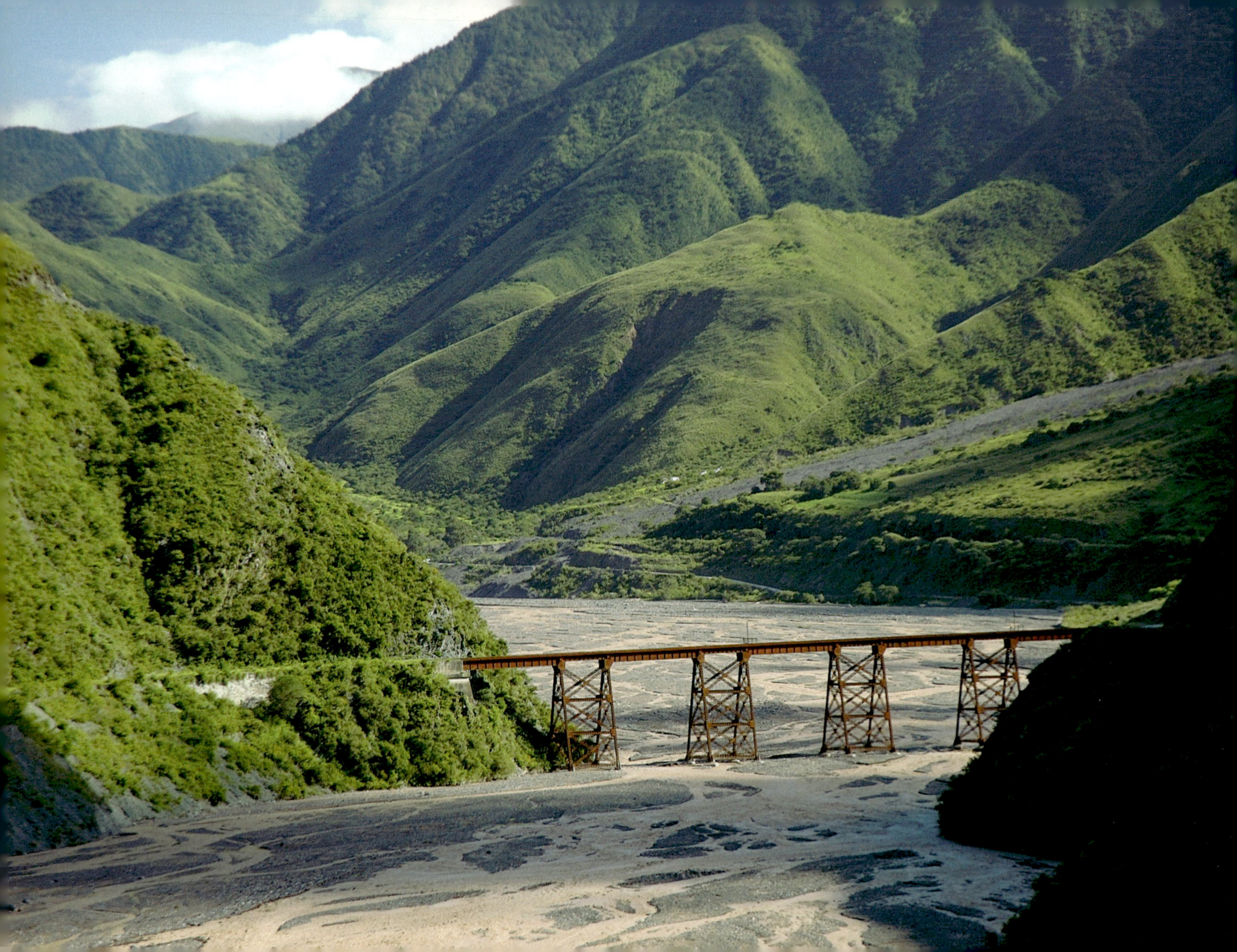

From Salta to Purmamarca via Quebrada del Toro and Puna

We head west, out of Salta on National Route 51. The road climbs slightly. The city lies behind but we travel in the midst of oats, tobacco or alfalfa fields; crops change with each season. The mountains get closer; the vegetation turns rich at the foot of the hills. It is here that it rains more frequently in the Valle de Lerma.

The last village in the valley before we enter the Quebrada del Toro is Campo Quijano, where we find a borax processing plant, a mineral brought down from the Puna. On leaving this village we find Río Blanco, a group of traditional colonial summer houses surrounded by seibos *(Erithryna falcata)* and ferns growing on stone walls.

We are now in the gorge and it is plain to see that it is a natural passageway crossing the Oriental Andes. It is, and has been, a ceaseless connecting road between the high plateau or Puna and the lower fertile valleys to the East, for the inhabitants of both regions.

The river flowing through this gorge is the Rio Toro, whose name, they say, comes from a Quechua word meaning mud. When one sees it swell in summer after heavy rainfall it is easy to understand why.

Quebrada del Toro in summer.
Toro Viaduct. (p. 90)

Pampa grass in the Río Toro,
near Estancia El Gólgota.

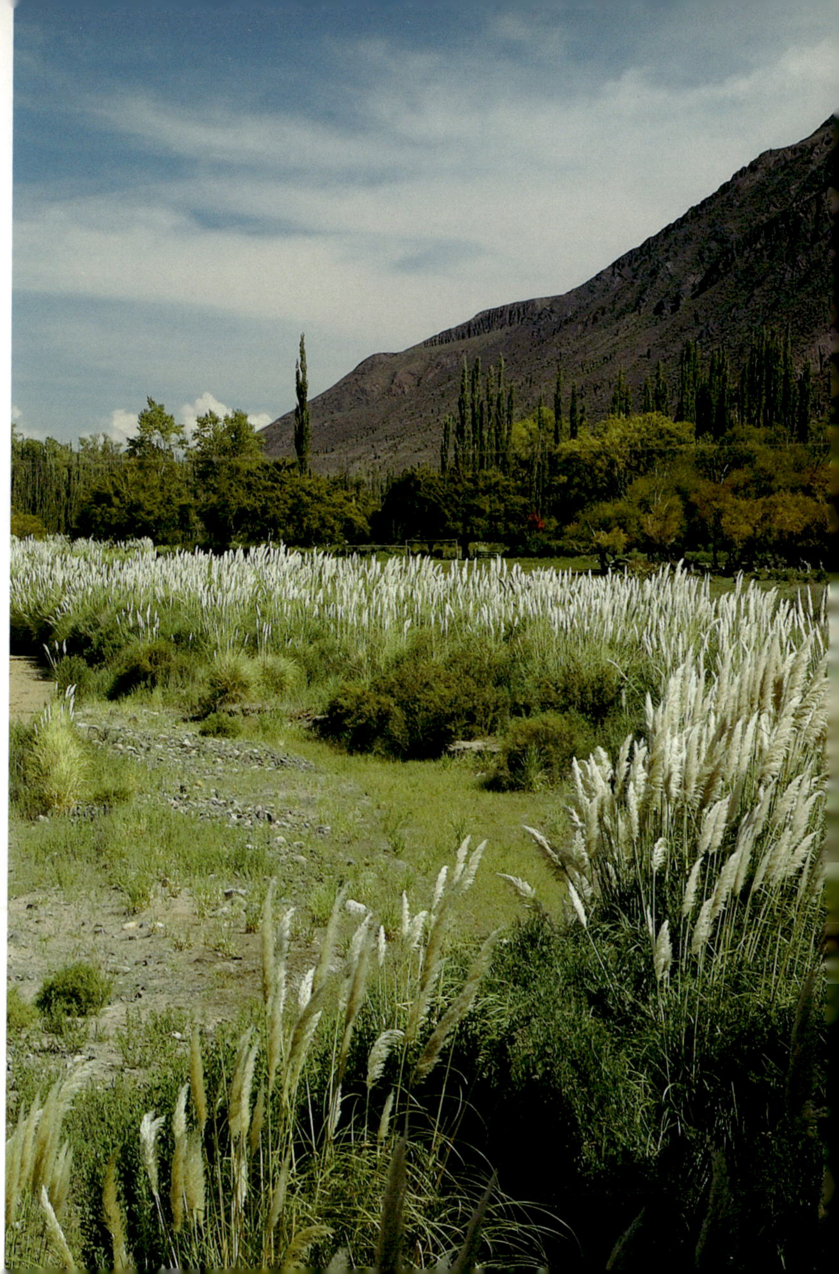

The railway crosses the road; it is the Ramal C14 that leads to Chile. Road and railway run sometimes side by side, sometimes on the opposite river bank, others the rails go higher than the road.These rails were built between 1921 and 1948, an incredible engineering task accomplished by Ing. Fontaine Maury. It is famous for being the third highest railway in the world, and because it climbs without the use of a ratchet wheel, using instead a zig zag system, going from 1187 m.a.s.l. in Salta to 4200 m.a.s.l. (13780 ft) in La Polvorilla.

Train to the Clouds crossing the Toro Viaduct; this is the first bridge in the gorge and also the longest. On the right we see the train on the Polvorilla Viaduct, set at 4200 m.a.s.l. and the highlight of the tour.

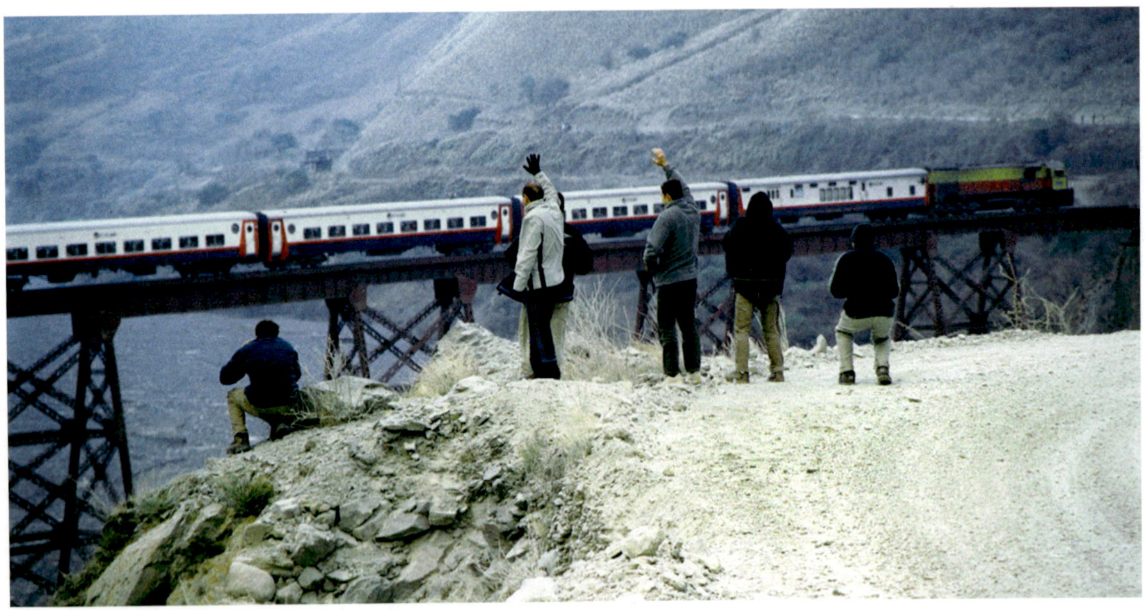

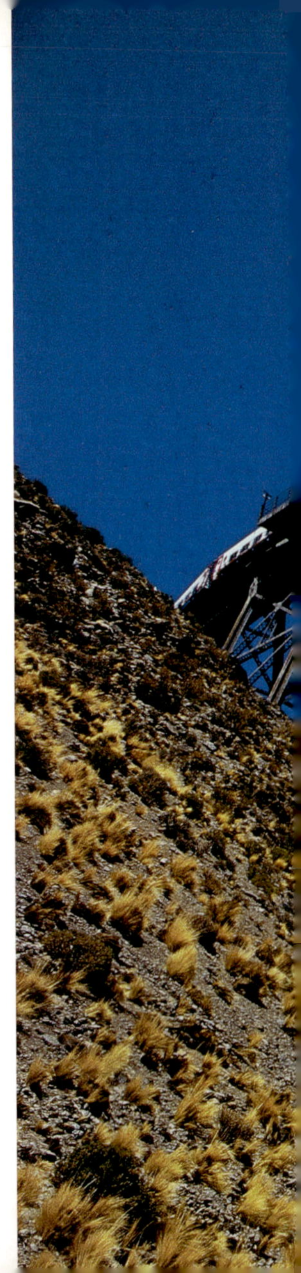

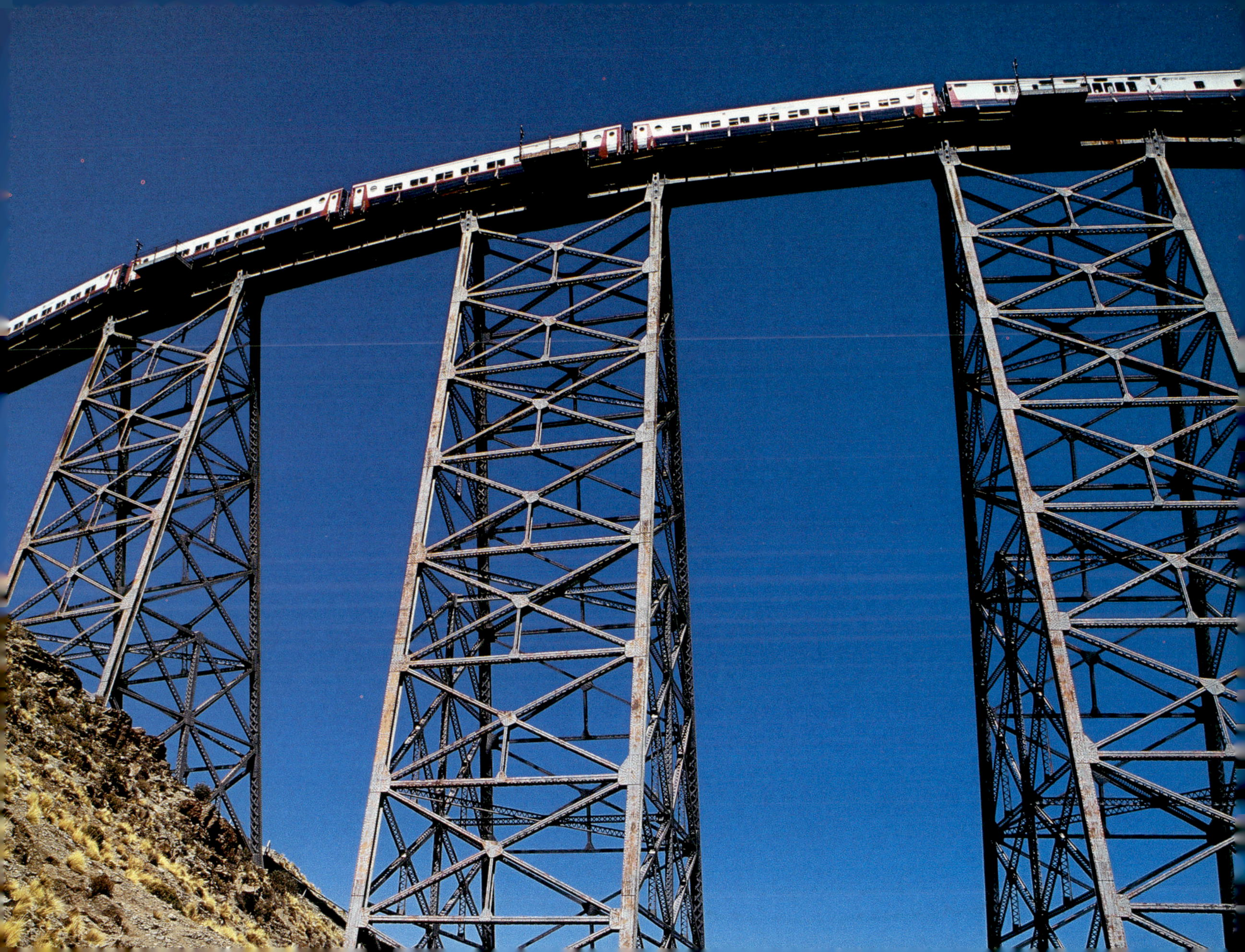

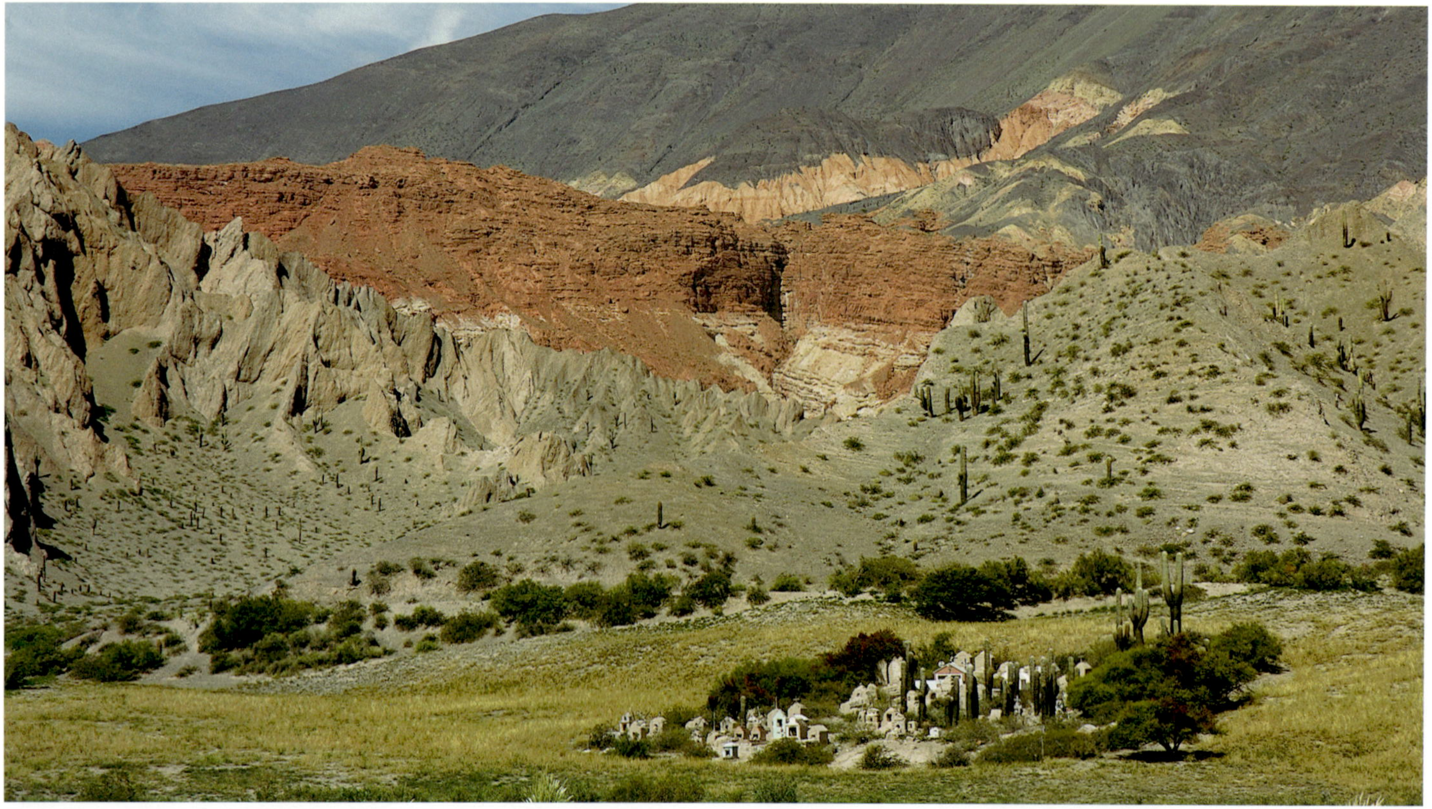

Quebrada del Toro. A cemetery.

This railway was made to transport nitrates from the mines in Chile over to Argentina, but when this construction ended, nitrates were replaced by artificial fertilizers, so its original use changed. The first time it ran as the tourist attraction named the "Train to the Clouds" was in July 1972.

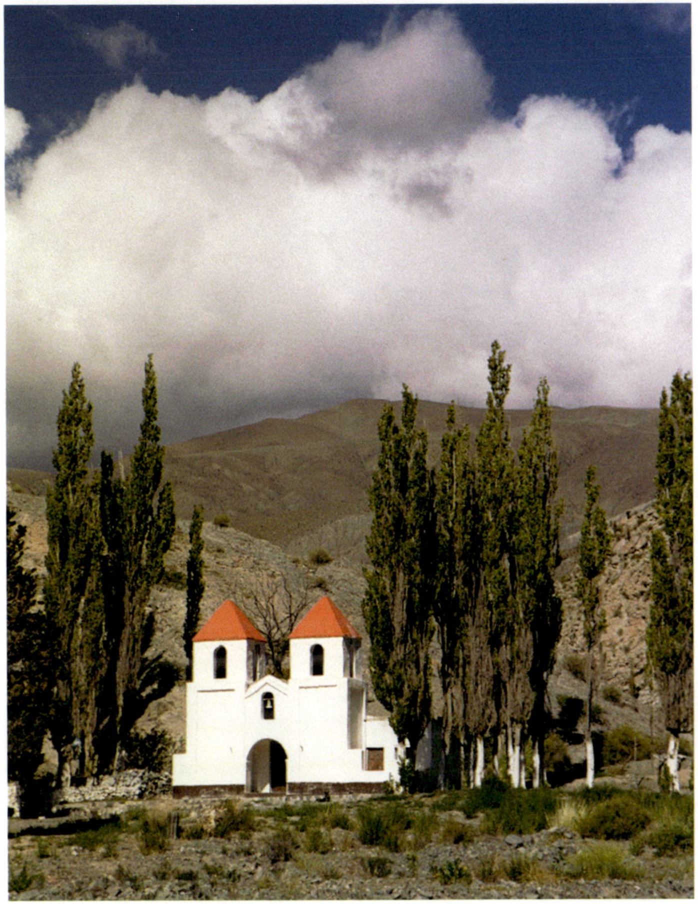

Church in Alfarcito. This village owes its name to the alfalfa meadows it grew to feed mules and cattle on their way up to the Puna.

The road goes by Alfarcito, where it climbs abruptly and the landscape changes; we drive by grasslands under which is damp sponge like ground. We arrive at Santa Rosa de Tastil, whose name makes reference to the pre–hispanic ruins located behind the village. They are Argentina's most important archeological site without any Inca influence. Belonging to the Atacama Culture they were abandoned pacifically by their inhabitants circa 1439 AD (by Eduardo Cigliano, an archeologist who researched this culture extensively).

After crossing Abra Blanca (4080 m.a.s.l.), San Antonio de los Cobres is the first town we find in the Puna. Its inhabitants work in the open mines of the region, mainly borax and salt; they also trade between the most remote Puna areas and the cities down in the valley.

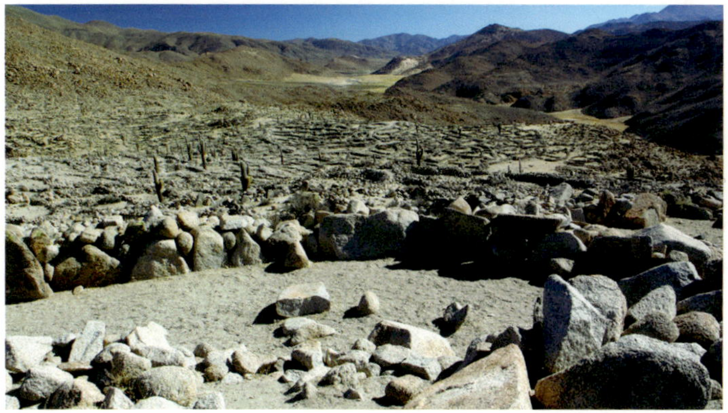

Tastil Ruins. Vista from the highest point.

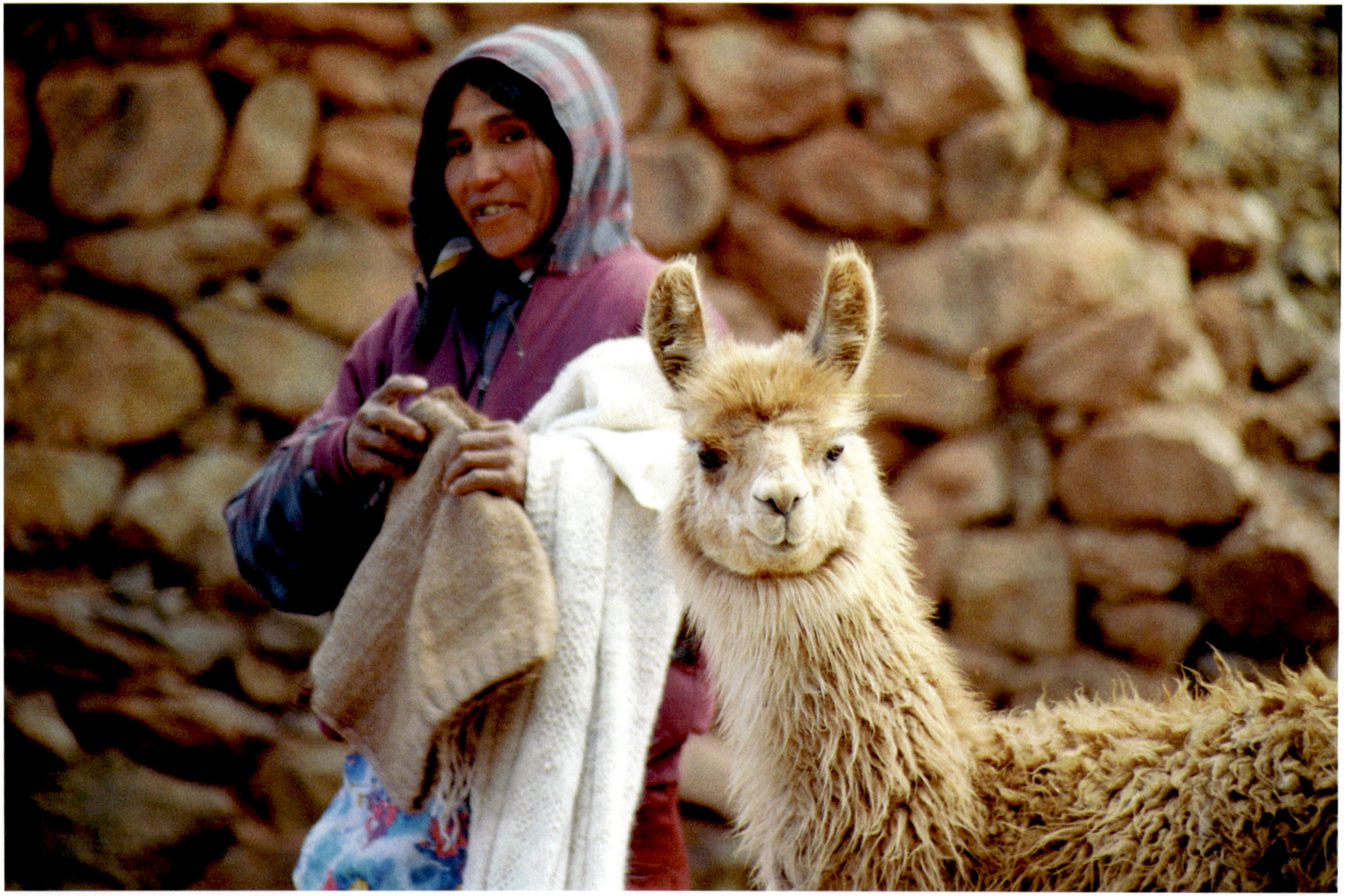

Lady, and her llama, selling wool crafts in San Antonio de los Cobres.

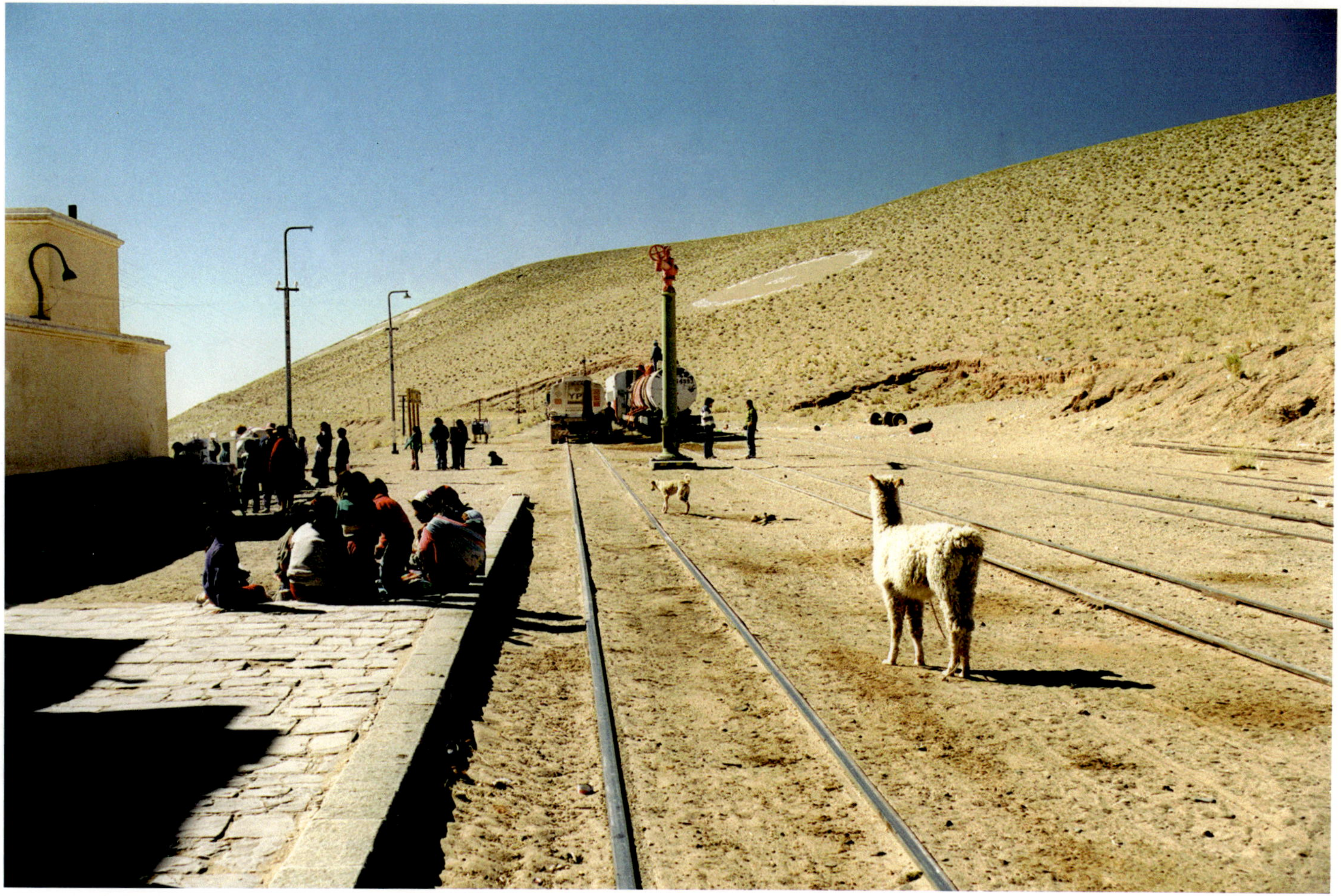

San Antonio de los Cobres Train station.

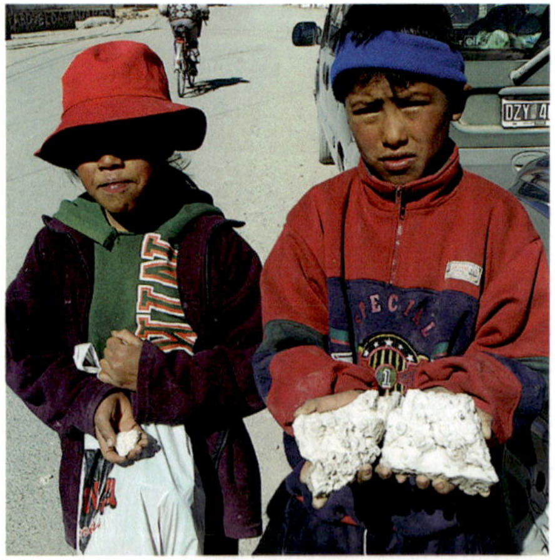

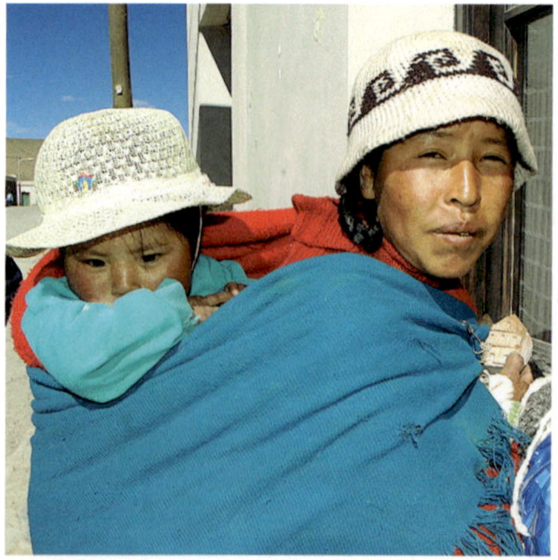

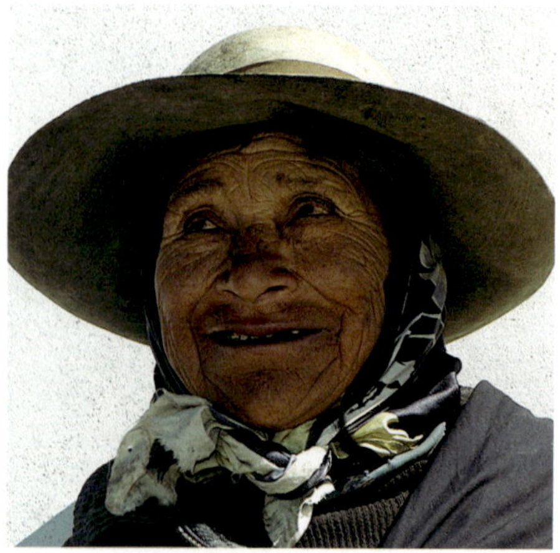

The Puna inhabitants belong to an Andean race, as we can see in their defined features. Long before the Spanish conquest they were influenced by two of the most important Andean cultures, the Tihuanacu and the Inca.

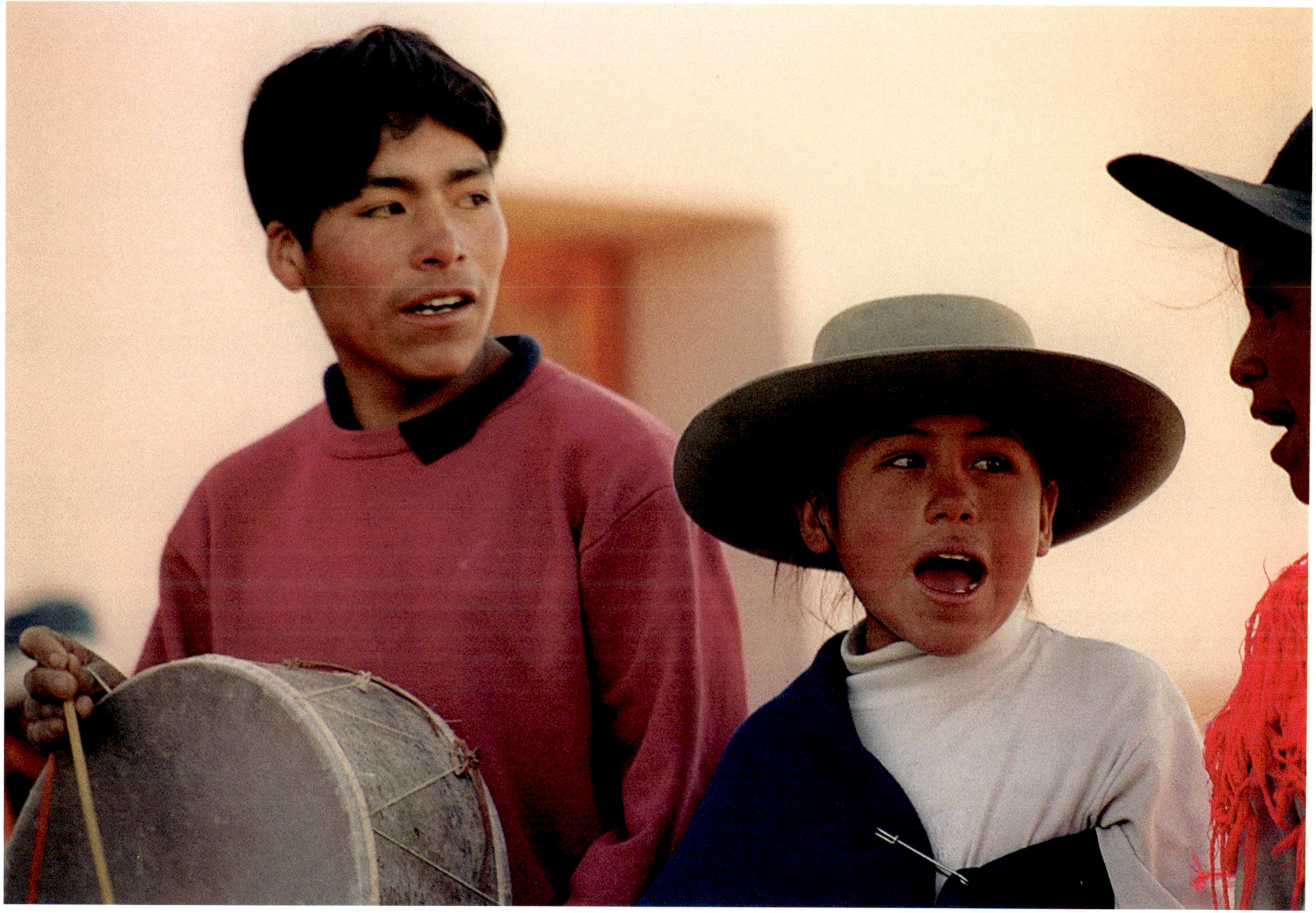

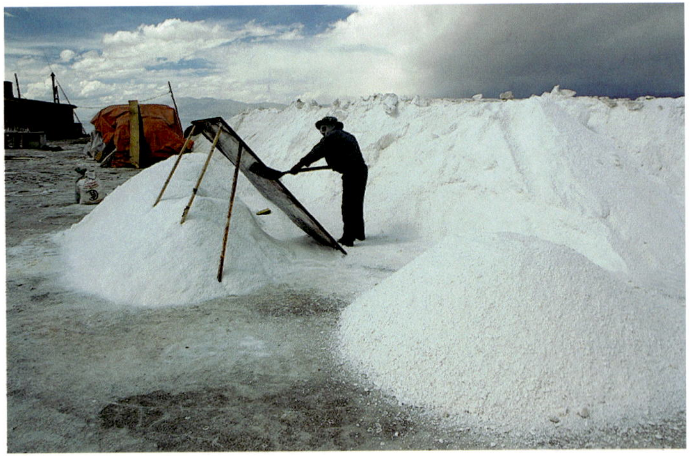

Salinas Grandes. Worker seiving salt.

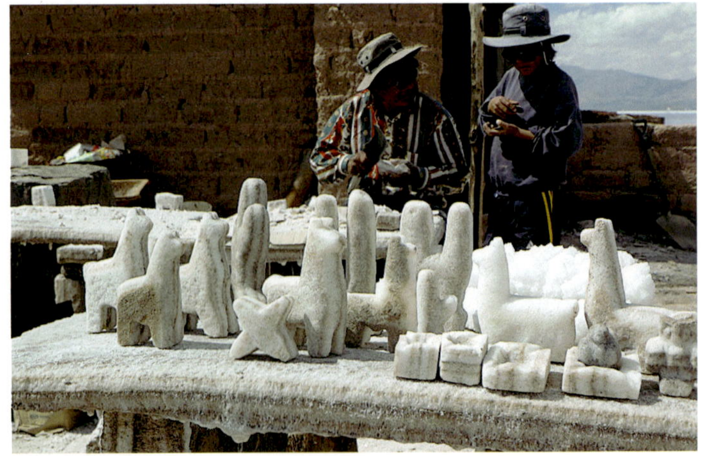

Salt handicraft sale.

National Route 40 leads to the north, lonely immensity overwhelms us while the small dwellings we see show that there is human life in this high plateau.

The Salinas Grandes cover the lowest part of this Puna basin. During ancient times they were lakes that even today, after heavy summer storms are covered with a few centimeters of water for a couple of days.

Sunset. The Occidental Andes as seen from the Puna.

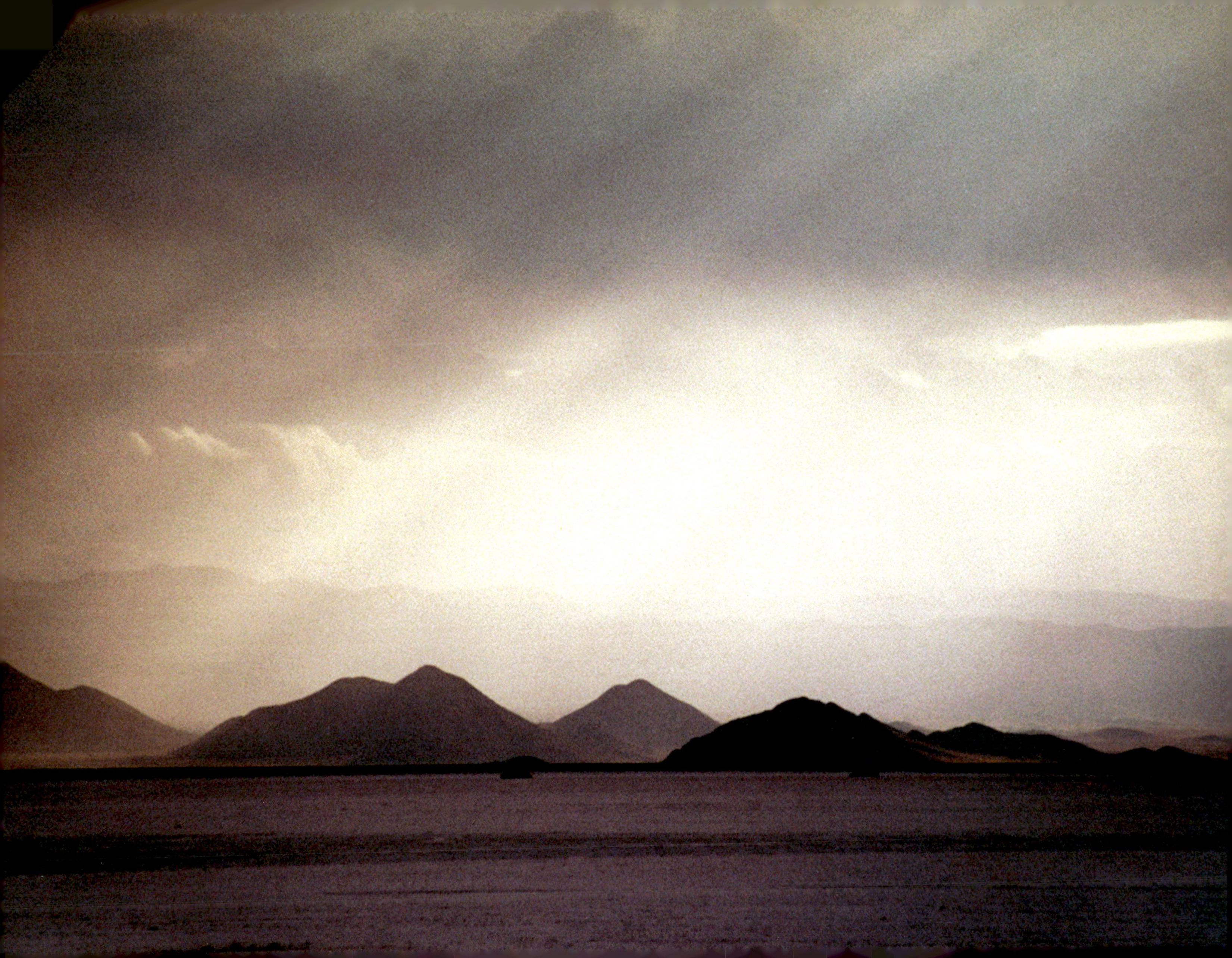

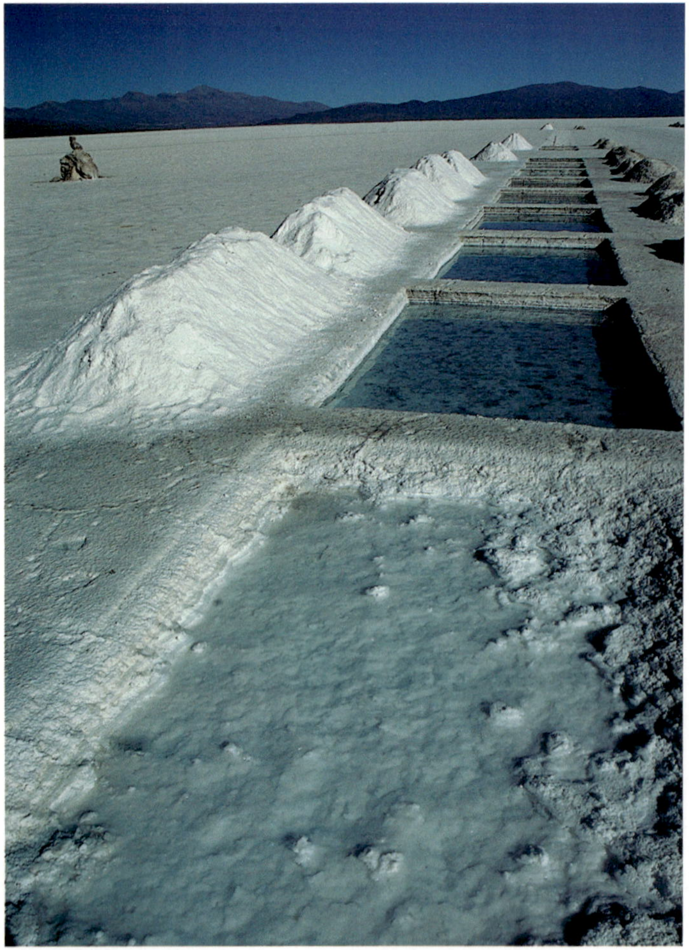

Hand made pools where the workers gather salt.

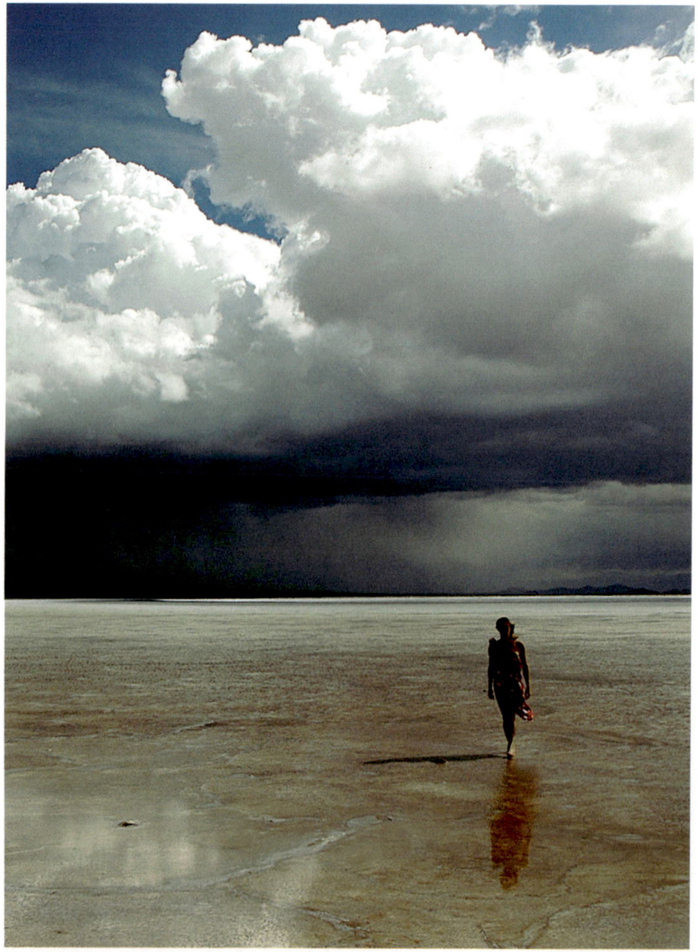

In summer and only during a few days, after a shower the Salinas are covered by a few centimeters of water.

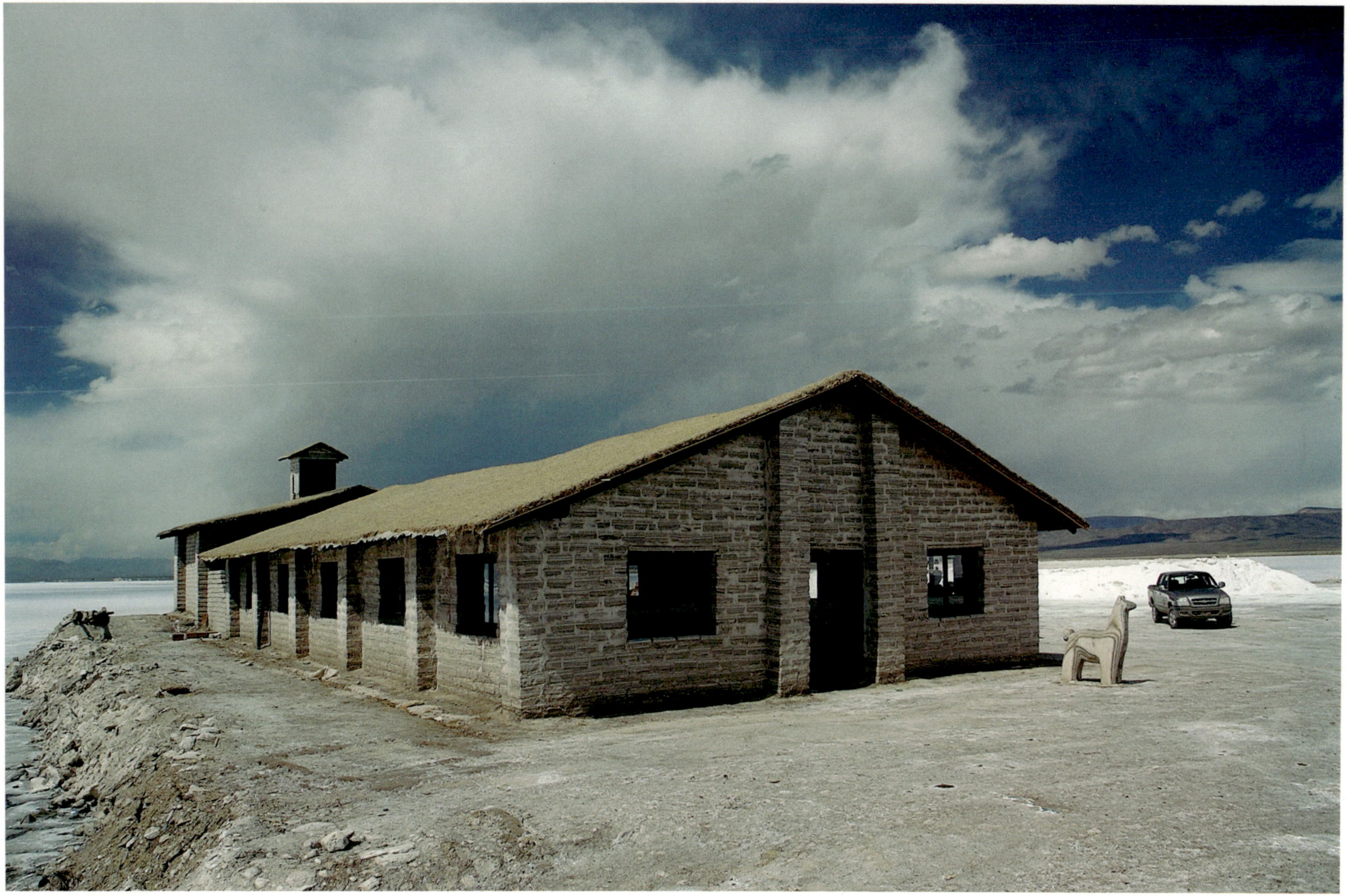

A coffee shop built with salt bricks.

The Puna is a high mountain plateau located between two mountain ranges. In northern Argentina, the Andes divided in two ranges: Oriental Andes and Occidental Andes. They both join later in the province of Catamarca, from where they go on south as one mountain chain. Between these two ranges we find the Puna, with an average height of 3800 m.a.s.l. (12470 ft). Here it rains very little, although there is rainfall on the surrounding mountain tops. This water eventually filters under the sandy soil and emerges in the center of each Puna pocket full of minerals, where it will forma a salt flat.

This Puna or Altiplano formation extends, with similar characteristics to the south of Ecuador.

After visiting this breathtaking place, our road heads East on National Route 52, climbing once again to reach an altitude of 4170 meters. There we encounter the typical colours the Eastern Andes. The Cuesta de Lipán slides down, and the landscape changes as fast as we loose meters.

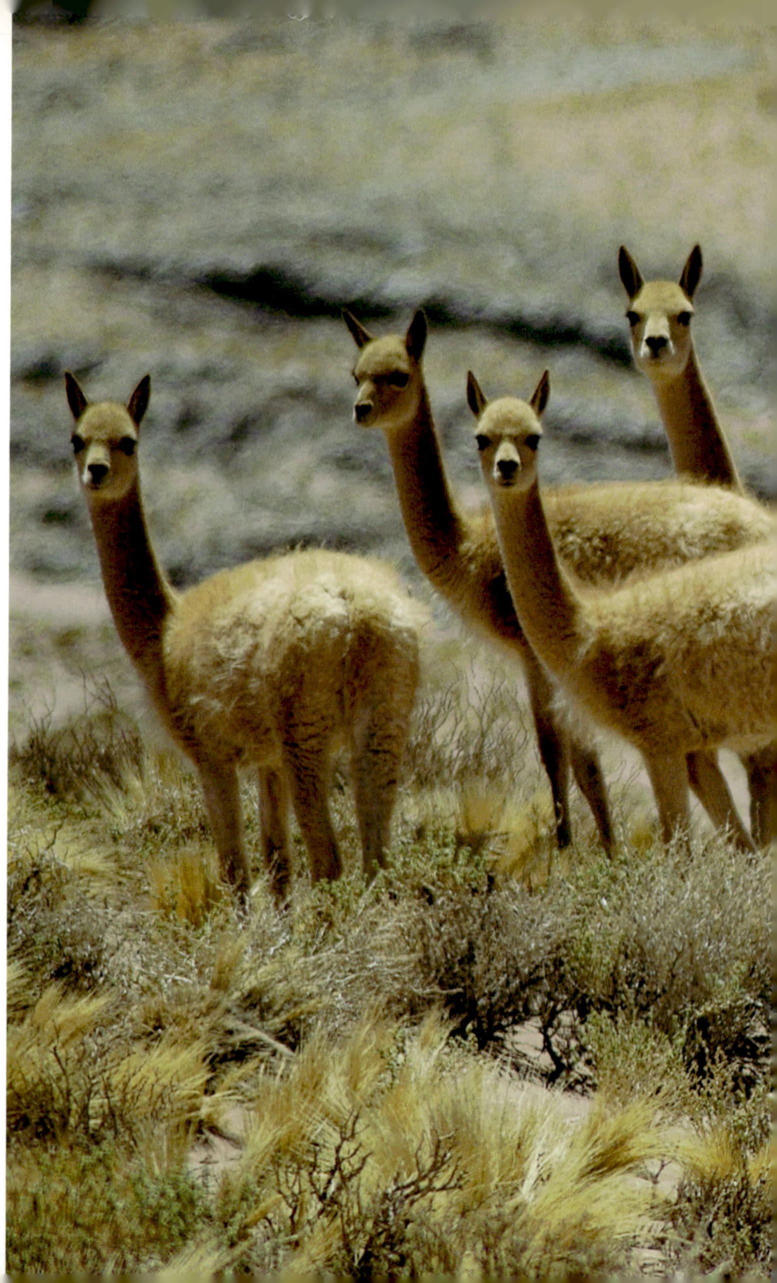

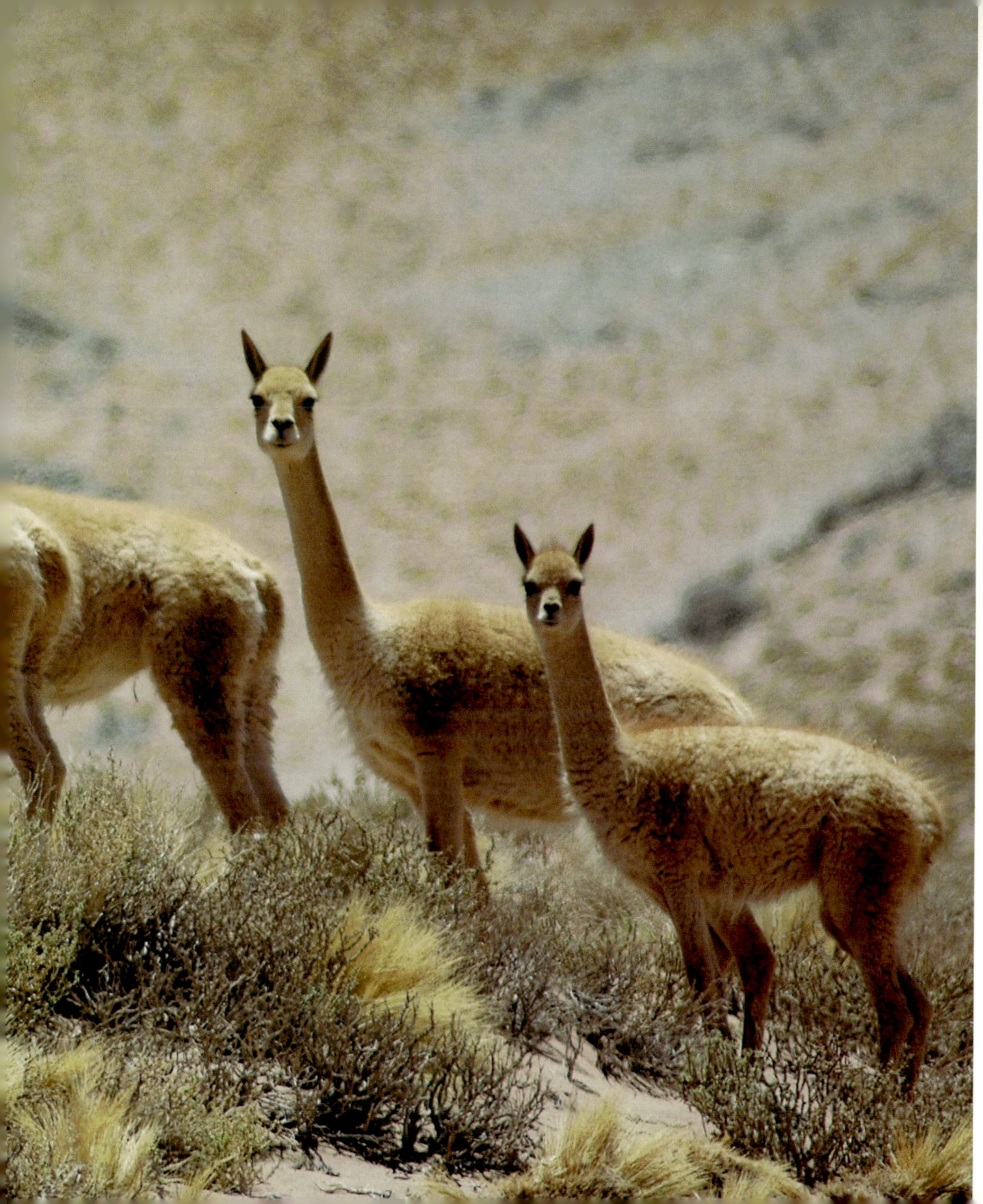

Vicuñas (Vicugna Vicugna). This is one of the four andean camelids. They are wild and an endangered species. They have been hunted for years for their fleece since the goods knitted with their wool are very valuable.

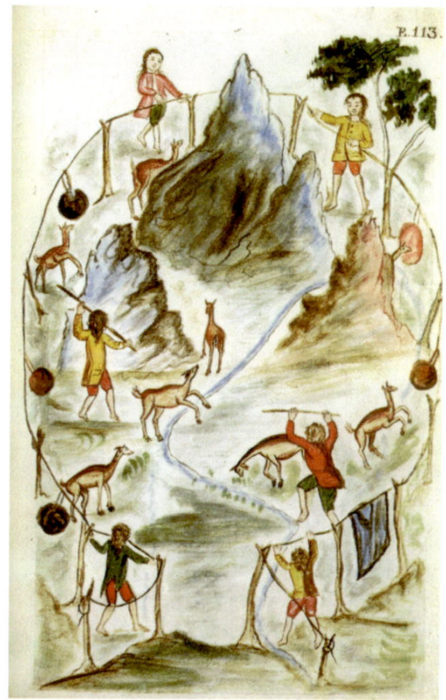

Martínez Compañón (1735–1797), Vicuña hunting.

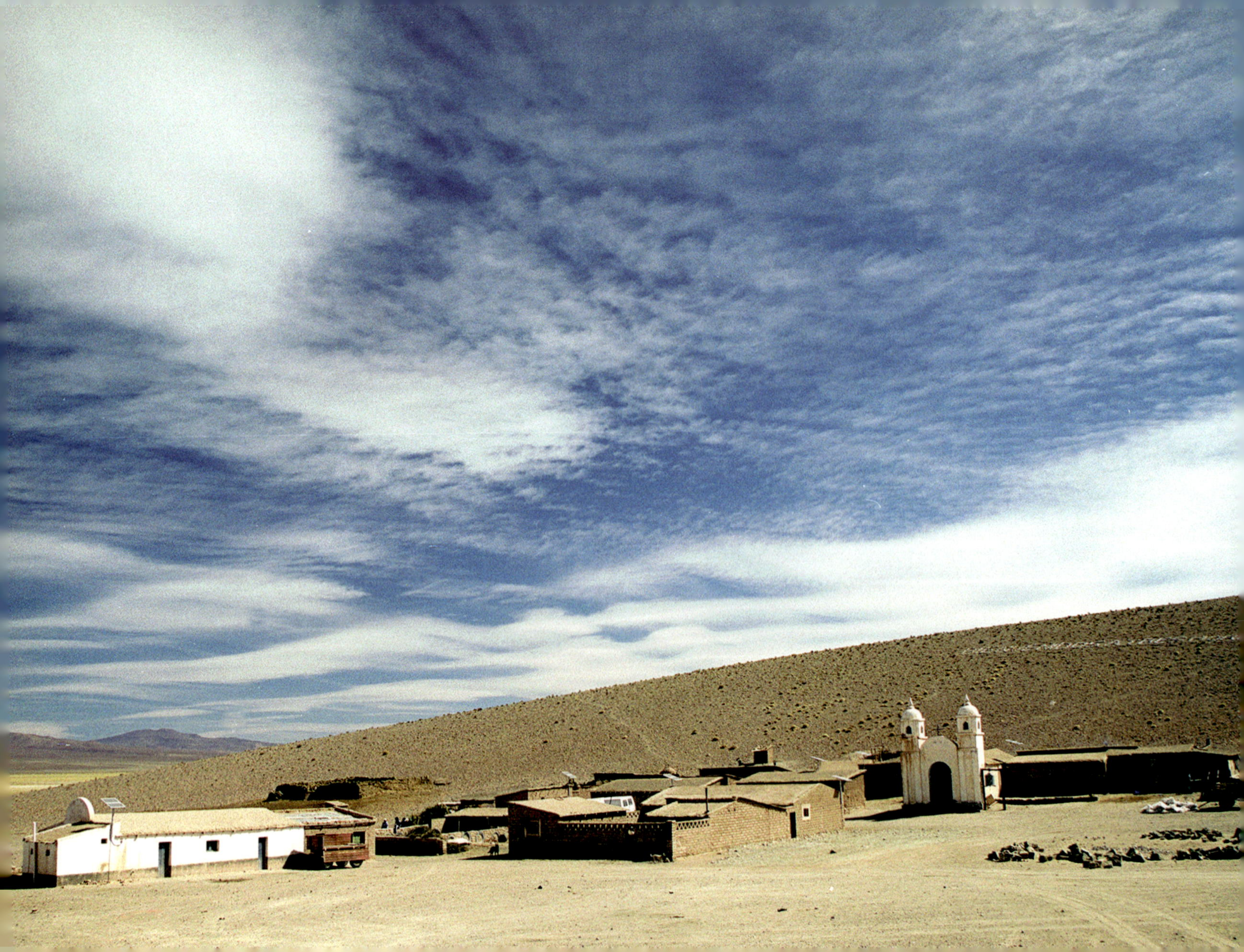

Below awaits the town of Purmamarca. Its proximity is announced by houses surrounded by fruit trees and corn, peppers and vegetable fields. The mountains display their entire palette of ocher, purple and green, and arriving in the afternoon allows us to see them at their best.

As we arrive in Purmamarca we find the main square full of local people selling their crafts. The plaza is surrounded by the most important buildings as in all Hispanic towns, only that here time has halted and the charm of past centuries endures.

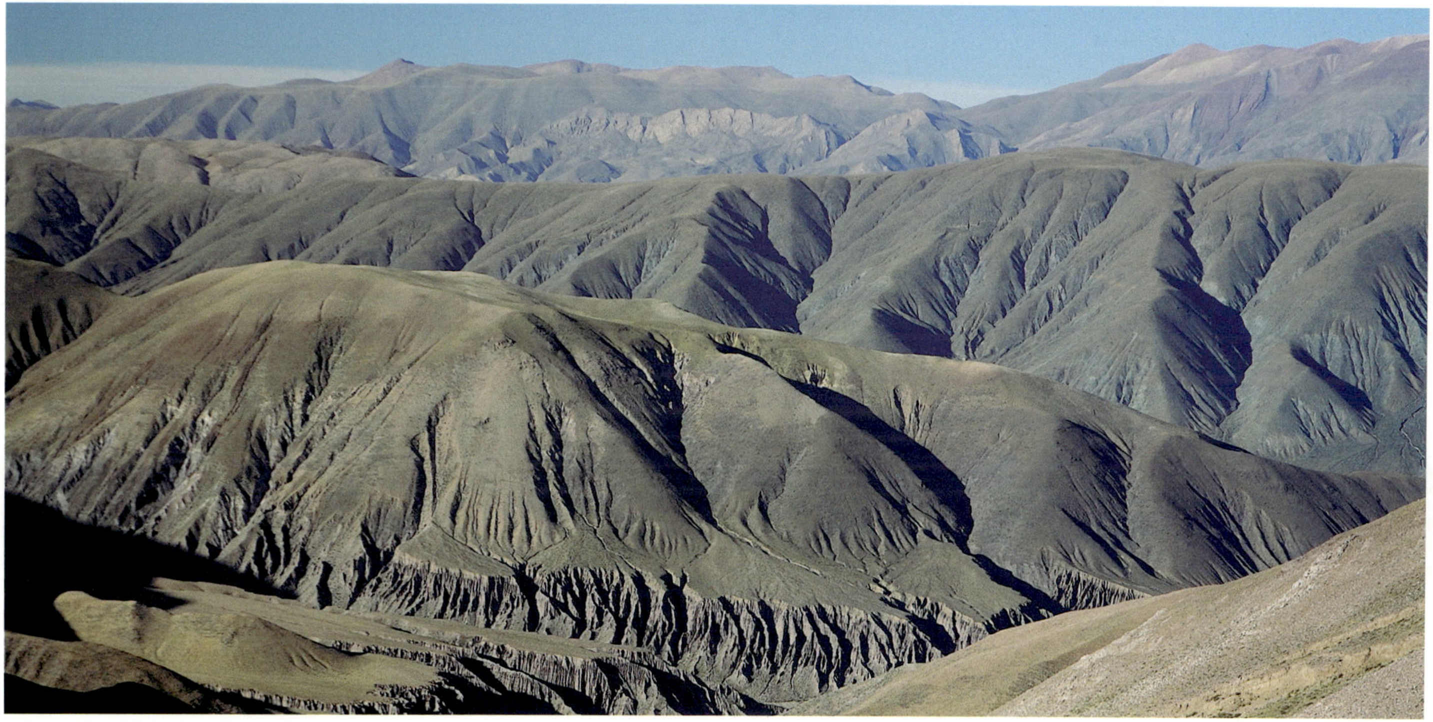

Cuesta de Lipán, view from the pass en route to Purmamarca.

Tres Morros, a small village by the Salinas. (p. 106)

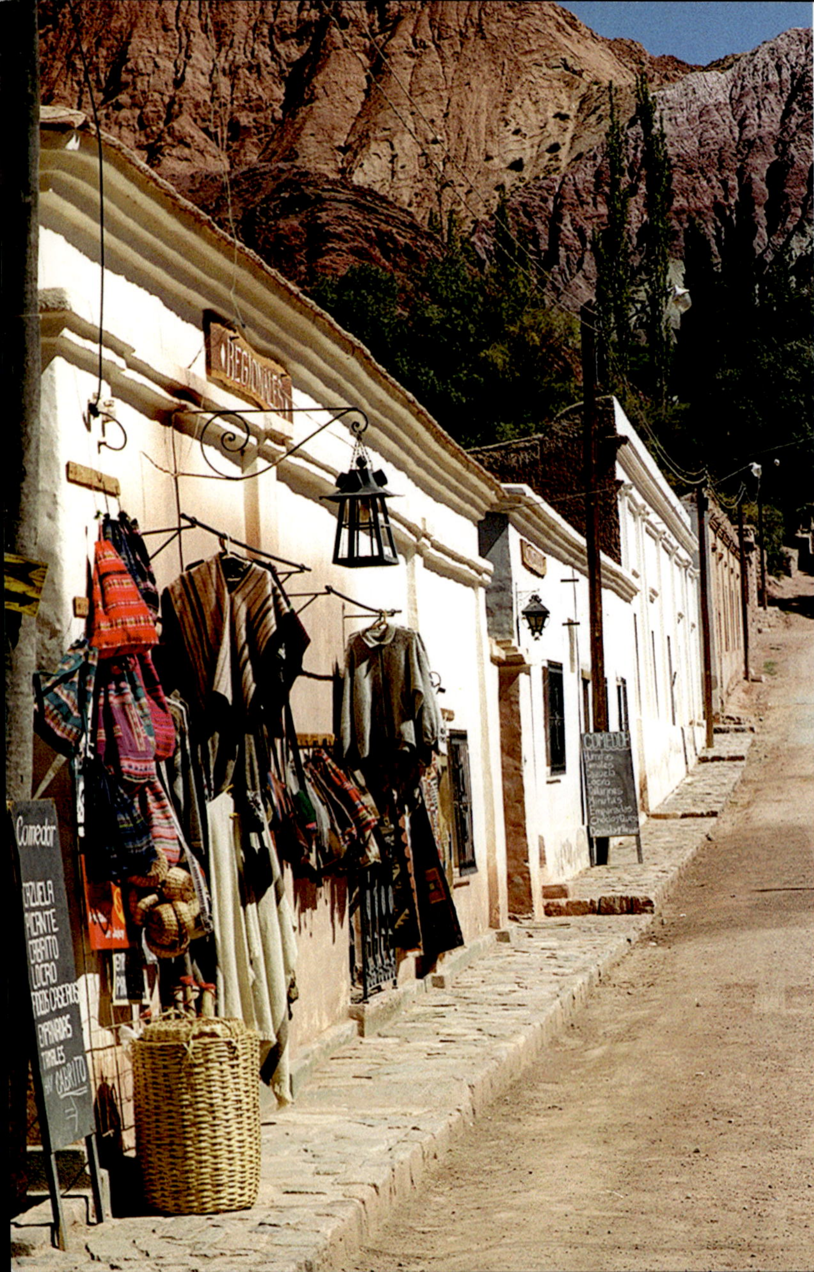

Quebrada de Humahuaca and Iruya

The Quebrada de Humahuaca was declared a UNESCO World Heritage Site in 2003, in order to protect its archeological and cultural legacy and unique landscape. This gorge owes its name to the Omaguaca tribe, its original inhabitants.

It is a natural corridor 170 kilometers long, that joins Argentina's North with the Puna or Altiplano, which spreads across the borders of Argentina, Chile, Bolivia and Peru; and vibrates to the rhythm of its people and their Andean traditions since Pre Hispanic times.

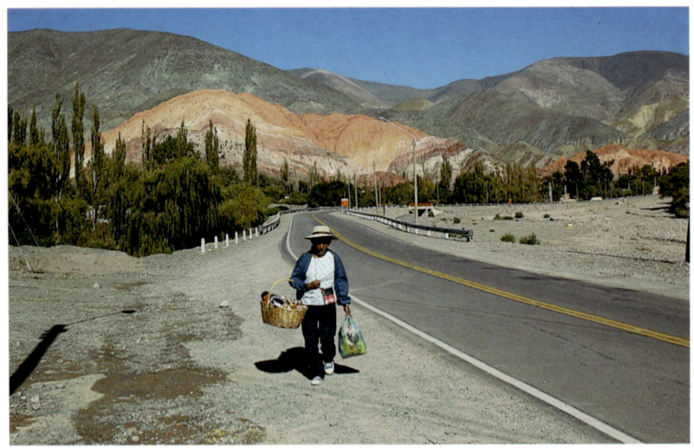

National Route 52, behind the Seven Colours Hill.

A little street in Purmamarca.

Lady under the arches of the old Cabildo.

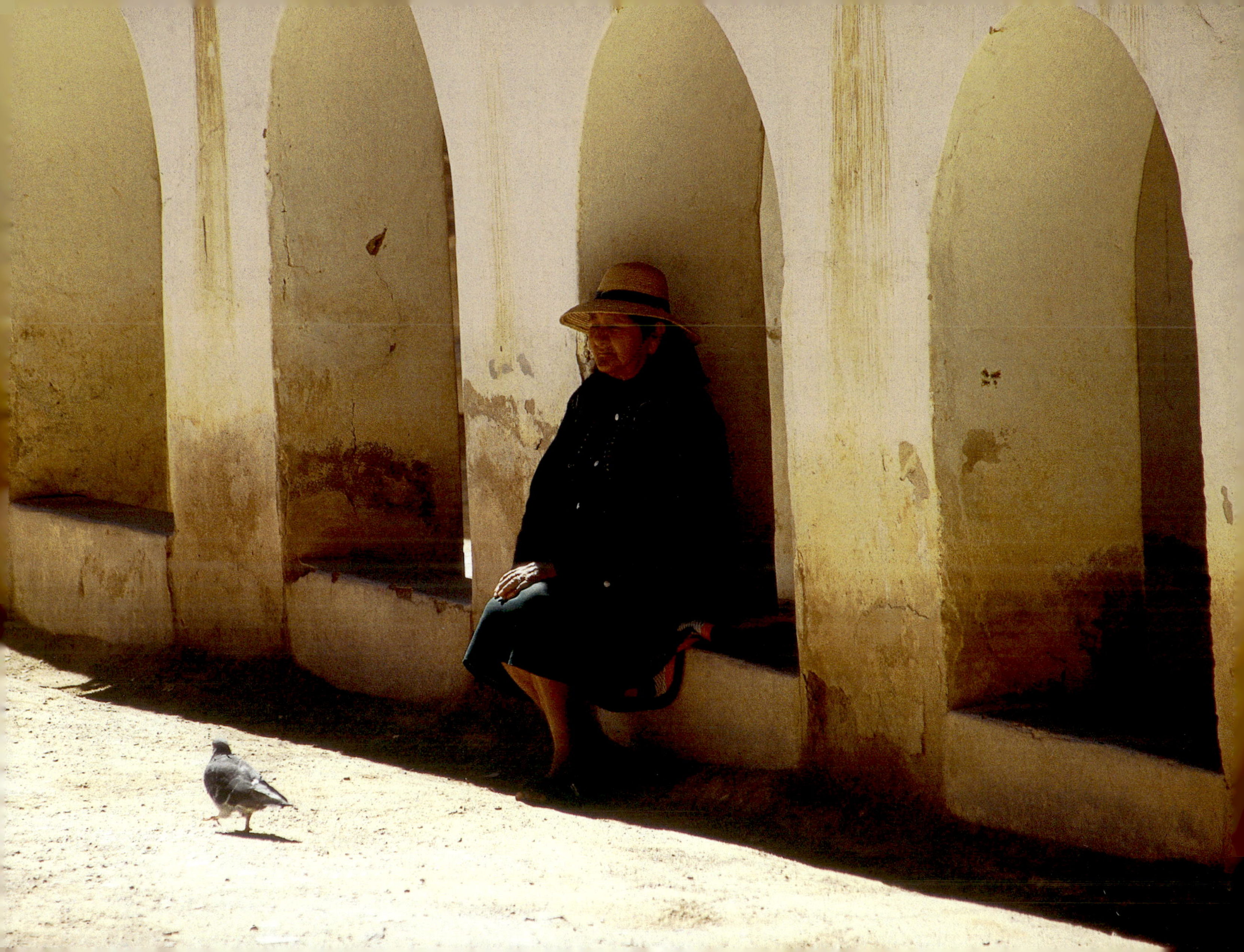

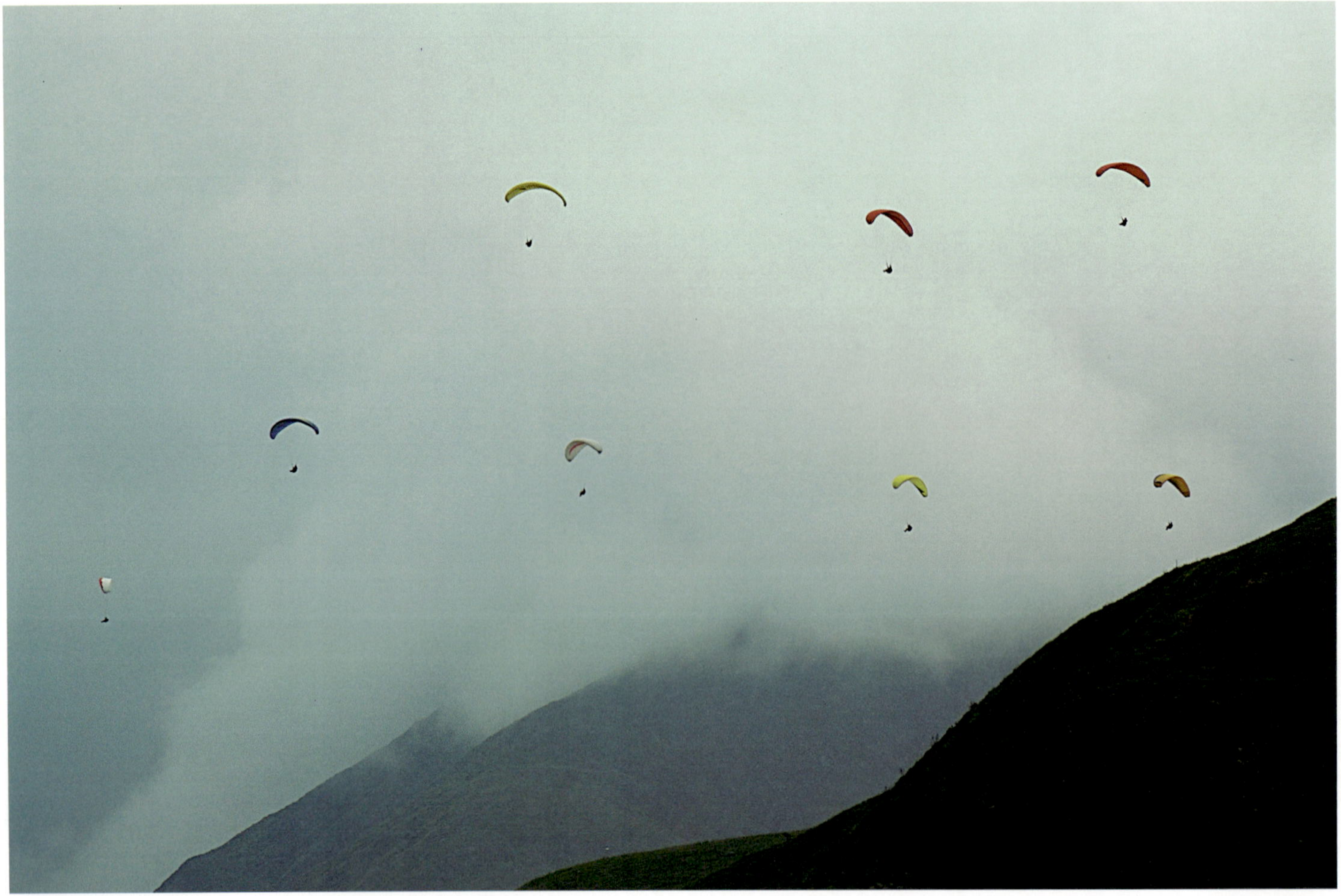

Paragliding in Volcán.

Ceramics, woven wool crafts, vegetable growing, trade and barter; llama, goat or sheep breeding…all of them every day activities in this northern corner of Argentina; which make it a place to travel through with wide open eyes.

From the city of San Salvador de Jujuy, we follow route 9 North, and near Yala the valley becomes a gorge. From here to Tres Cruces the road runs along the Río Grande.

Near Volcán we are already at a height of 2000 m.a.s.l. (6560 ft), so when down in the valley it is cloudy, this is where we drive through the clouds. Up to this altitude we find trees growing on protected mountain sides, after here only grass lands; and as we go further up, cacti, thorny shrubs and the twisted Queñoa *(Polylepis australis)* tree on the high mountain.

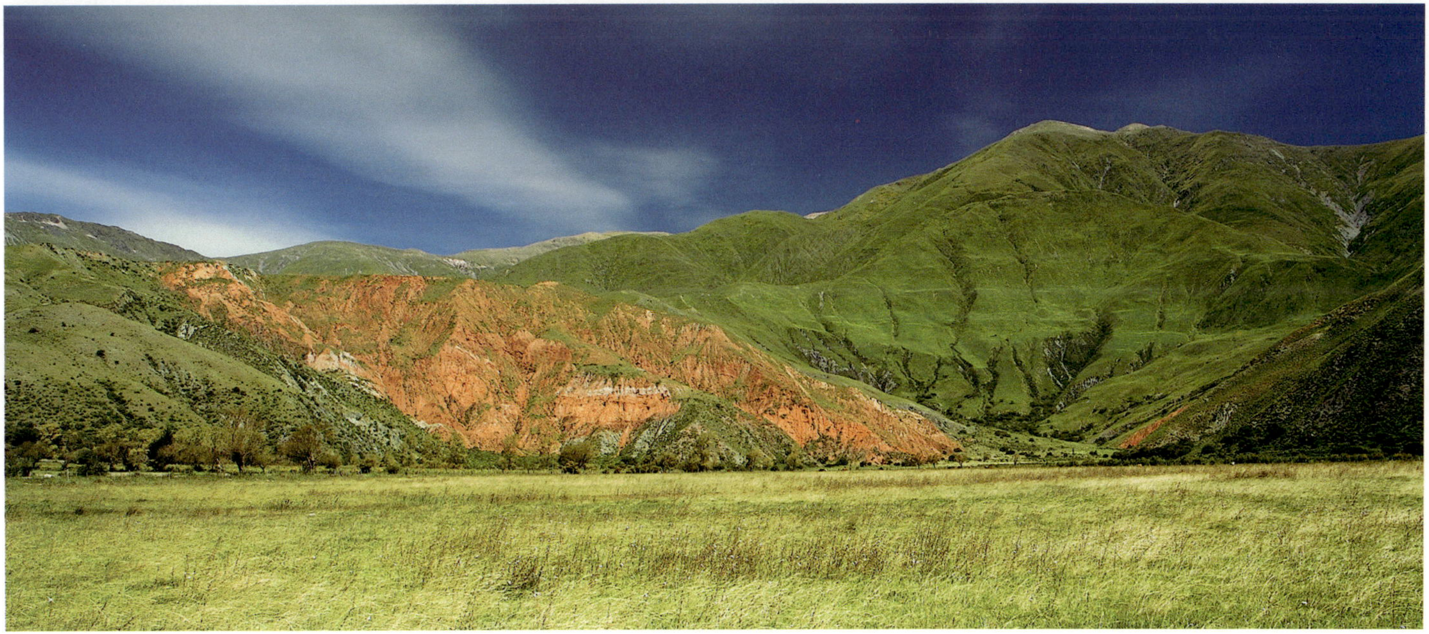

Volcán. The colours appear.

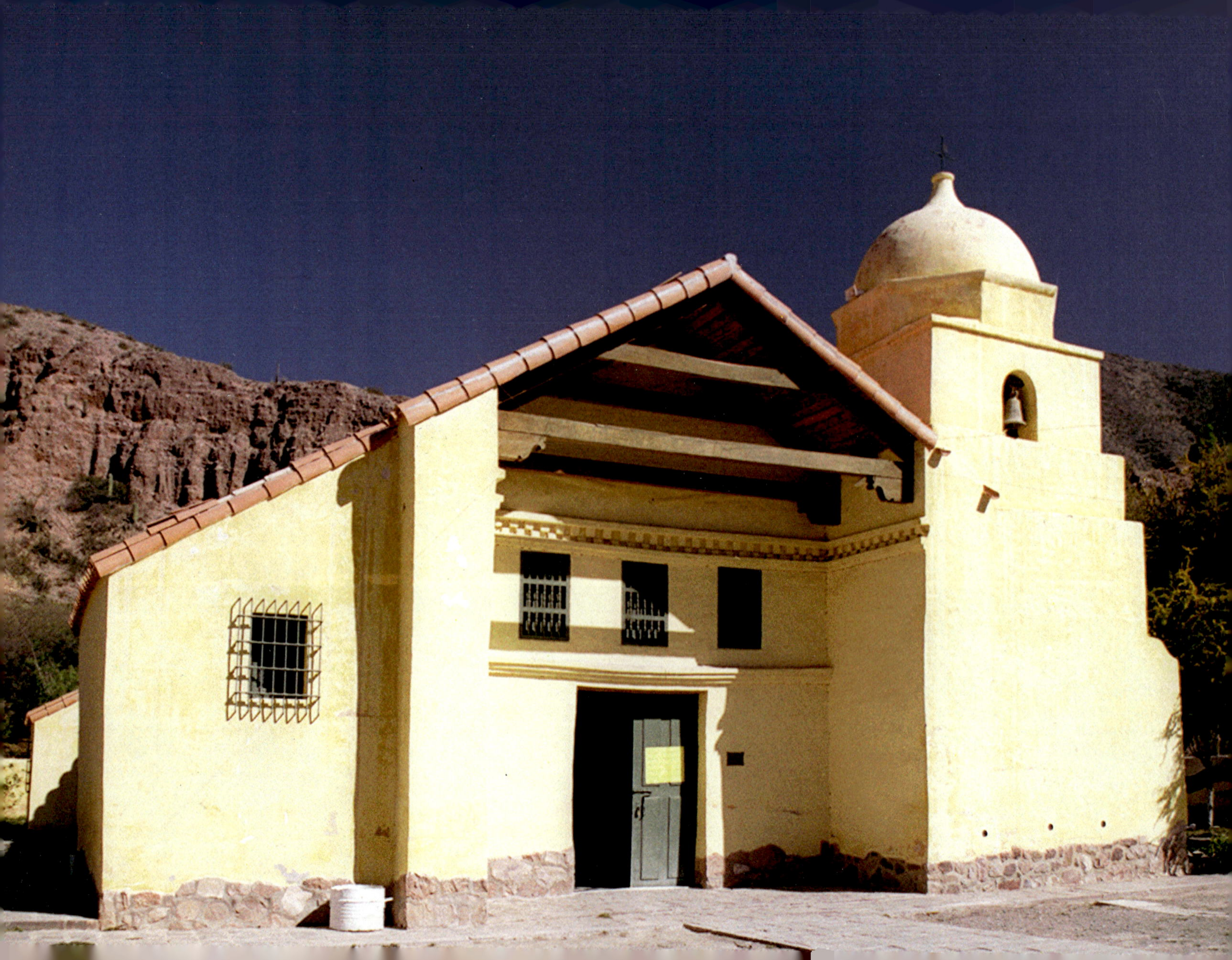

As we drive along, in Tumbaya we see the first cardones *(Trichocereus sp.)* standing tall on impossible slopes. If we go by this town during Easter perhaps we will see a procession coming down from the hills to the tempo of the sikuris.

The gorge runs in between the Zenta Range to the East and the Oriental Andes to the West; the latter hide the Puna in their heights. Following the Cuesta de Lipán from Purmamarca, we can drive up there.

Purmamarca, located where the Purmamarca and Grande rivers meet, stands by the famous Mountain of the Seven Colours. It is one of the towns with most character of the area. Here we will find the Santa Rosa de Lima Church and the smallest town hall in Argentina; today the local library.

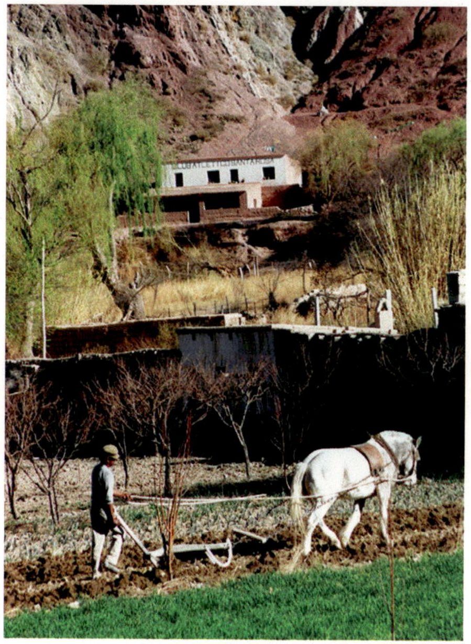

Purmamarca. Tilling the soil.

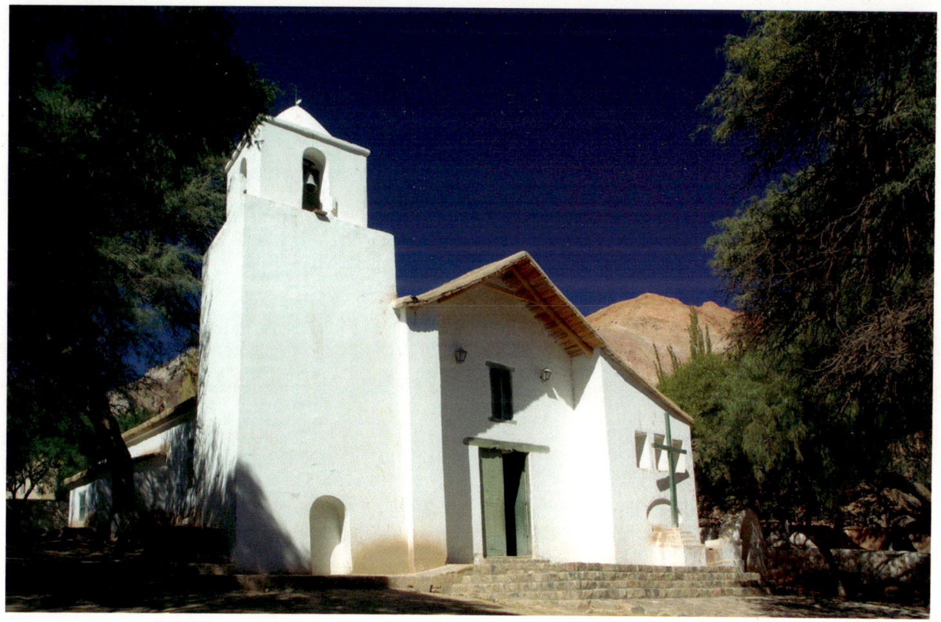

Purmamarca. Santa Rosa de Lima Church, 1648.

Tumbaya Church, 1796. It guards paintings of the Cuzco School. . (p. 113)

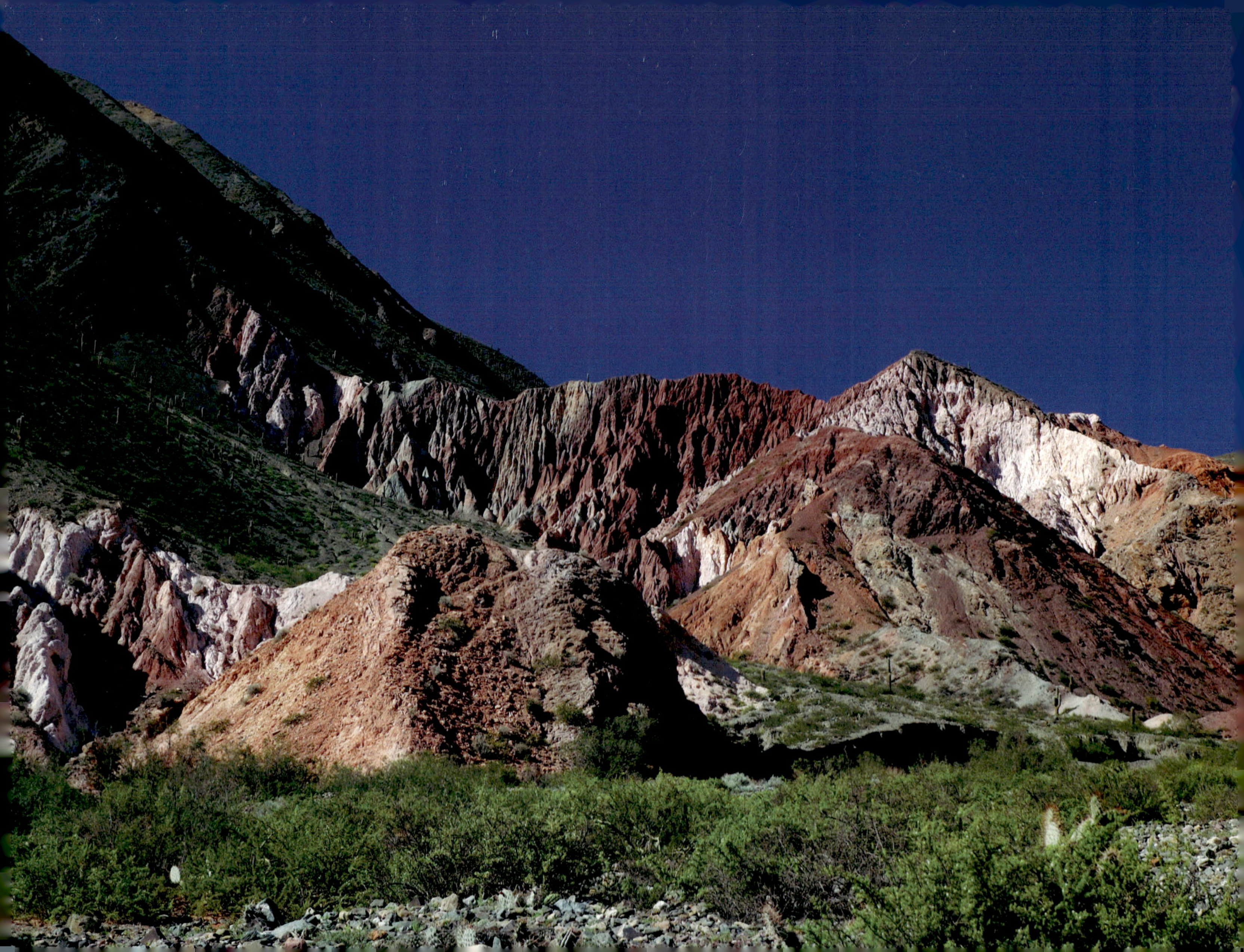

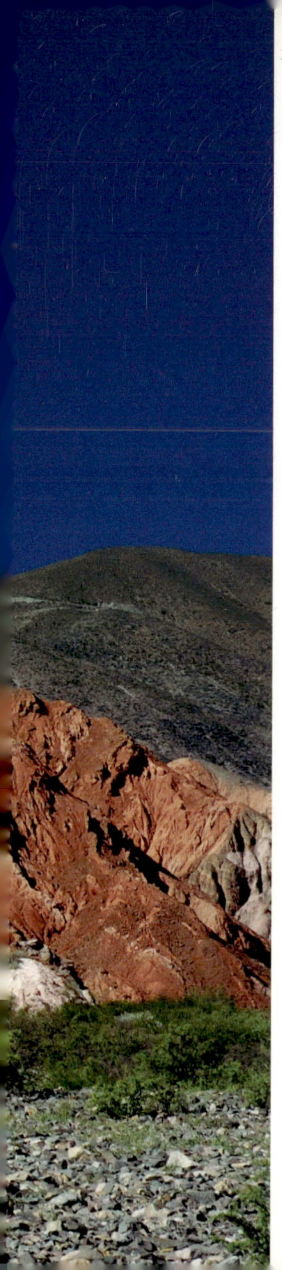

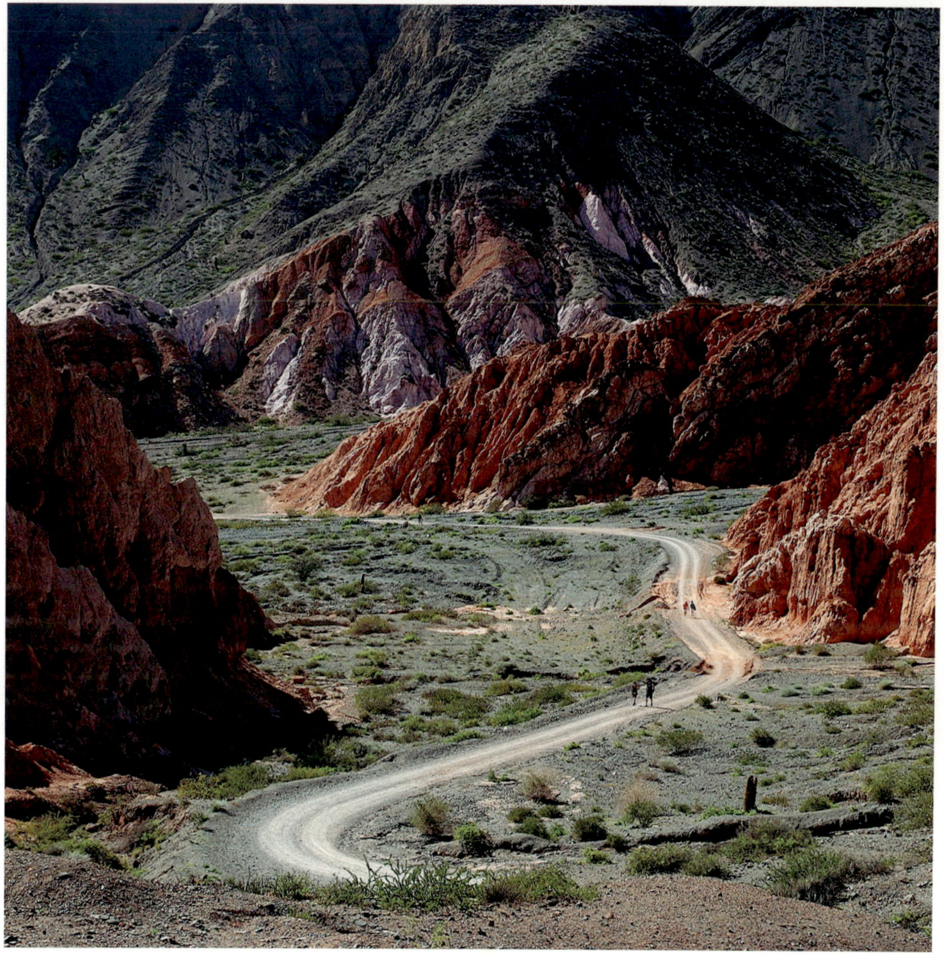

Paseo de Los Colorados, a great walk in Purmamarca.

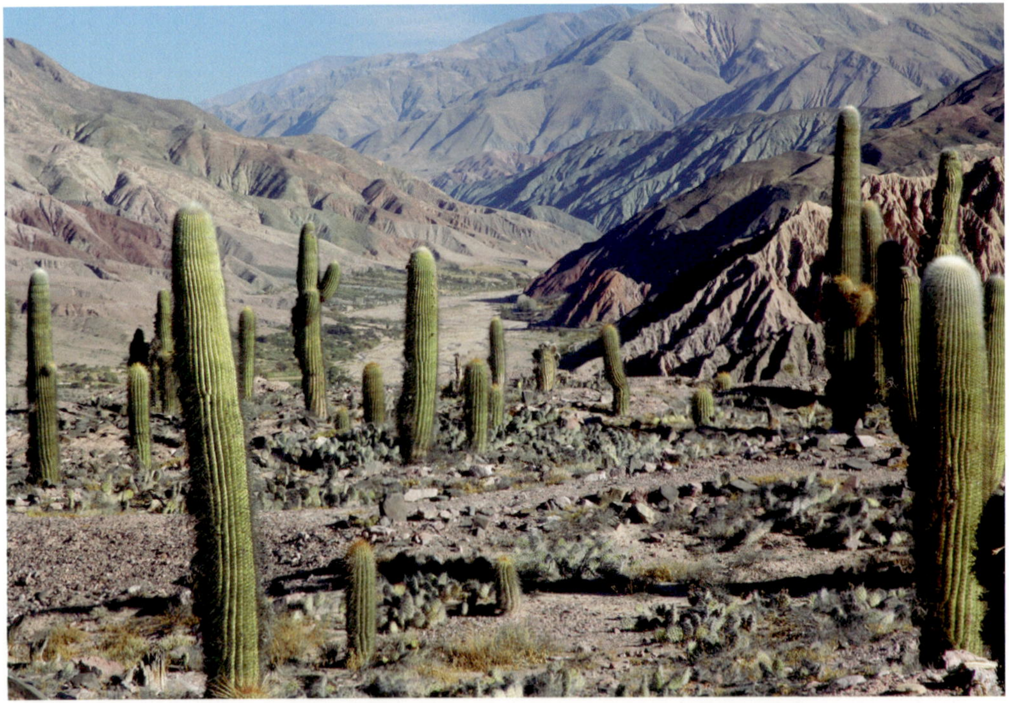

Pucará de Hornillos Ruins.

Our road goes on to the North; the Posta de Hornillos reminds us of colonial times when this road connected Peru with the port of Buenos Aires. This crossing was done on horse back or oxen drawn carts, and here in the mountains where the trail got too steep, transport continued with a mule caravan.

Chapel in the Posta de Hornillos. This place was used as general quarters during the Independence wars. (p. 117)

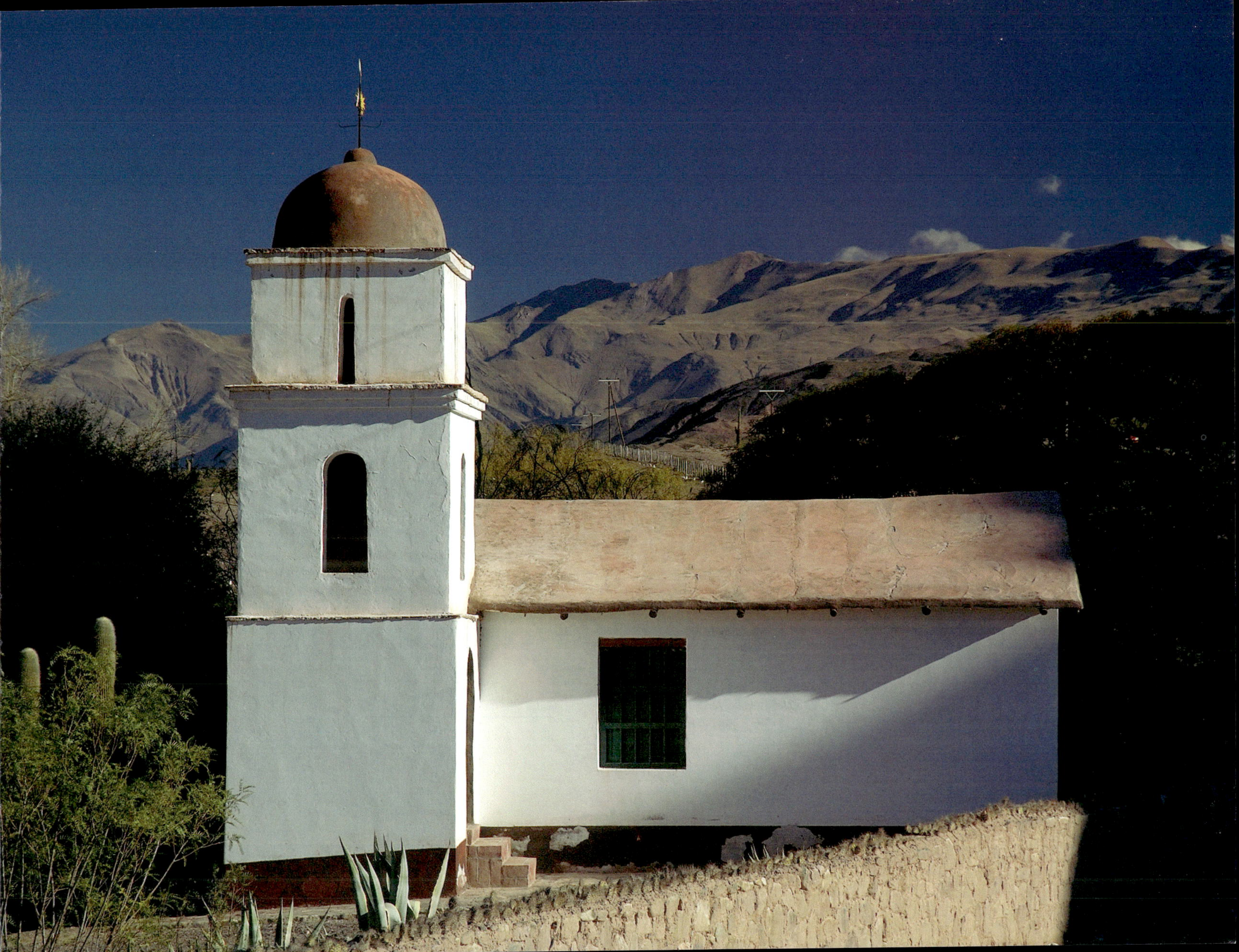

Maimará is another village with a beautiful location; near the river it has green houses for growing carnations and vegetables.

We drive on to Tilcara, located at the foot of its Pucará, which has partially restored ruins.

Pucará means fortified lookout, and it is one of many in the Quebrada, all strategically located to control anyone who dared pass through here. Tilcara, Perchel, Juella, Yacoraite… all of them names to look up on the map, to discover and learn about.

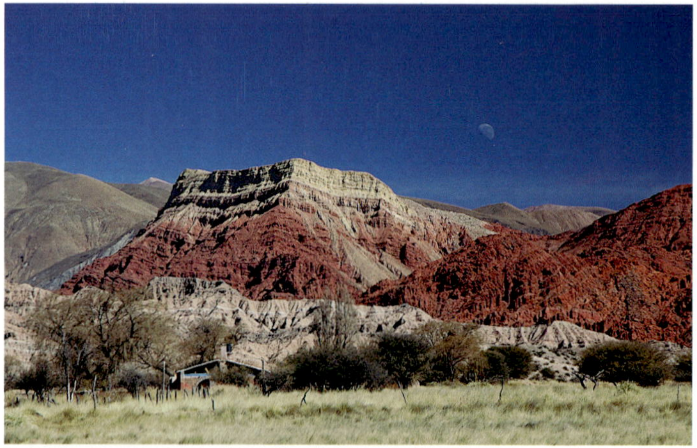

Yacoraite. This hill is called Pollera, which means skirt.

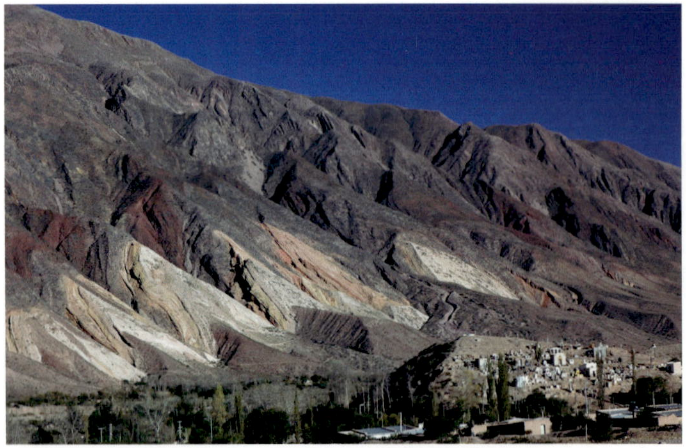

This mountain is known as The Painter's Palette. Maimará.

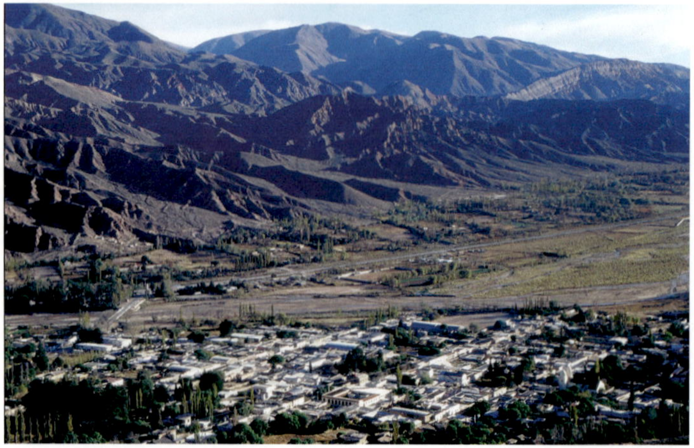

The town of Tilcara.

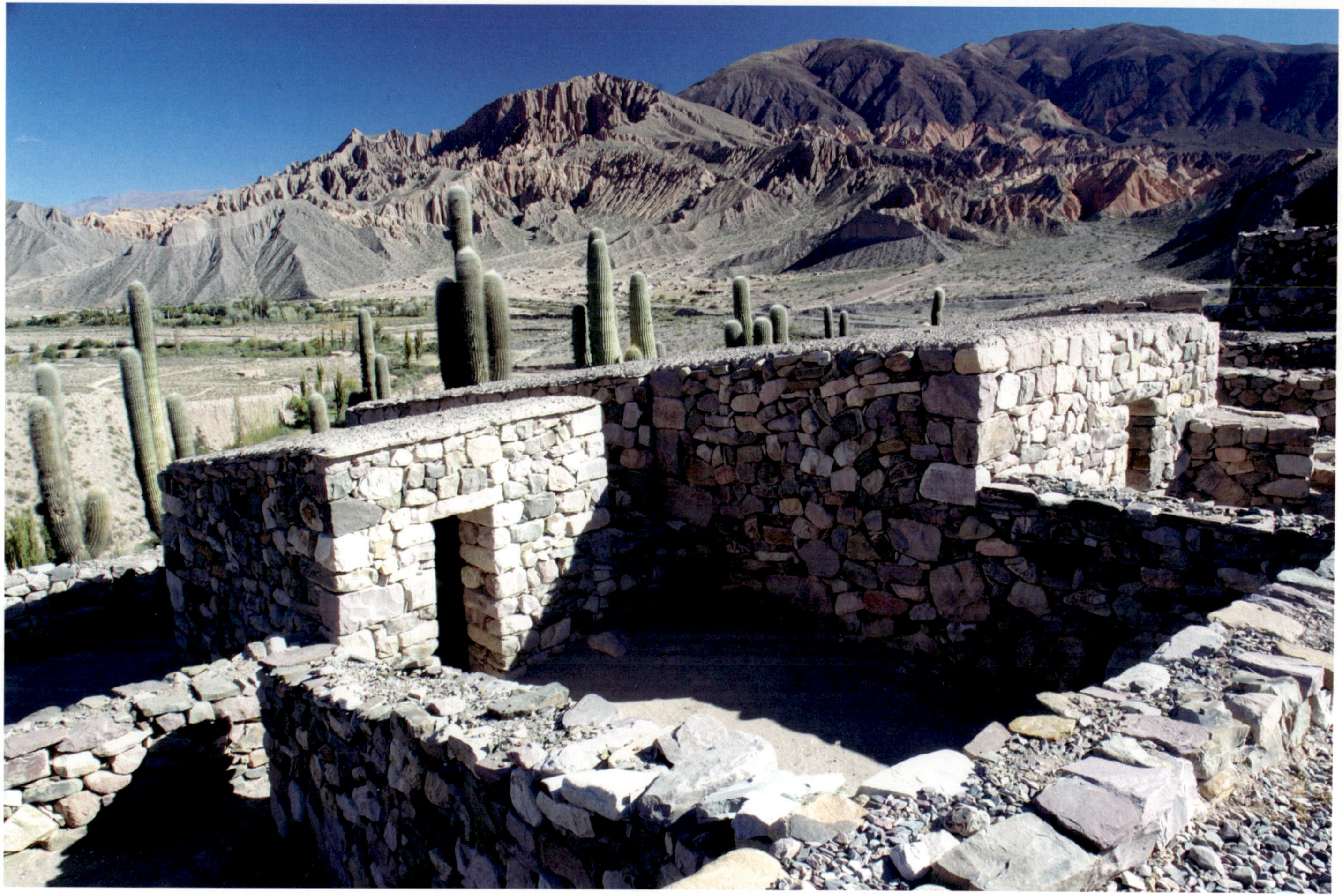

The Pucará, or fortified city in Tilcara.

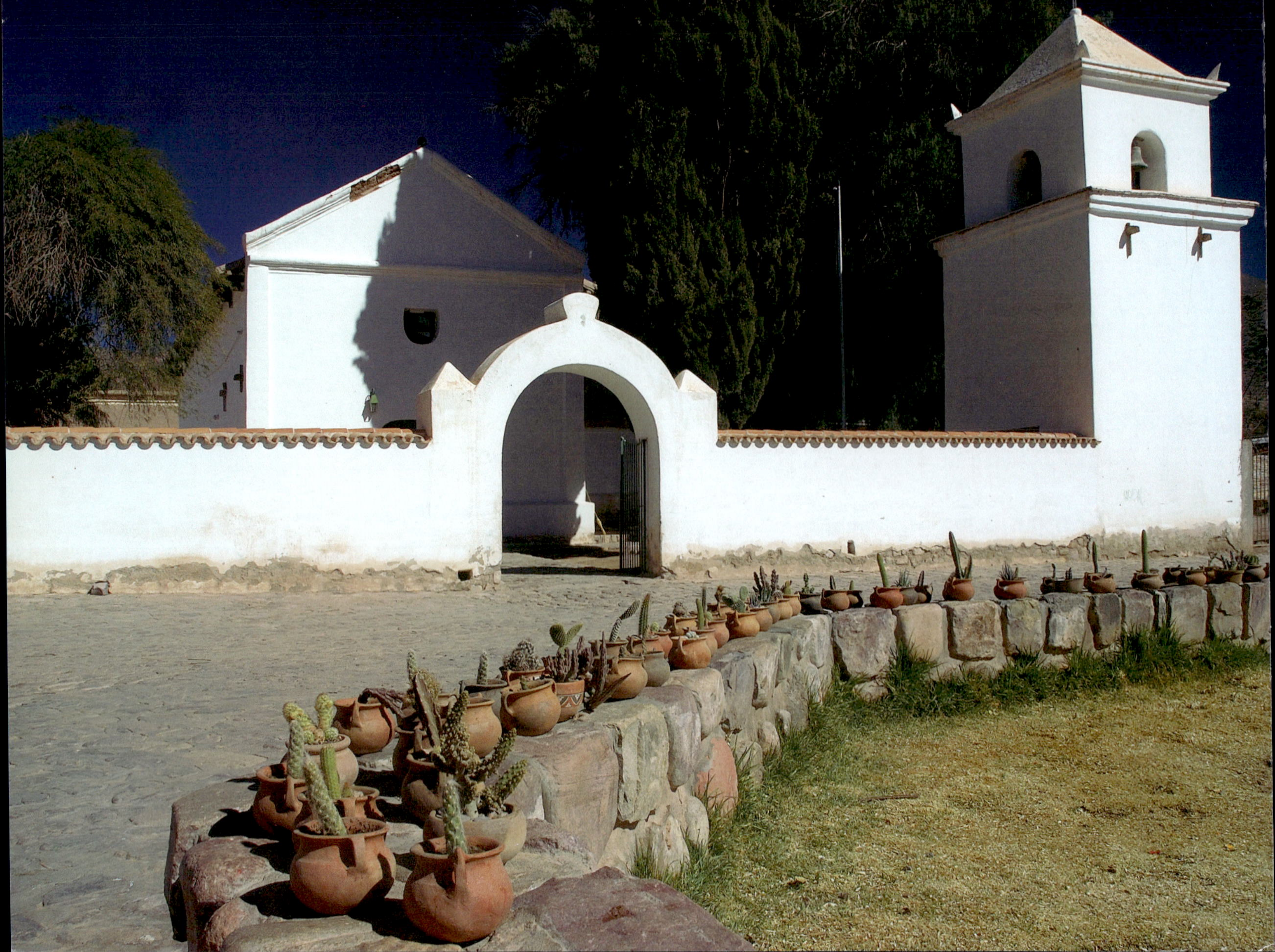

Before reaching Huacalera we cross the Tropic of Capricorn, at 23º27' south. The landscape changes, the gorge becomes wide and dry. Leaving the main road we go down towards the river and drive into Humahuaca, the biggest town in the area, founded over the ruins of an old Inca Tampu. At the marketplace we can find goods from Chile, Bolivia and Argentina. The streets are cobbled and narrow; the houses different from other towns of the region.

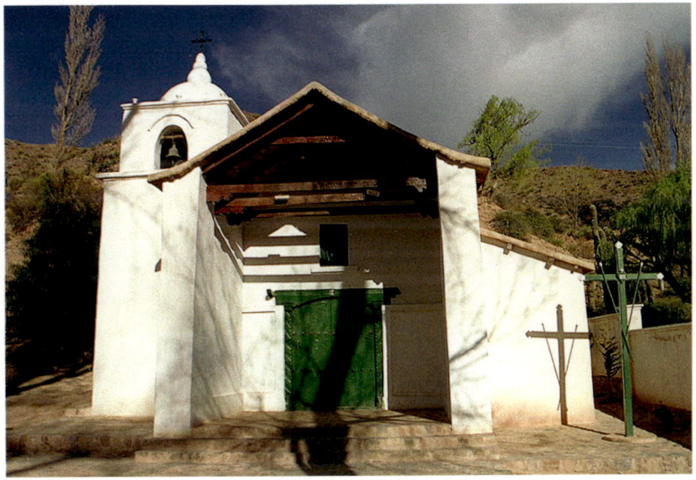

Huacalera Church, 17th century.

Uquía. San Francisco de Paula Church, 17th century. (p. 120)

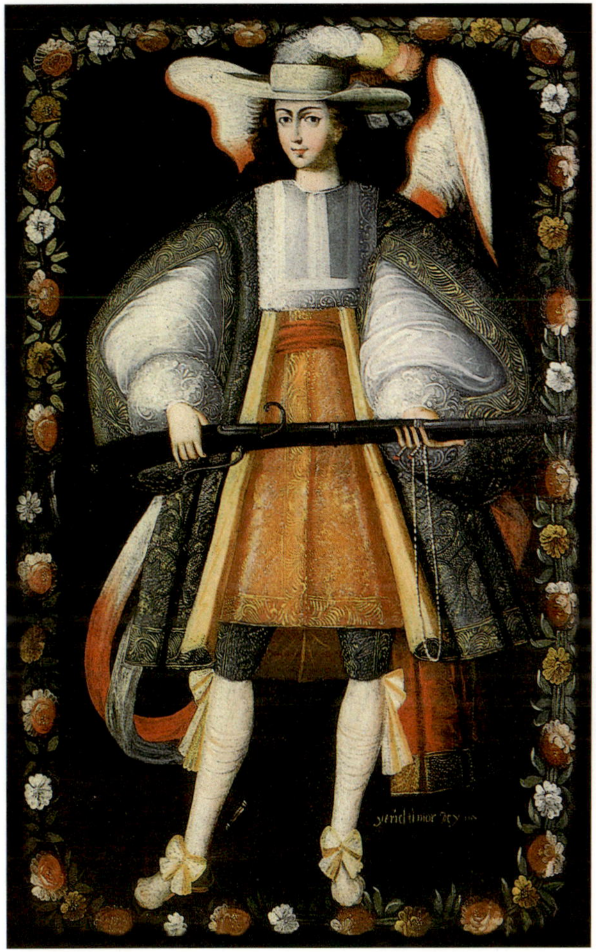

Yeriel Angel in the church of San Francisco, Uquía, 17th century.

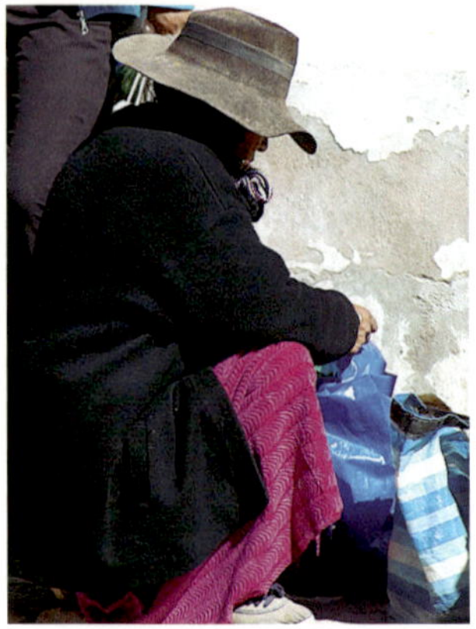
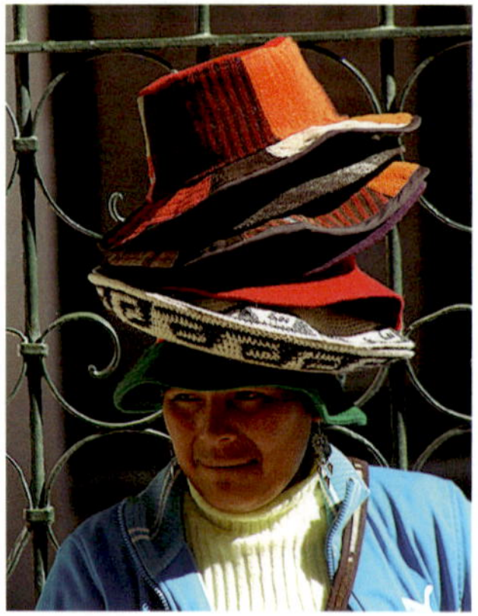

Humahuaca. Ladies selling coca and hats.

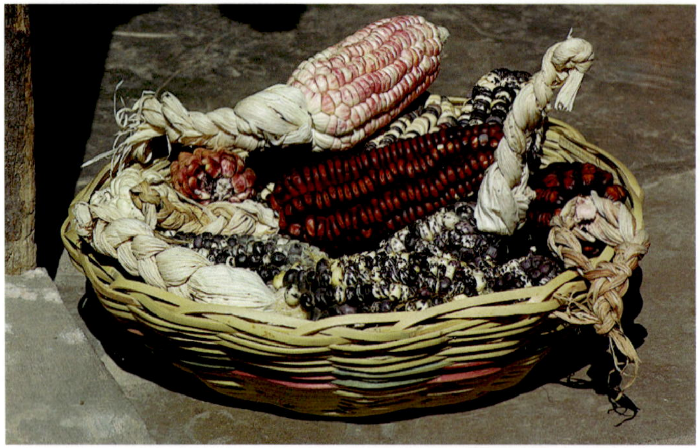

Corn.

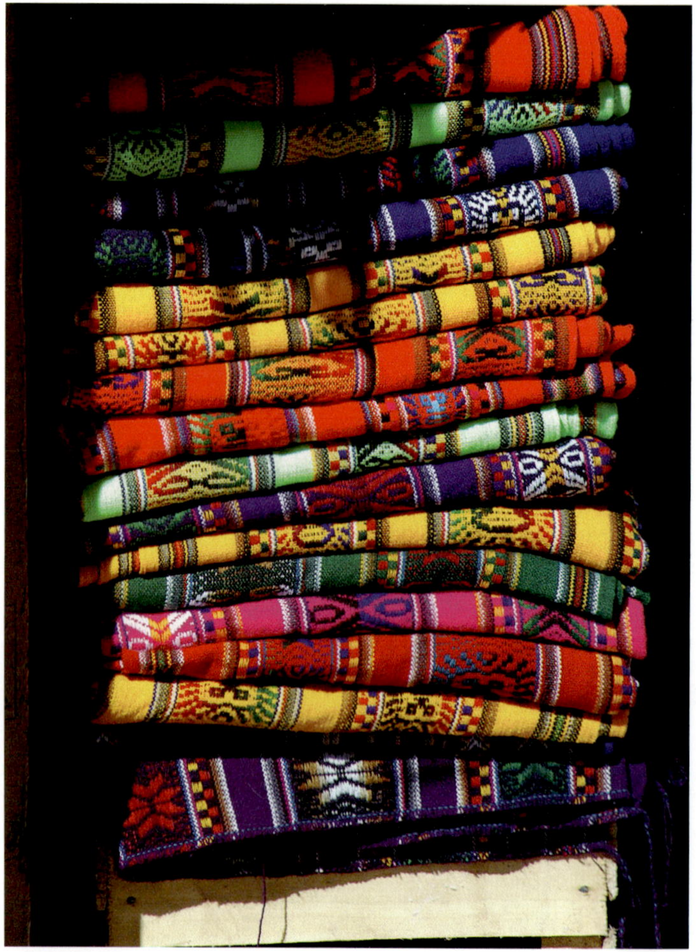

Aguayos.

In the Quebrada de Humahuaca, the fusion of European and Andean cultures is ever-present. We find it in festivals, misachicos and during Carnival; all of them decorated with colours, music and wind.

As the seasons change, everything else does. Rain and mud tainted rivers bring fertility to the fields on the river banks, allowing farmers to grow flowers and vegetables. Then, sun and winter frosts… Empty fields… The North Wind blowing as dry as the Puna… Festivities venerating the Pachamama… Then, celebrations asking for rain so that it may start all over again.

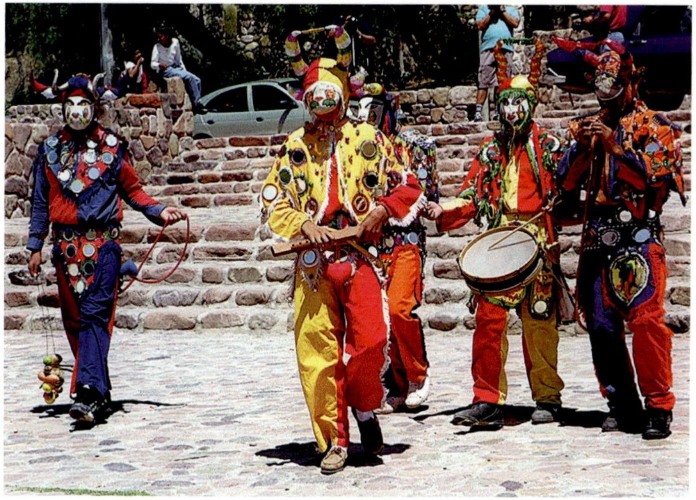

Carnaval in Humahuaca. A festival full of cultural syncretism.

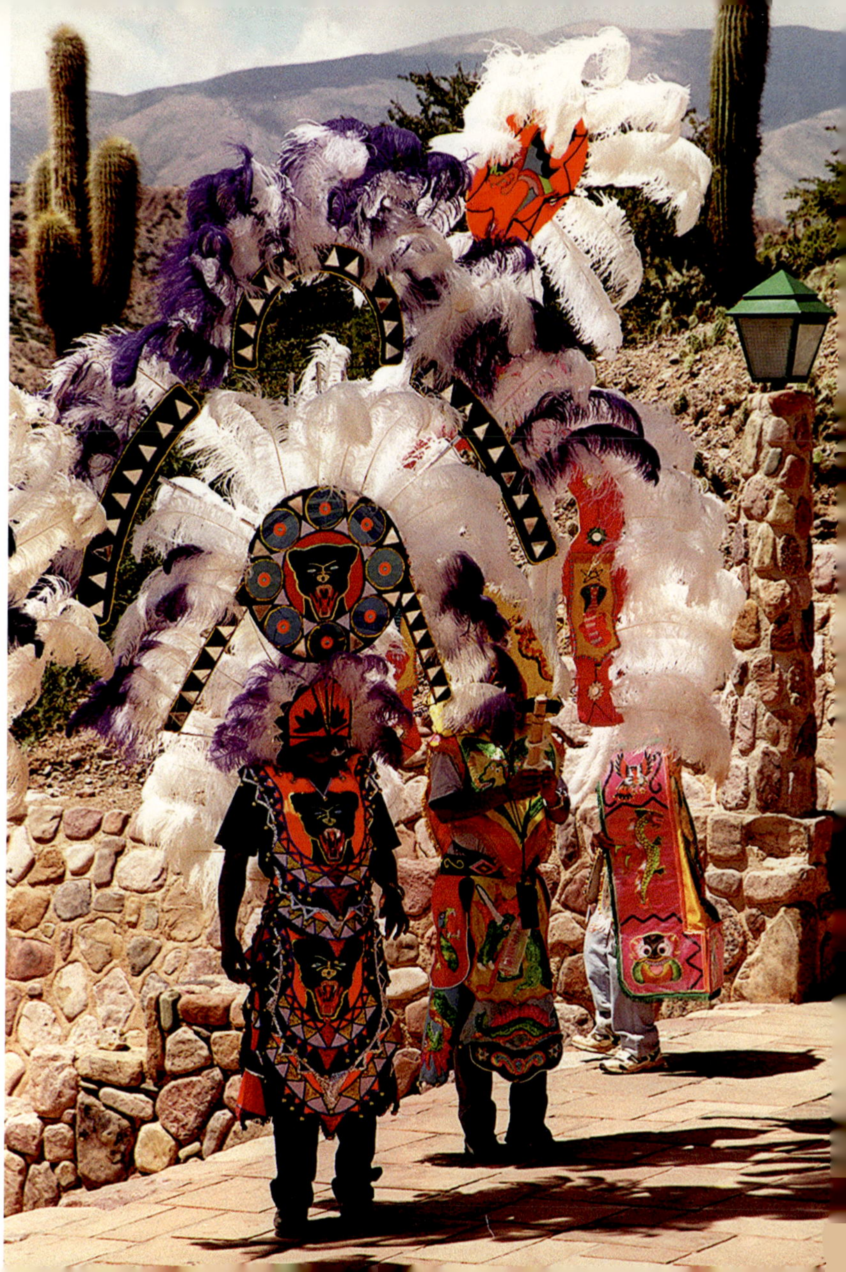

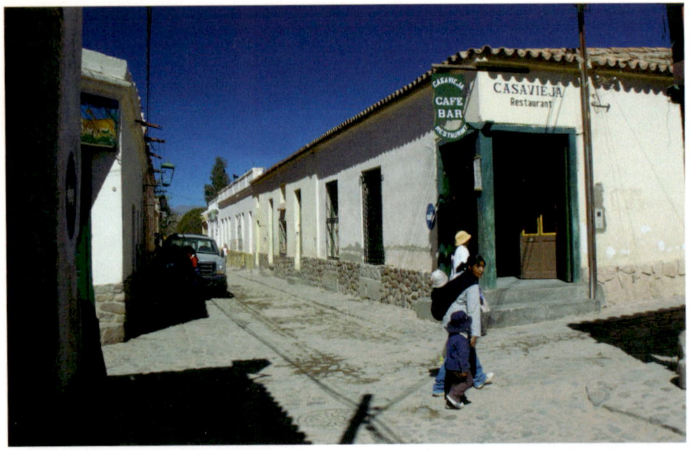

Humahuaca Street.

124

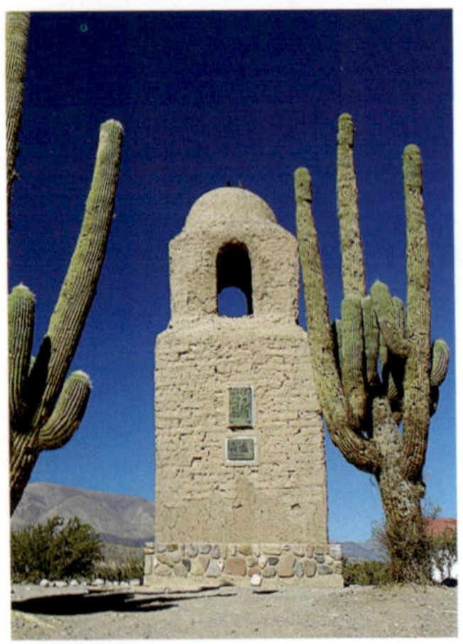

Santa Barabara turret, 19th century. The Spaniards used this place as a fortress.

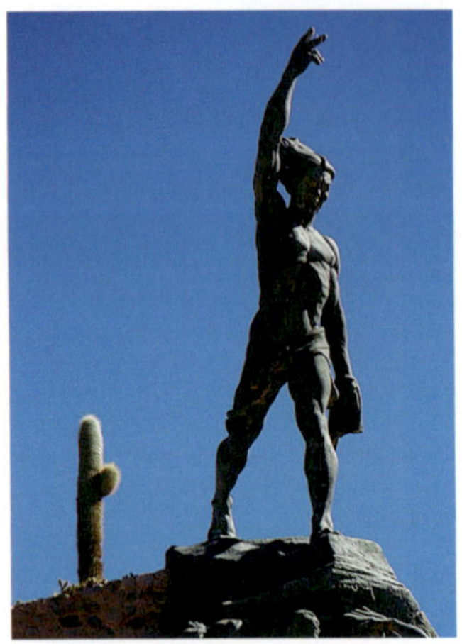

Independence Monument, built in 1950.

A few kilometers after Humahuaca we reach a sign indicating a turnoff to the right, towards the Zenta Range. Amongst other enticing names, it reads Iruya. Iruya is a hidden gem; going there along a road of a thousand hairpin curves is a gift to oneself.

We twist along mountains of grasslands and wind polished stones, cross the little village of Iturbe. Since the train from Buenos Aires to La Quiaca does not run anymore, the old train station serves today as a football field for the children of this town that has multicoloured doors and windows to liven up the adobe walls of the small houses.

Further ahead the road crosses the river and for a time we drive inside a minor course. This is because in this land of steep mountains, sometimes one can only travel along the river bed, since the rest of the landscape is to steep and unstable to set a road on it. As we climb the road gets narrower, we find houses but they are now made of stone and have straw roofs.

But for a willow or poplar planted years ago, there are no trees, only grasslands. We left the cardones behind in the Quebrada; here it is too high for them. To our right a colossus looms above everything, it is El Morado, named because of the colour of the soil at its summit. With luck, we will see vicuñas or a guanaco proudly looking down on us.

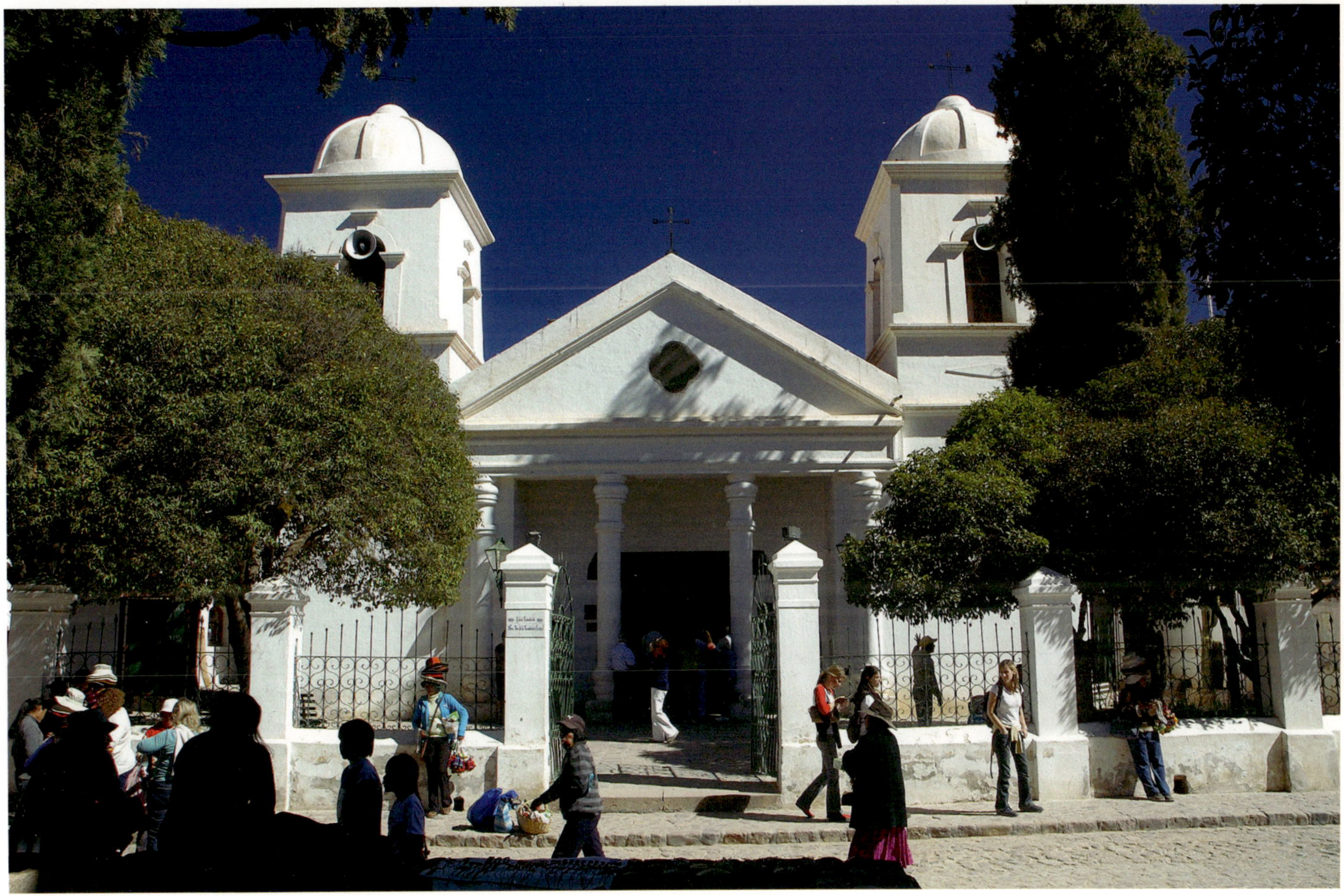

Humahuaca Cathedral, 1641. Consecrated to Our Lady of the Candelaria.

We arrive at the Abra del Condor, a pass at 4000 m.a.s.l. (13123 ft), from where we start our way down immersed in amazing scenery. We are in the midst of the Zenta Range, where mountains slope down at all angles eroded by water from summer downpours.

Finally we arrive at Iruya, that according to locals its name comes from the indigenous word Iruyoc, "land of pastures". The houses seem to be hanging from the mountains and the stone streets climb up at impossible angles.

In the surrounding mountains live communities that have not altered their way of life in years, they live off the trade between the tropical forests to the East and the dry high lands to the West. One can only reach these places on foot or by mule. Every now and then they come to Iruya with their llama wool, Andean potatoes or seeds, honey and fruit from other climates. Then it is a party day in Iruya, there is barter, music, dancing and a mass held in the San Roque Church.

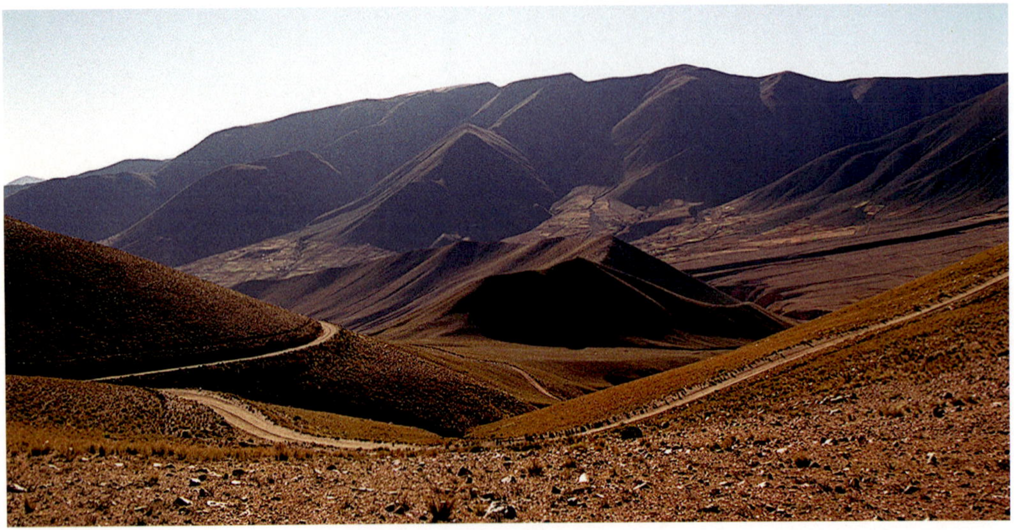

Looking East from Abra El Condor, at 4000 m.a.s.l.

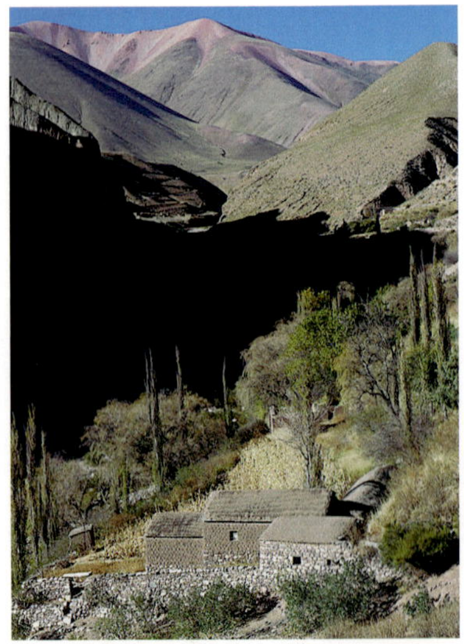

Stone houses on the road to Iruya.

San Roque Chruch in Iruya. *(p. 127)*

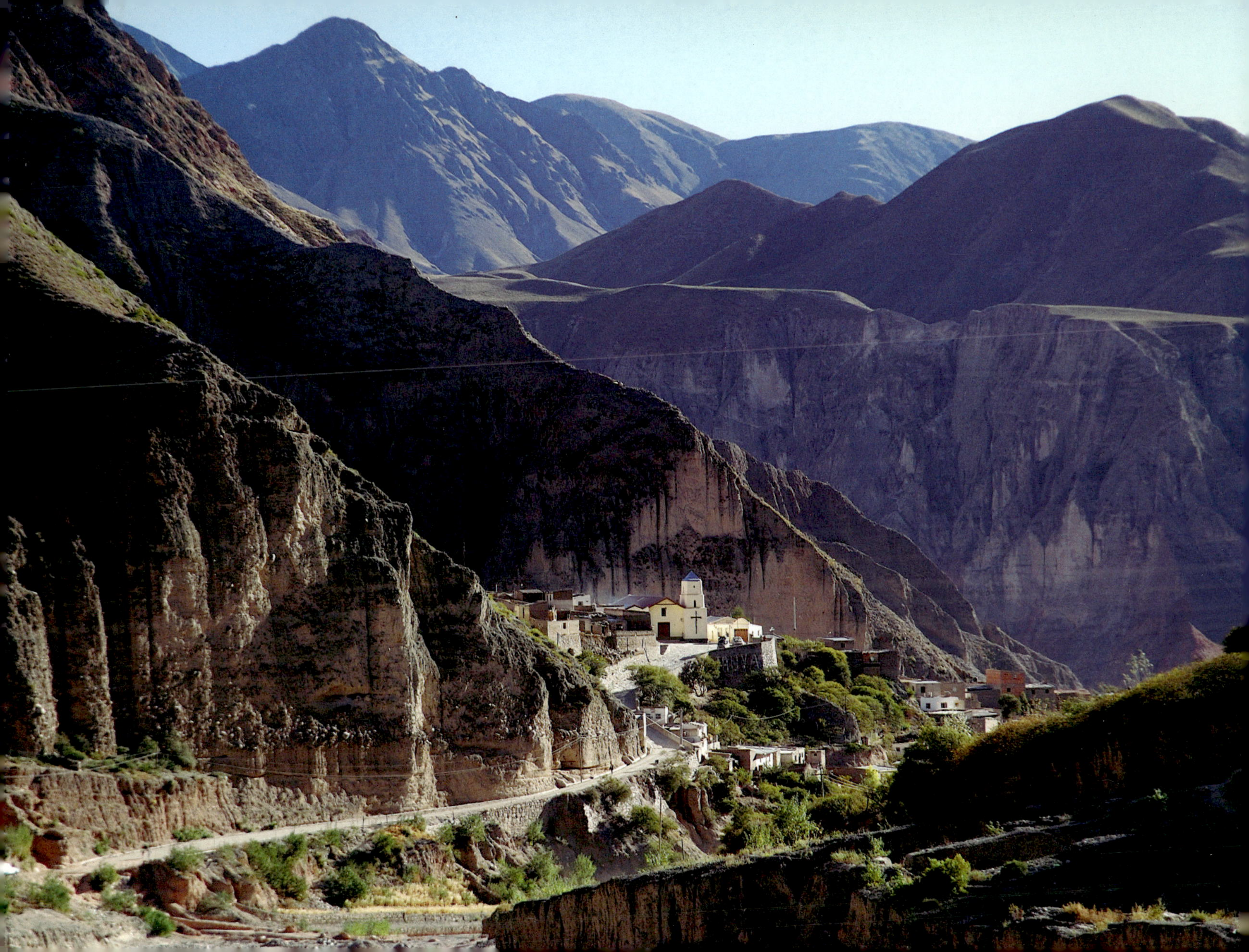

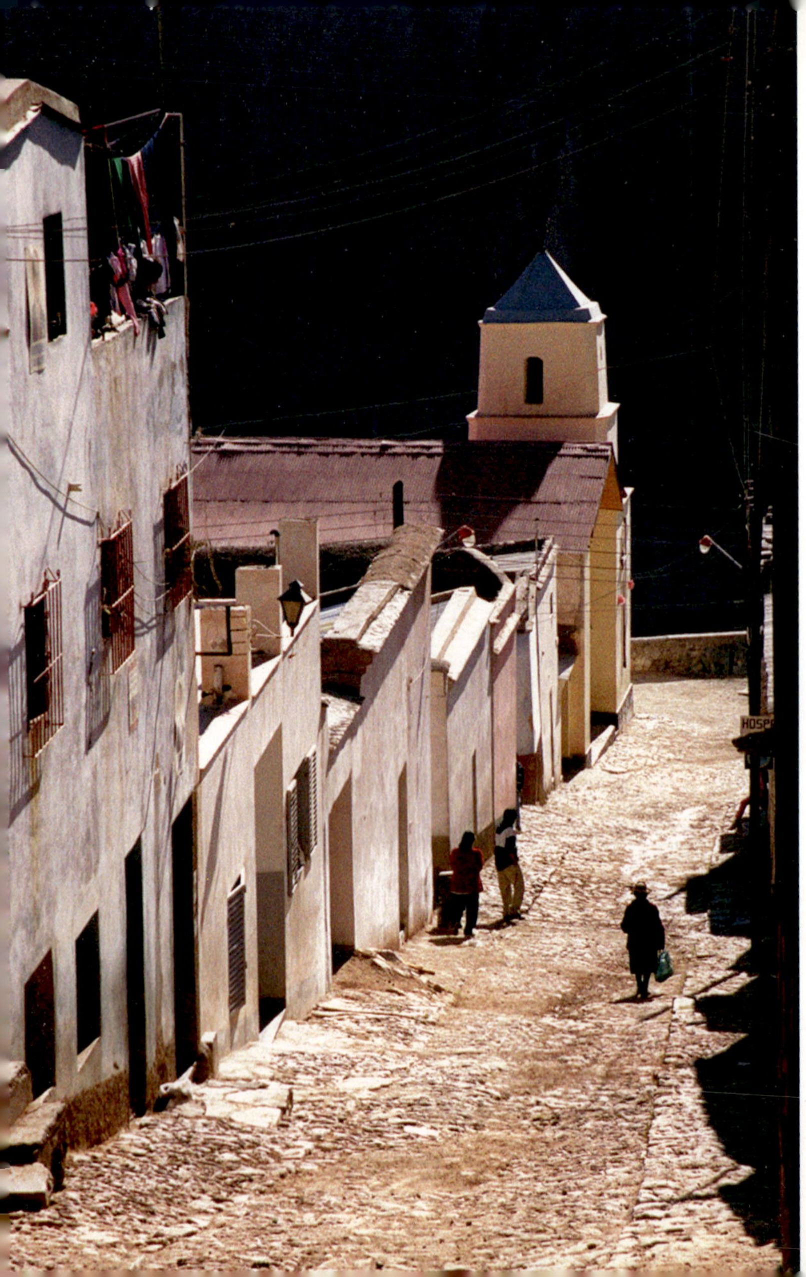

Index

Introduction 2
From the City of Tucumán to Quilmes via Tafí del Valle 4
From Cafayate to Salta via Quebrada de las Conchas 26
City of Salta and San Lorenzo 42
From Salta to Cachi via Cuesta del Obispo.
Route 40 to Cafayate. 58
From Salta to Jujuy via Camino de Cornisa 80
From Salta to Purmamarca via Quebrada del Toro and Puna 90
Quebrada de Humahuaca and Iruya 108

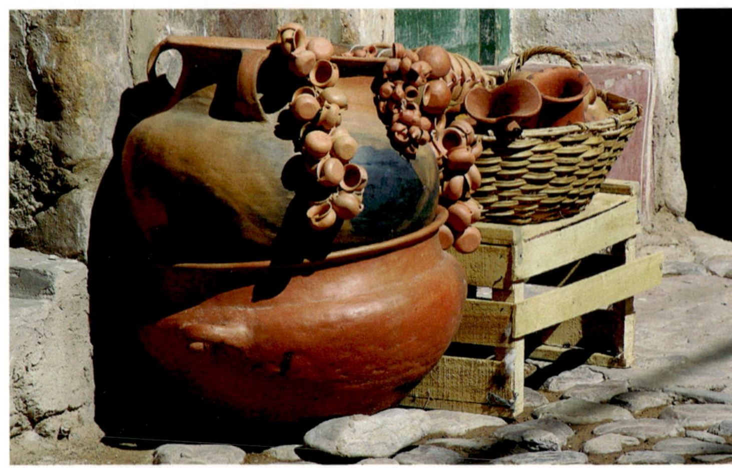

A street in Iruya.